When Washington Shut Down Wall Street

When Washington Shut Down
Wall Street

THE GREAT FINANCIAL CRISIS
OF 1914 AND
THE ORIGINS OF AMERICA'S
MONETARY SUPREMACY

William L. Silber

PRINCETON UNIVERSITY PRESS

PRINCETON AND OXFORD

Copyright © 2007 by Princeton University Press

Requests for permission to reproduce material from this work should be sent to Permissions, Princeton University Press

Published by Princeton University Press, 41 William Street, Princeton, New Jersey 08540

In the United Kingdom: Princeton University Press, 3 Market Place, Woodstock, Oxfordshire OX20 1SY

Library of Congress Cataloging-in-Publication Data

Silber, William L.
When Washington shut down Wall Street : the great financial crisis of 1914 and the origins of America's monetary supremacy / William L. Silber.
   p. cm.
Includes bibliographical references.
ISBN-13: 978-0-691-12747-7 ((hardcover) : alk. paper)
ISBN-10: 0-691-12747-6 ((hardcover) : alk. paper)
  1. Currency crises—United States—Case studies. 2. Currency question. 3. World War, 1914–1918—Finance. 4. McAdoo, William Gibbs, 1863–1941 5. Gold standard. I. Title.
  HG3903.S54 2007
  332.0973'09041—dc22   2006013076

British Library Cataloging-in-Publication Data is available

This book has been composed in Sabon

Printed on acid-free paper. ∞

pup.princeton.edu

Printed in the United States of America

10 9 8 7 6 5 4 3 2 1

For

Talia	Joseph
Leora	Joshua
Danielle	Jacob
Arianna	Jack
Rebecca	Evan

and

Lillian

With Love

It is impossible to be sure that a decision in August 1914 to suspend gold payments, even with the purpose of subsequently resuming them, would not have given to at least our immediately subsequent financial history a very different turn from that which it actually took.

Alexander Noyes, *The War Period of American Finance, 1926*

Contents

Acknowledgments

Historical research requires the help of dedicated individuals who pay attention to the details. I would like to thank my research assistants Yang Lu, Steven M. Pawliczek, and Josh Sullivan for helping to collect data and archival material. They cheerfully accommodated my numerous requests to revisit the same documents. Bruce Kirby of the Library of Congress, Nancy Paley of JP Morgan Chase, and Steven Wheeler of the New York Stock Exchange went out of their way to provide source material. This project could not have been completed without their enthusiastic assistance.

I imposed the task of reading my work in progress on a number of colleagues and friends. Adam Brandenberger, Allan Meltzer, Anna Schwartz, Thomas Sargent, Joachim Voth, Paul Wachtel, and Eugene White read the manuscript and offered thoughtful comments. I especially appreciated the memos they wrote that bristled. Steve Cecchetti, author of an excellent new textbook on money and banking, read the book in one sitting. I benefited from his enthusiasm and perceptive suggestions. I inflicted the first draft of every chapter on Dick Sylla. He took time away from his work on Alexander Hamilton to give me encouragement, advice, and lessons in grammar and history. Niall Ferguson read the manuscript as though it were his own. He explained what I really said in the eyes of a professional historian. I thank him for being a role model. My friend, David Weisbrot, a distinguished biologist, commented with his usual intellectual curiosity. I will miss his input in the future. Kenneth Garbade read and reread every single sentence and forced me to purge the fuzzy logic from every argument. He imposed a standard of rigor that, after more than thirty years of friendship, I recognize as a sign of affection. I have received far more than I have given during our lifetime collaboration.

The conversational style of this book benefited from years of training by the master of exposition, my late coauthor, friend, and mentor, Larry Ritter. The prose would have been clearer had he been able to comment. Peter Dougherty, the Director of Princeton University Press, and my editor, picked up some of the slack. And so did my wife, Lillian. She read all of the chapters and cleansed the manuscript of every misplaced metaphor she could find (I slipped in a few after her final review). The errors that remain reflect a stubborn streak that I try to suppress only moderately.

When Washington Shut Down Wall Street

The Legacy of 1914

THE GREAT WAR threatened the United States with financial disaster. During the last week of July 1914, Europeans began to liquidate their Wall Street investments and transfer gold to Europe to pay for the war. Foreign investors owned more than 20 percent of American railroad securities, the largest category of securities traded on the New York Stock Exchange.[1] Under the gold standard, they could demand the precious metal in exchange for the proceeds of their stock sales. The biggest gold outflow in a generation imperiled America's ability to repay its debts abroad. Fear that the United States would abandon the gold standard pushed the dollar to unprecedented depths on world markets.

The European assault on American finance brought danger and opportunity. In 1914 the United States was a debtor nation with a history of financial crises. Failure to meet its foreign obligations could sink American dreams of world monetary leadership. If it passed the test, however, the United States could jump to the head of the class.

Less than three weeks after the outbreak of the European conflict, Woodrow Wilson reviewed a road map for America's march to world financial supremacy. Henry Lee Higginson, an investment banker in Boston, wrote to the president on August 20, 1914, that "England has been the exchange place of the world, because of living up to every engagement, and because the power grew with the business. Today we can take this place if we choose; but courage, willingness to part with what we don't need at once, real character, and the living up to all our debts promptly will give us this power; and nothing else will. I repeat that it is our chance to take first place."[2] Wilson sent Higginson's letter to Treasury Secretary William G. McAdoo with the following covering message: "Here is a letter which is no doubt worth your reading whether you think the suggestions are practicable or not."[3]

McAdoo had, in fact, launched a plan to defend American financial honor before he received Higginson's letter from Wilson. This book traces William G. McAdoo's battle for American financial credibility during four months in 1914, from the end of July through the middle of November, a brief period that changed the course of U.S. financial history. McAdoo's strategy turned the financial crisis into a monetary triumph, and the story of his success provides a blueprint for crisis control that merits attention today.

In 1914 most developed countries—including Austria, Belgium, Britain, France, Germany, Italy, Japan, and Spain—could rely on central banks to fight their financial battles.[4] Even Czar Nicholas II had the Imperial Bank of Russia. The United States, without a central bank since 1836, after Andrew Jackson scuttled the Second Bank of the United States, resembled a headless financial giant. The Federal Reserve System, authorized by Congress on December 23, 1913, remained on the drawing board. It could have been a classic power vacuum, especially with President Woodrow Wilson distracted by his wife's fatal illness.

McAdoo seized the opportunity to confront the panic. He maintained America's commitment to the gold standard while every other country of the world, save for Britain, abandoned it because of the war. The boost to the dollar's credibility helped America challenge Britain as the financial capital of the world. November 11, 1914, the day the dollar's discount disappeared on world markets, and four years to the day before the Armistice, marks the turning point in America's battle for international financial leadership. In January 1915 the New York capital market replaced London as money lender to the world. Argentina, Canada, and China, traditional British clients, visited Wall Street to raise capital.[5] By the time America entered the world conflict in 1917, foreign governments issued more than $2.5 billion of dollar-denominated securities in New York.* A decade would pass before the transfer of financial power was complete, but a tectonic shift in monetary supremacy had begun.

How important was the gold standard at the outbreak of the Great War? John Maynard Keynes said that London's position as the world's leading financial center would surely be jeopardized if Britain suspended gold payments. He advised the British government that "we should not repudiate our external obligations to pay gold until it is physically impossible for us to fulfill them."[6] Keynes knew that capital markets forgive a country that suspends specie payments during wartime as long as it resumes its obligation after the emergency has passed.[7] But a financial superpower must meet a higher standard.[8]

Britain ruled world finance in 1914. Two characteristics—the pound sterling as international money and London as global moneylender— qualified Britain for the world financial crown. The pound served as the currency of choice for international transactions, just as the dollar does today, and borrowers throughout the world visited the City of London,

---

* Chapter 9 shows that America's role in world finance between 1915 and 1917 compares favorably with Britain's record immediately prior to 1914.

rather than Wall Street, to raise capital. The war would force London, at least temporarily, to stop supplying capital abroad but, according to Keynes, it could continue as king of international finance by insuring that sterling remained as good as gold. Britain signaled its intention in August 1914 to continue as the world's financial superpower by following Keynes's advice.

Treasury Secretary McAdoo recognized America's opportunity to shine by remaining true to gold, just like the world's monetary superpower. The United States had hoped to join the international financial elite since the turn of the twentieth century. McAdoo's entrepreneurial skill would turn the dream into reality.

William Gibbs McAdoo was born in Marietta, Georgia, in 1863.[9] He moved to Knoxville, Tennessee, in 1877, when his father became a professor of history and English at the University of Tennessee. McAdoo entered the University of Tennessee in 1879 and joined the debating society. The upperclassmen saddled McAdoo, a freshman with "a chip on his shoulder," with defending the unpopular side of every issue.[10] He enjoyed the limelight and knew that he wanted to be a lawyer. His heart settled on studying at the University of Virginia in Charlottesville, the best law program in the country from where McAdoo sat. That was before he discussed it with his father, William G. McAdoo Sr.

During the Christmas holidays in 1881 young Will McAdoo worked in the U.S. Circuit Court at Knoxville. He was then offered a permanent job as deputy clerk in the U.S. Circuit Court at Chattanooga. His father urged him to take the job "to learn law from actual contact with the courts."[11] In May 1882 McAdoo left Knoxville for Chattanooga, one year shy of his college degree. He never got to Charlottesville.

McAdoo was admitted to the bar in Chattanooga but did not practice law for very long. His father's advice to study law by apprenticeship imprinted a pragmatic gene deep inside his brain. It altered his life.

William McAdoo abandoned his fledgling legal career for the business world. To overcome his abbreviated academic training, McAdoo mastered the details of every prospective venture. At age thirty, before launching a plan to electrify the Knoxville Street Railroad, he learned how to calculate electric power and how dynamos are set up. Despite McAdoo's preparation, the venture failed and wiped out his life savings.[12] Ten years later, before he undertook to build a railroad line under the Hudson River, he investigated an abandoned tunnel dressed in rubber hip boots and yellow oilskins and brandishing an oil lantern. This time McAdoo's groundwork succeeded. As president of the Hudson & Manhattan Railroad Company, he inaugurated passenger rail service between Manhattan and New Jersey in 1908. After McAdoo became Woodrow Wilson's treasury secretary in 1913, his practical bent helped to avert the monetary crisis that began with the outbreak of war in the summer of 1914.

How did McAdoo manage the crisis?

The absence of a central bank hampered America's defenses. McAdoo tried to get the Federal Reserve System up and running to combat the danger. Benjamin Strong, governor-elect of the powerful Federal Reserve Bank of New York and a leading figure during the formative years of the central bank, wanted to protect the new currency system from the crisis. He blocked McAdoo's push for an early opening of the Federal Reserve Banks. The reversal, however, set the stage for McAdoo's improvisational skills. He rushed tons of gold to treasury offices around the country to trumpet America's commitment to redeem dollars in the precious metal.[13] He orchestrated a rescue of New York City from the brink of bankruptcy, introducing the "Too Big to Fail" doctrine in American finance.* McAdoo's pragmatism could have produced a jigsaw puzzle of confusion. Instead, his entrepreneurship created a formula for crisis control that belongs in every policy maker's playbook.

Failure to respond promptly to a crisis spells disaster. A financial panic spreads like an epidemic. On July 31, 1914, McAdoo shut the New York Stock Exchange for an unprecedented four months to hamper British sales of American securities. The British could not drain American gold without the dollar proceeds from sales of U.S. stocks and bonds. On August 3 he flooded the country with paper currency to prevent a repetition of the bank runs that had embarrassed America only a few years earlier, during the Panic of 1907. Banks had been forced to suspend the convertibility of their deposits into currency when they could not meet depositor demands for cash during October 1907. Banks avoided suspending their obligations in 1914 by offering depositors the emergency currency dispensed under McAdoo's orders.†

William McAdoo knew, however, that these finger-in-the-dike measures could not remain in place forever. Shutting the stock exchange immobilized the capital market, and unlimited supplies of emergency currency tempted inflation. McAdoo recognized that he needed an exit strategy to replace these powerful weapons before they disrupted the economy. He understood that the gold drain could be reversed by promoting American exports of agricultural goods to offset European sales of U.S. securities. On August 14, 1914, McAdoo met with businessmen

---

* Chapter 7 describes how McAdoo helped New York City meet its maturing bond obligations to British and French investors.

† McAdoo implemented the emergency currency provisions of the Aldrich-Vreeland Act. The legislation had been passed in May 1908 to avoid a repetition of the Panic of 1907. This is the only time the Aldrich-Vreeland Act was used. Chapters 3 and 4 provide a detailed explanation.

at the Treasury to arrange for "sufficient ships to move our grain and cotton crops to European markets."[14] The conference created the Bureau of War Risk Insurance, which supported the dollar's redemption in the foreign exchange market. As 1914 drew to a close, the flood of emergency currency receded and the New York Stock Exchange reopened. McAdoo had tamed the crisis without inflicting collateral damage.

How did the summer of 1914 change history?

A suspension of the gold standard in 1914 would have been a setback to American dreams of international financial leadership. The Panic of 1907 had already damaged U.S. credibility. A panic in 1914 would have been the second act in an American financial tragedy. Alexander Noyes, the contemporary business editor of the *New York Times*, appropriately highlighted the drama: "It is not too much to say that as a matter of financial history, the United States stood during those two or three weeks of August at the parting of the ways."[15] Suspending the gold standard would have relegated the dollar to second-class status, and sterling would have remained the undisputed money of choice for international finance.

Europe needed American capital to fight the Great War, but excess capital does not equate to a new monetary standard. Oil-rich Saudi Arabia helped finance American deficits during the 1970s, but the Saudi riyal never challenged the U.S. dollar as the international medium of exchange. Moreover, Britain did not need an abundance of capital after the war to retake first place as moneylender to the world. Financial institutions, such as banks and insurance companies, lend money by mobilizing the savings of others, committing only a few cents of their own in the process. Britain had the financial machinery and expertise to do the same.

America would have dominated world finance during the last half of the twentieth century even if it had abandoned gold in August 1914. The financial burden of the Second World War and the erosion of the British Empire doomed sterling. However, the 1920s and the 1930s would have evolved quite differently had William G. McAdoo not enhanced American financial credibility at the outbreak of the Great War.

With New York wounded by failure in 1914, London could have avoided setting a timetable for restoring a fully operational gold standard after the war. Britain could have followed Keynes's advice in 1925 and not pushed sterling into its prewar parity with the dollar.* Keynes felt that battling New York for world financial supremacy in 1925 imposed too great a cost on the British economy. He wrote to a director of the Bank of England: "Are you sure that you want London to be at any

---

* Keynes did not oppose the gold standard per se but wanted to avoid the deflationary consequences of forcing a return to the prewar parity of $4.8665 per pound sterling. Chapter 9 discusses Keynes's position in detail.

time the dumping ground of unlimited cheap American money liable to be withdrawn at a day's notice?"[16] Keynes was right. Sterling's return to gold forced Britain into a deflationary straightjacket that exacerbated the Great Depression.[17]

What can 1914 teach us about crisis management?

McAdoo succeeded in August 1914 because he did not hesitate to bludgeon the crisis with a sledgehammer. He wielded powerful weapons—suspending stock trading for four months and flooding the country with emergency currency—that could have injured America. His exit plan, stimulating agricultural exports with the Bureau of War Risk Insurance, avoided lasting damage to the economy. McAdoo could apply massive force because he had implemented a plan to restore normal functions. Failure to include a strategy for withdrawal either promotes toothless emergency weapons, like a placebo to treat a serious disease, or imposes unnecessary costs.

McAdoo brought more than a blueprint and sledgehammer to the crisis. Walter Lippmann, the political commentator and nationally syndicated columnist, described McAdoo as someone who is "swift to note and swift to move. He picks his course quickly, moves fast upon it and with great audacity. . . . Instinctively he prefers the bold and the decisive to the prudent and the tepid course."*

Not everyone has the courage to act, even when they know what to do. Leadership matters. The 1970s witnessed the greatest peacetime inflation in the United States. The Federal Reserve System had been in operation for more than half a century when inflation spiraled out of control. Arthur Burns, a former Columbia University economist and president of the National Bureau of Economic Research, sat at the helm of the Federal Reserve System for nearly the entire decade. He had been appointed chairman of the Federal Reserve Board by President Richard Nixon in 1970. Economists knew how to stem the inflation that threatened to destroy American economic stability. According to Milton Friedman, the problem was not lack of knowledge but, rather, lack of leadership:[18] "The explanation for [the Great Inflation] is fundamentally political, not economic. . . . I believe that Arthur Burns deserves a lot of the blame, and he deserves the blame because he knew better."[19]

The American financial system could have survived the summer of 1914 even if McAdoo had done nothing. The gold drain would have disappeared as the war forced Britain to America's doorstep for provisions.

* Lippmann's description (1927, 113) first appeared in an essay dated June 1920, when McAdoo's name was bandied about as the Democratic Party's presidential nominee. McAdoo withdrew his name from consideration, in part, out of deference for the ailing incumbent, Woodrow Wilson; see "A News Report, June 20, 1920," *Papers of Woodrow Wilson* (1991, 438–39).

But the clarity of hindsight ignores contingencies that failed to materialize. Alexander Noyes, in his retrospective a decade later, emphasized the point: "It should not be forgotten that the financial outlook for the United States seemed desperate, even to a great part of the banking community, at the time when maintenance of gold payments was agreed on. . . . [I]t is impossible to be sure that a decision in August 1914 to suspend gold payments, even with the purpose of subsequently resuming them, would not have given to at least our immediately subsequent financial history a very different turn from that which it actually took."[20]

McAdoo's imprint—decisive leadership combined with a road map for crisis control—turned a potential financial disaster into a monetary triumph.

CHAPTER ONE

The Opening Salvo

LATE THURSDAY AFTERNOON on July 30, 1914, two days after Austria declared war on Serbia, America's banking elite marched into the headquarters of the Morgan bank at 23 Wall Street. Following a chaotic decline of 6 percent in stock prices during the day, J. P. Morgan Jr. had summoned A. Barton Hepburn, chairman of the Chase National Bank; Francis L. Hine, president of the First National Bank; and Benjamin Strong Jr., president of the Bankers Trust Company and future governor of the Federal Reserve Bank of New York.[21] J. P. Morgan Sr. had called a similar meeting on October 24, 1907, during the height of that year's panic.[22] The death of Morgan Sr. in 1913 meant that Wall Street now lay in the untested hands of Morgan Jr.

No notes survive from Thursday's meeting, but the front page of the next day's *New York Times* carried a headline that read: "Bankers Here Confer on War: Closing of Stock Exchange Not Necessary, Meeting at Morgan Offices Decides." After the meeting, J. P. Morgan Jr. left for a yachting party, and Henry Davison, a key Morgan partner schooled in the 1907 crisis by Morgan Sr., escaped from lower Manhattan's humidity to his Long Island retreat.[23]

On the morning of the reassuring headline, however, the governing board of the New York Stock Exchange voted to close less than fifteen minutes before the scheduled ten o'clock opening bell. The New York Stock Exchange remained shut from July 31 until December 12, 1914, longer by four months than any other suspension in the Big Board's 200-year history. According to Henry Noble, president of the New York Stock Exchange, "If at any time up to July, 1914, any Wall Street man had asserted that the stock exchange could be kept closed continually for four and one-half months he would have been laughed to scorn."[24]

What happened between the Thursday afternoon meeting at Morgan's offices on July 30 and Friday morning that forced Henry Noble to announce the suspension of trading?

War among the Great Powers—Britain, France, Germany, and Russia—remained in doubt when the exchange closed. The main headline in the August 1 *New York Times* read: "Czar, Kaiser and King May Yet Arrange Peace."[25] In contrast, on October 24, 1907, when Morgan Sr. ordered that the exchange "must not close one minute before its usual time,"[26] the New York Stock Exchange never suspended trading even though the crisis was well underway.[27] Did J. P. Morgan Jr. carry that much less influence than his father?

The press softened the slight to Morgan Jr.'s reputation by reporting that dramatic overnight developments forced the exchange to review the decision to stay open on July 31: "There had been no call for the meeting [of the exchange's governing board], and the understanding was that the Exchange would open as usual . . . but the discovery that the market was loaded down with big selling orders and almost bare of buying orders . . . alarmed the brokers so much that they hurried upstairs to urge a reconsideration of the decision to remain open."[28] Exchange president Henry Noble confirmed this account in his 1915 retrospective on the crisis: "Many members of prominent firms appeared in the [meeting] room to report that orders to sell stocks at ruinous prices were pouring in upon them from all over the world and that security holders were in a state of panic."[29]

The facts contradict this version of events.

SLOW DANCE TO WAR

The spark that ignited World War I, the assassination in Sarajevo of Austria's Archduke Franz Ferdinand and his wife, the Duchess of Hohenberg, smoldered for a month. Gavrilo Princip, a Bosnian-Serb nationalist, shot the archduke and his wife on June 28, 1914. Earlier that morning, the royal couple had escaped an attempt on their lives when the archduke deflected a bomb thrown at his car.

The day after the murder, the *New York Times* headline explained: "Heir to Austria's Throne Slain with His Wife by a Bosnian Youth to Avenge Seizure of His Country."[30] The seizure of Bosnia occurred in 1908 when Austria-Hungary annexed both Bosnia and Herzegovina, angering ethnic Serbians living in the region. Bosnia's Serbs wanted to be united with the neighboring Kingdom of Serbia.* On June 30 the *Times* front page announced: "See Serb Plot in Royal Murders: Killing of the Archduke and His Wife Believed to Have Been Planned in Belgrade." The *Times* added melodrama by publishing the archduke's final

---

* In 1878 the Treaty of Berlin awarded the former Turkish provinces of Bosnia and Herzegovina to the empire of Austria-Hungary "to occupy and administer." In 1908 Austria-Hungary annexed the provinces. A number of secret societies (including the Black Hand) emerged within the Kingdom of Serbia and in the Austrian province of Bosnia to agitate for Bosnia's independence (see Remak 1959, 30ff.).

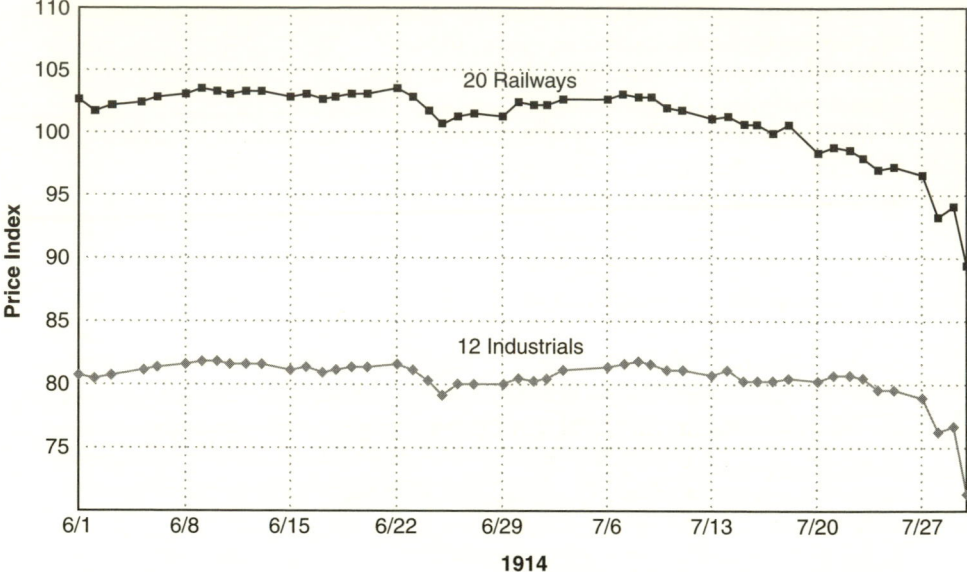

Figure 1.1. Stock Prices on the New York Stock Exchange, June and July 1914.

Data Source: *Wall Street Journal.*

words to his wife: "Sophie, remain alive for our children."[31] Nevertheless, the crisis slipped to the back burner until the July 23 Austrian
Ultimatum to Serbia demanding punishment of those responsible for
the crime in Sarajevo.

Figure 1.1 shows the lazy path of stock prices on the New York Stock
Exchange from the beginning of June until the last week of July, confirming investor indifference.* European investors owned more than $4 bil-
lion of U.S. railroad securities in 1914, representing more than 20 percent
of the largest category of securities on the New York Stock Exchange.[32]
They could have driven down stock prices by selling only a small fraction
of their holdings. Stocks ignored the June 28 assassination perhaps because the recent Balkan wars had left mostly local scars. Bulgaria, Serbia,
Greece, Romania, and Turkey had fought in 1912 and 1913 without
arousing the Great Powers. The murder of the archduke did not disturb
European investors until it was almost too late.[33]

---

* Figure 1.1 shows the index of twelve industrial stocks and twenty railroad stocks, as
published in the *Wall Street Journal.* The industrial index, currently called the Dow Jones
Industrial Average, was expanded to thirty stocks in 1928. The railroad index, currently
called the Dow Jones Transportation Average, was renamed in 1970 to reflect its broader
composition.

On July 24, 1914, the front page of the *Times* reported a European showdown: "Austria Ready to Invade Serbia, Sends Ultimatum." The Ultimatum, delivered to the Serbian government in Belgrade at 6 p.m. on Thursday, June 23, demanded "The punishment of all accomplices in the murder of Archduke Francis Ferdinand and the suppression of all societies which have fomented rebellion in Bosnia."[34] The diplomatic confrontation provoked European investors. The *Wall Street Journal* reported "sales of American securities by European holders who have been frightened by the strained relations obtaining between [Serbia] and Austria-Hungary."[35] Prices fell by half of 1 percent on July 23 and by 1 percent the following day.

When Austria declared war on Serbia on Tuesday, July 28, stock prices registered the largest setback of the year to date—a decline of 3.5 percent.* The declaration of war triggered reports of German and Russian troop mobilization. On Thursday, July 30, prices sank another 6 percent, the biggest one-day drop since March 14, 1907, during a "rich-man's panic."[†] The *Wall Street Journal* attributed the collapse that began in the last hour of trading to news that "Germany had demanded of Russia an explanation for the massing of troops on the frontier, setting a twenty-four hour time limit for a reply."[36] The report did not, however, prevent the "business as usual" edict from Morgan offices on the afternoon of July 30, 1914.

Would the closing rout have been extended the following morning? No one knows for sure because the New York Stock Exchange Governing Board voted to close on July 31 at 9:45 a.m., but the evidence suggests prices would have stabilized.

---

* The 3.5 percent drop on July 28 is large by conventional measures of statistical significance, but the previous week's declines are not. The daily standard deviation of returns during the first six months of 1914 measured .642 percent for the index of twelve industrial companies and .597 percent for the index of twenty railroads. Thus, changes in industrial stock prices are significant if they move by more than 1.26 percent per day (1.96 times .642) and railroad price movements are significant if they move by more than 1.17 percent per day (1.96 times .597). The two-day return, from the close on July 22 through the close on July 24, potentially relevant because the Austrian ultimatum was delivered at 6 p.m. local time (while the New York Stock Exchange could still react), is also not statistically significant.

† The decline on March 14, 1907, of 8.29 percent in the industrials (see Siegel 1998, 183) was called a rich-man's panic by A. Barton Hepburn, president of the Chase National Bank: "It is a rich man's panic and the results, however serious, will not be disastrous" (*New York Times*, March 15, 1907, 2). Sprague (1910, 241) applies the phrase to the entire month of March 1907. Stock price declines during 1903 were also labeled a rich man's panic (see *New York Times*, November 8, 1903, WF2). On July 30, 1914, the index of twelve industrial stocks declined by 6.9 percent and the index of twenty railroad stocks declined by 5 percent. Both declines are statistically significant.

European investors wanted to sell their U.S. stocks on the morning of July 31, 1914. The press reported that at least $100 million of American securities were thrown onto the market by foreign investors.[37] But more than enough American buyers stepped into the breach. The *Wall Street Journal* reported:[38] "Most of the brokers in the Street had large volumes of buy orders and much disappointment was expressed by bargain hunters that the Exchange failed to open."* Who were the bargain hunters? The *New York Times* headline "Shorts Eager to Buy" gave the answer.[39] The "shorts"—traders who had sold stock the previous week at high prices but did not own the shares they sold—wanted to buy at low prices so that they could deliver the stock they sold. The *Times* emphasized their anxiety by adding that the shorts "feared that the Stock Exchange would not reopen until stock prices rose again."[40]

Why did the New York Stock Exchange Governing Board vote to close at 9:45 Friday morning, July 31, if stocks were not about to crash? Saturday's newspapers reported that Treasury Secretary William G. McAdoo "issued a statement in which he approved of the closing of the Stock Exchange."[41] In fact, McAdoo did much more than just approve. On the morning of July 31, J. P. Morgan Jr. had called another meeting of Wall Street's bankers to discuss overnight developments. At 9:30 he telephoned McAdoo. The treasury secretary told him to close the exchange.[42] Morgan then relayed the message to the governing board only minutes before the opening bell.

The decision to remain open on Thursday afternoon had originated with the bankers at Morgan offices. The reversal at the New York Stock Exchange on Friday morning came from Washington. McAdoo wanted the exchange shut and J. P. Morgan made it happen.

McAdoo did not disclose his telephone call with Morgan until many years later,[43] but within days the *New York Times* publicized Treasury's

---

* Additional evidence that prices would have stabilized on July 31 comes from the Consolidated Stock Exchange. The Consolidated Stock Exchange, in business since 1875, opened as usual, at 9:30 a.m., on the morning of July 31, 1914. It closed at 10 a.m. after the New York Stock Exchange announced it would not open. The Consolidated Stock Exchange specialized in trading odd lots (units of less than 100 shares) of NYSE-listed companies. Six stocks traded between 9:30 and 10:00 a.m. on the exchange. Two rose in price, two fell, and two were unchanged (see Silber 2006). European investors would not have directed their sell orders to the Consolidated Exchange—only a few hundred shares of each stock usually traded during the first half hour—but with selling pressure in the air, buyers would have lowered their bids while waiting for the New York Stock Exchange to open. The stability of opening prices on the Consolidated Stock Exchange confirms the press reports that buyers had emerged in the marketplace.

sentiments as though it had been eavesdropping on the conversation: "It would not surprise officials in Washington if Mr. McAdoo used his influence in New York to keep the New York Stock Exchange closed for some time. No direct proposal of this kind may be made but he is expected to show that the Government does not look kindly upon the reopening of the exchange at this time."[44]

Why did Treasury Secretary McAdoo shut the exchange on July 31 and keep it closed for an unprecedented four and one-half months?

HONORING THE GOLD STANDARD

William G. McAdoo learned the value of silence early in his career. Three months after he was admitted to the bar at Chattanooga in January 1885, he won his first court case by offering a number of convincing arguments in favor of his client. Later that day, the tall and wiry young attorney walked up the street with Judge Trewitt, a wise old jurist who had presided in the case. McAdoo recalls: "I was all puffed up with success and I hoped the Judge would compliment me . . . but he did not say a word. Finally, I said: 'Judge, how did I try my case?' He stopped, turned towards me and said with great emphasis: 'My boy, never prove a case but once.' "[45]

Judge Trewitt's message, one convincing argument is sufficient, paid dividends years later when McAdoo visited J. P. Morgan Sr. to raise money for his Hudson & Manhattan Railroad Company. McAdoo had already completed building the tunnels connecting Manhattan and Hoboken, New Jersey, and now needed financing to inaugurate passenger rail service. It was 1906 and a favorable nod from Morgan Sr. could make all the difference. McAdoo arrived at Morgan's office with inner trepidation: "I feared that I would be unable to convince this emperor of finance and would be responsible for a failure." Morgan greeted McAdoo cordially and listened to his presentation. At the end McAdoo recalled: "I finished what I had to say and waited. He seemed to be willing to hear more, but I remembered from long ago Judge Trewitt's advice. . . . It is very easy to talk a good proposition to death. After a moment of silence Mr. Morgan asked a few pertinent questions . . . [but] did not say a word of approval or disapproval." Some days later Morgan agreed to take $1 million in preferred stock. The financing was a success and the tunnels opened for business on February 25, 1908.[46]

McAdoo took Judge Trewitt's advice to Washington. On August 1, 1914, his press release approved the closing of the New York Stock

Exchange but said no more.[47] Most people assumed he approved the shutdown to avoid a crash.* He did not want to reveal his main concern.

McAdoo did not care about stock prices. He worried only about the identity of the buyers and sellers.[48] He knew that Europeans, primarily British and French investors, would try to sell their U.S. stocks in New York, the only marketplace in the world still open on the morning of July 31.† And he also knew that American investors would have snapped up the bargains, perhaps because they had sold short, as reported in the press. Stocks had already declined by 10 percent since the European crisis began.[49]

McAdoo worried that British and French investors would take the dollar proceeds of their stock sales and withdraw gold from the American banking system, as was their right under the gold standard. With banks holding only a fraction of their deposits in reserves, there simply was not enough gold to go around. National banks had a total of $1,003 million in gold or gold equivalents as of June 30, 1914.[50] European sales of 25 percent of their $4 billion in American securities would have swept away the gold like a deadly avalanche.

Under the gold standard, paper currency and bank checking accounts could be exchanged for gold at a fixed price. In 1914, before dollar bills in the form of Federal Reserve notes came into existence, circulating currency came from the U.S. Treasury and from certain commercial banks. The U.S. Treasury issued paper currency called gold certificates, silver certificates, and U.S. notes (greenbacks). The Treasury promised to redeem all of its paper currency in gold bullion or gold coin, like the famous twenty-dollar coin called the double eagle, at subtreasury offices around the country at a rate of $20.67 in paper currency per ounce of gold. The double eagle contained slightly less than an ounce of gold.

---

* A number of prominent economic and financial historians said prices would have declined. Sprague (1915, 513), in a follow-up to his classic 1910 study of crises under the National Banking System, applauds the decision to close the exchange: "If the stock exchange had not closed on Friday, July 31, it is certain that the decline in the price of securities during the day would have been so extreme as to have occasioned numerous failures of brokers and their customers and presumably much loss to the banks as well." Friedman and Schwartz (1963, 172) accept Sprague's account of the crisis. Chandler (1958, 55), in his celebrated biography of Benjamin Strong, extends Sprague's observation: "A general money panic would almost certainly have occurred if the Exchange remained open with falling security prices, widespread calling of loans collateralized by securities, and large foreign sales increasing the burden of foreign payments." See Silber (2006) for evidence to the contrary.

† Montreal, Toronto, and Madrid closed on July 28; Vienna, Budapest, Brussels, Antwerp, Berlin, and Rome closed on July 29; St. Petersburg, the Paris Bourse, and all the South American countries were shut on July 30; and London closed on the morning of July 31 before New York (Noble 1915, 9). An exception: "The Paris *Parquet* remained . . . open to a certain extent up to the impending evacuation of Paris by the Government on September 2nd" (Keynes 1914, 461).

Commercial banks chartered by the Office of the Comptroller of the Currency in the U.S. Treasury issued paper currency called national bank notes. Banks promised to redeem their national bank notes in "lawful money"—either gold coin or any paper currency issued by the U.S. Treasury (which could then be turned into gold at a local subtreasury office).[51] Thus all types of currency could be exchanged for gold at the rate of $20.67 per ounce.

Bank checking accounts, the dominant means of payment even in 1914, could also be converted into gold.[52] A person could cash a check at a local bank and receive a dollar of currency for each dollar in a checking account. Banks held reserves in the form of "lawful money," gold coin or Treasury currency, to insure that they could pay out cash on demand. Thus checking deposits could be exchanged for gold at the rate of $20.67 per ounce, either directly, by receiving a double eagle from the bank, or indirectly, by exchanging the Treasury paper currency received at the bank into gold at the local subtreasury office. Banks were required to hold only a fraction of their deposits in reserves, 25 percent for the large New York banks.[53] A bank did not want to hold more reserves than necessary because reserves do not earn interest. They rarely needed more because deposits and withdrawals tended to balance each other.

The gold standard prevented a country from depreciating the value of its currency by printing more than it could promise to redeem in gold. It held the price level in check like a giant anchor. In 1914 the British pound had been tied to gold for about 200 years.[54] The value of the pound in 1914 was not that much different from its value in 1714, when Sir Isaac Newton was in charge of the British mint.[55] Countries adhering to the gold standard could borrow money in world capital markets at relatively low interest rates.[56] Lenders were confident they would not be repaid in depreciated currency.

The gold standard provided protection against inflation but not against crises. Banks could not pay gold on demand if everyone wanted to cash in at the same time. Crises frequently forced countries to abandon the convertibility of their currency into gold. It was understood that a country could leave the gold standard during wartime, without a lasting penalty to its reputation, as long as it returned after hostilities ended.[57] The capital markets recognized that combatants needed flexibility to finance a war. Britain suspended the convertibility of its currency during the Napoleonic Wars and America did the same during the Civil War.[58]

The Austrian Ultimatum of July 23, 1914, sent European investors fleeing from dollars into the safety of gold. During the last week of July, American gold exports to Europe exceeded $25 million, a larger outflow in a week than in all but three months between 1900 and 1914.[59] Gold exports would grow as Europe foraged for resources to fight the war.

McAdoo could have short-circuited the European run on America's store of precious metal by suspending the gold standard. His problem was American neutrality. The United States did not enter the war until April 1917. In August 1914, America had no excuse for abandoning its commitment to gold. Moreover, a suspension would damage America's financial credibility at a time when the United States could least afford the setback. America stood at the brink of launching a new currency arrangement—the Federal Reserve System. McAdoo shut the New York Stock Exchange on July 31, 1914, to buy time. He wanted to prevent European investors from forcing America off the gold standard.

McADOO'S DILEMMA

Congress had passed the Federal Reserve Act on December 23, 1913, to protect America against financial crises. The United States had been without a central bank since 1836, after Congress failed to override President Andrew Jackson's veto of the bill that would have rechartered the Second Bank of the United States. America paid for its seventy-five year experiment in financial anarchy with a crisis-prone banking system. The panics of 1873, 1884, 1893, and 1907 had embarrassed American financial institutions.[60] Administrative delays had kept the Federal Reserve System on the drawing board for more than eight months. The original legislation had omitted crucial details to avoid endless congressional debate, including the precise number of Federal Reserve districts—the act specified between eight and twelve—and the location of the district Reserve Banks. On July 31, 1914, America needed an institution like the Bank of England, the Bank of France, or the Imperial Bank of Germany to help combat the financial crisis.

McAdoo knew that a central bank could protect the country's gold stock. He recalled the hearings he had conducted in January 1914 while touring the country as chairman of the Organizing Committee under the Federal Reserve Act. The act had established an organizing committee to implement the new currency system. McAdoo had come to New York on January 6, 1914, to hear the views of bankers and businessmen about the location of the individual Federal Reserve Banks.[61] He had heard J. P. Morgan argue in favor of a powerful Federal Reserve Bank of New York. But the words that stuck in his mind came from Max May, vice-president at the Guaranty Trust Company in charge of foreign exchange operations.

May said that it was important to have a strong bank in New York because "the purpose of the Act is to control the money markets of the United States, and also those of Europe, to some extent. To influence Europe the bank must be large."[62] May added: "This was a most important feature inasmuch as it involved control of the international gold movement."[63]

McAdoo then asked: "How is the movement controlled now?"[64] In response, May said: "Mostly, we lock the stable after the cow is stolen. . . . After the gold has moved out of the country the money rates go up to make them higher than Europe, where the gold is flowing."[65]

McAdoo regretted how easily Max May could parody America's impotence. In Britain, the Bank of England could try to prevent an outflow of gold by raising the interest rate before the damage was done. The Bank of England had, in fact, doubled its rate from 4 to 8 percent on July 31, 1914.[66]

McAdoo needed the Federal Reserve System to help fight America's financial battles, and he used the press release that approved the closing of the New York Stock Exchange to reinforce that view: "After a conference with the President, Secretary McAdoo expressed the belief that there should be no further serious delay in getting the new reserve bank system fully organized. . . . The international character of the Federal Reserve banks under the new law is broad and flexible in the matter of dealing with gold coin and bullion."[67]

Shutting the exchange on July 31 was a lot easier than keeping it shut. The Panic of 1873 had closed the New York Stock Exchange for the longest period to date—ten days.[68] McAdoo would need more time than that to organize the Federal Reserve System. Determined opposition to a quick opening would arise from Benjamin Strong, soon-to-be named first governor (chief executive officer) of the Federal Reserve Bank of New York, and from Paul Warburg, a Wall Street financier nominated to the Federal Reserve Board by President Wilson. They worried about endangering the birth of the new currency system.* Some businessmen believed "that the organization of the Reserve System [should] be deferred until the return of more normal conditions."[69]

McAdoo delegated the job of padlocking the exchange to its president, Henry Noble. Noble worked hard at the job but almost destroyed McAdoo's objectives. Meanwhile, the treasury secretary walked a tightrope: he had to organize the Federal Reserve System to smother the monetary crisis without endangering the system's viability.

McAdoo did not know then that he would have to defeat the crisis alone.

* Chapter 8 details the battle of McAdoo versus Strong and Warburg.

LAUNCHING THE FEDERAL RESERVE BOARD

William G. McAdoo should have had no trouble establishing the new currency system. The Organizing Committee created by the Federal Reserve Act consisted of the secretary of the Treasury, the secretary of agriculture, and the comptroller of the currency. Since two of the three members of the Organizing Committee satisfied a quorum and since the comptroller of the currency served under the treasury secretary, McAdoo could easily have had his way. Moreover, the Federal Reserve Act authorized the treasury secretary himself to determine when to open the Reserve Banks. Why didn't McAdoo just pick a date?

The Federal Reserve System came in thirteen separate pieces—a board located in Washington, D.C, and twelve individual Federal Reserve Banks spread throughout the United States. The individual Reserve Banks were real banks with assets and liabilities, just like commercial banks, except their only customers were the banks who were members of the system. In fact, the member commercial banks technically owned the Federal Reserve Banks and actually elected their directors. The Federal Reserve Banks needed office space, vaults, and staff, among other things, before opening for business. McAdoo had to negotiate the opening date for the Reserve Banks with the officers of those institutions—a conflict that would last months.

The Federal Reserve Board, the government's watchdog within the system, needed only people to begin operation. The legislation specified that the Federal Reserve Board should consist of seven individuals appointed by the president, including the secretary of the Treasury and the comptroller of the currency as ex officio members.* The Federal Reserve Act designated the secretary of the Treasury as chairman of the Federal Reserve Board. McAdoo would occupy the same position as Paul Volcker and Alan Greenspan did during the last quarter of the twentieth century.†

To establish the board, President Wilson had submitted five nominees for confirmation in the Senate on June 15, 1914.[70] The Senate Banking

---

* Ex officio means that the treasury secretary and the comptroller serve as members of the board by virtue of their positions rather than by explicit appointment by the president to a term of office on the board. The president designated a governor of the board from among one of his five appointees to the board. The governor acted as the chief operating officer of the Federal Reserve Board. He also chaired the meetings in the absence of the treasury secretary.

† Neither Greenspan nor Volcker served as treasury secretary. The Federal Reserve Act was amended in the 1930s to separate the two positions. In a curious omission, the Federal Reserve Board's website (www.federalreserve.gov/bios/boardmembership.htm) fails to include McAdoo among its list of chairmen. Instead, it lists Charles S. Hamlin as the first chairman. McAdoo was, in fact, the chairman; Hamlin occupied the position of governor.

Committee quickly confirmed Adolph Miller, an economics professor at the University of California; W.P.G. Harding, a banker from Birmingham, Alabama; and Charles Hamlin, a Boston lawyer serving as an assistant treasury secretary. The two remaining nominations, Edward Jones, a close friend of the president's from Chicago and a director of the International Harvester Company, and Paul M. Warburg, a partner in Kuhn, Loeb, the powerful New York banking house, met considerable resistance in the Senate Banking Committee. They remained unconfirmed a week before the outbreak of the Great War.[71]

McAdoo had mostly himself to blame for the administration's predicament. He had lost Wilson's ear on potential candidates for the board to Colonel Edward M. House, the president's close friend and adviser. McAdoo had tried to dominate the new currency system even before it had been signed into law. He had met with Wilson on December 20, 1913, three days before the bill was passed, and wrote him a note afterward: "The immediate success of the new system depends almost wholly upon this Board. It must be composed not only of able men, but men who are in sympathy with purposes of the bill and the aims of the administration, and it is *essential* that they shall be acceptable to your Secretary of the Treasury."[72]

Wilson met with House two days later and said that he did not sympathize with McAdoo's desire for a board that would work in harmony with him.[73] The president wanted to remove the Federal Reserve Board from McAdoo's control.

Wilson did not think poorly of McAdoo; quite the opposite. In March 1914, McAdoo, seven years younger than the president and a widower with grown children, became engaged to the president's daughter Eleanor, twenty-five years younger than McAdoo. Wilson wrote to his intimate friend and confidante, Mary Allen Hulbert, in Paris: "Dearest Friend, Has the cable brought you news of Nellie's engagement to Mr. McAdoo, the Secretary of the Treasury? Of course it has. That is what the Paris edition of the *Herald* is for. The dear girl is the apple of my eye: no man is good enough for her. But McAdoo comes as near being so as any man could. I am therefore content, not that she is to leave us for him, but that she should have such prospects for happiness."[74]

McAdoo tendered his resignation to Wilson upon the engagement: "Mr. President, I think in the circumstances that I ought to resign after my marriage, and I should like you to think that my resignation is at your disposal, to take effect at your convenience."[75]

McAdoo hoped that Wilson would reject his offer to resign, but he had fallen under Eleanor's spell and would have accepted his fate. He had written to Ambassador Walter Page in London: "You can imagine what a happy man I am. As I tell all my friends, the days of miracles are not yet over, or I certainly could not have succeeded in winning the love of this wonderful girl, because she certainly is an unusually fine and lovable character. There aren't enough appropriate superlatives in the English language for me to give you a just description of her."[76]

Wilson did not disappoint McAdoo when he responded to his resignation offer: "You were appointed Secretary of the Treasury solely on your merit. No one imagined at the time that the present situation would arise. . . . You are now organizing the Federal Reserve Banks and engaged in other matters of vital public interest. Your resignation would be a serious blow."[77]

Wilson refused McAdoo's resignation but also refused to follow his recommendations to the Federal Reserve Board. Wilson knew how persuasive McAdoo could be and felt that the new currency system needed an independent voice to succeed. In June 1913, while the legislation to establish the Federal Reserve System still languished in the House Banking and Currency Committee, McAdoo tried to substitute a bill that would have made the central bank a bureau within the Treasury. Carter Glass, chairman of the House Banking and Currency Committee, complained to Wilson and convinced the president that to do so would make the bank a political tool.[78]

During the 1930s Congress would further insulate the central bank from politics by passing legislation to remove the treasury secretary and the comptroller of the currency from the Federal Reserve Board. An independent central bank helps to neutralize the tendency of politicians to spend first and pay later, a process that would depreciate the value of the currency without a vigilant central bank. The evolution of an independent Federal Reserve System in the United States confirms the wisdom of Wilson's original decision.

McAdoo's desire to dominate the Federal Reserve damaged his influence with the president. But McAdoo could not help trying to be a hero. He craved public approval even for his business ventures. As a young entrepreneur, McAdoo risked his life savings trying to bring electricity to the Knoxville Street Railroad. He felt proud that the citizens of Knoxville applauded his efforts, even though the failed venture left him penniless.[79] After moving to New York, McAdoo successfully tunneled under the Hudson River to provide passenger rail service connecting New York City with New Jersey. As president of the Hudson & Manhattan Railway Company, he created the corny slogan, "Let the Public Be Pleased," and demonstrated its sincerity by printing and publicly distributing 100,000 complaint forms.[80]

McAdoo had practiced socially responsible entrepreneurship long before it became fashionable. According to syndicated columnist Walter Lippmann, McAdoo is "the kind of man who likes enterprises more than profit."[81] When he became treasury secretary, McAdoo jumped at the opportunity to lead America to financial prominence. After he lost the battle to handpick members of the Federal Reserve Board, McAdoo buried his pride to help salvage Wilson's appointments.

Edward Jones of Chicago and Paul M. Warburg of New York remained unconfirmed in mid-July 1914, a month after the president had submitted their names. On July 11, the Senate Banking Committee voted 7–4 to reject Jones, a director of the International Harvester Company and former trustee of Princeton when Wilson headed the university. Farmers had sent letters to their senators protesting Jones's appointment because his company, then under indictment for antitrust violations, allegedly charged exorbitant prices for farm equipment. Warburg, a partner at the New York banking firm Kuhn, Loeb and an expert on central banking practice, had asked Wilson on July 6 to withdraw his name from consideration. Warburg resented the Senate Banking Committee's request for his (and Jones's) testimony, while the committee bowed to the reputation of Wilson's three other nominees.

Wilson refused to accept the setbacks. The *New York Times* headlined a battle: "For Open Fight on Warburg and Jones."[82] Senator Gilbert Hitchcock, Democratic senator from Nebraska and acting chairman of the Senate Banking Committee, voted against Jones, despite pressure from Wilson. The confrontation escalated. When the president questioned a statement released by the Senate committee, he provoked Hitchcock into saying: "If the President is correctly quoted, and if he doubts the accuracy of that statement, the confidential print of the testimony of Mr. Jones is at his disposal as are all confidential papers."[83]

Hitchcock's problem with Warburg was procedural: "The reason the Committee declines to take action on Mr. Warburg [is that] we can't get any definite information about him. All the Committee knows is that Mr. Warburg came to this country from Germany where his father was a leading banker and that his connection with Kuhn Loeb & Co. has enabled that firm to be eminently successful in European affairs. Mr. Warburg is said to be making between $300,000 and $500,000 a year from his connection with this firm. There are a number of questions the Committee would like to ask him. Unless we have this opportunity of questioning Mr. Warburg we will take no action whatever on his case."[84] "Radical" congressman Joe Eagle expressed his concern in less polite terms. He said that the problem with Warburg was that "he is a Jew, a German, a banker and an alien."[85]

On July 23, the day of the Austrian Ultimatum to Serbia, sustained opposition in the Senate forced Wilson to withdraw Jones's name from consideration.[86] The defeat in the Senate was a personal rebuke to Wilson, who had stuck by his good friend Edward Jones to the end. Warburg's continued refusal to meet with the Senate Banking Committee dimmed his prospects as well. Warburg's loss would damage Wilson, but spelled even more trouble for the Federal Reserve Board.

Warburg had been preparing for the job of central banker ever since he settled in the United States in 1905. On January 6, 1907, he published an article in the *New York Times* Annual Financial Review entitled "Defects and Needs of our Banking System."[87] Later, he helped Senator Nelson Aldrich, chairman of the U.S. National Monetary Commission, formulate the "Aldrich Plan" for a central bank.[88] Warburg favored a strong and independent central bank. When McAdoo launched his plan in mid-1913 to make the central bank a division of the Treasury, Warburg undermined the effort. He denounced the scheme in the "Mauretania Memorandum," and showed it to Wilson's adviser, Colonel Edward House, who happened to be sailing to Europe with Warburg on the *Mauretania*.[89]

The *New York Times* offered the following headline when trouble over the Warburg nomination first surfaced: "Call for Warburg as Balance Wheel."[90] The *Times* article explained: "The fear seems to be that unless men of high financial standing and great personal experience [such as Warburg] are included in the Board's membership, Mr. McAdoo and Mr. Williams [comptroller of the currency] will dominate its policy." The *Times* call for Warburg as a "balance wheel" was an understatement, as Warburg would soon become McAdoo's antagonist.[91]

Paul Warburg's pride prevented him from submitting to an inquisition by the Senate Banking Committee, but his desire to be a central banker sparked a plan. On July 23, the same day that President Wilson withdrew the name of Edward Jones from consideration by the Senate, Warburg penned the following letter to McAdoo: "Dear Mr. Secretary: May I hand you herewith copy of a paper which I wrote for the Senator. It contains: (1) A statement to the effect that my attitude does not involve any denying on my part the prerogative of the U.S. Senate; (2) The suggested basis of an agreement. The latter is in the form of a statement to be made by Senator Hitchcock preliminary to my appearing before the committee. . . . I hope that the Senator will be able to establish without much delay whether an agreement substantially on these lines will be feasible or whether any further attempt of reconciling the two sides must be definitely abandoned." Warburg added a postscript to McAdoo's letter: "I have not informed the Senator that I am communicating with you."[92]

What gave Warburg the confidence to conspire with McAdoo?

McAdoo had already demonstrated that he was a team player. After Wilson sided with Carter Glass's version of the currency bill in mid-1913 (perhaps with an assist from Warburg), McAdoo lobbied enthusiastically for Glass's legislation. Glass complimented him when recounting the fight to establish the Federal Reserve: "[McAdoo] was adept at persuading men [and did] effective missionary work to overcome obstructionists within Congress threatening to undermine the currency bill."[93]

McAdoo had also demonstrated his intolerance for prejudice of any kind. In 1909, as president of the Hudson & Manhattan Railroad, he followed a policy of equal opportunity employment well before it became the law of the land. He had said to his general superintendent, E. T. Munger: "Of course I want to run the road as economically as possible, but I am opposed to doing it at the expense of justice. Let's employ women as ticket sellers on the downtown lines and give them the same wages as men."[94] In 1911 McAdoo accepted the chairmanship of the National Citizens Committee. The committee's objective was to terminate an 1832 treaty with the Russian government because of Russia's discriminatory practices towards Catholics and Jews.[95] On December 6, 1911, the committee held a mass meeting in Carnegie Hall and adopted a resolution asking Congress to abrogate the treaty with Russia. McAdoo went to Washington with a subcommittee to present the resolution to Congress and to President Taft. McAdoo's subcommittee included Jacob Schiff, the senior partner of Kuhn, Loeb and Paul Warburg's brother-in-law.

On July 29, five days after Warburg had sent his note to Senator Hitchcock, with the Machiavellian copy to McAdoo, Hitchcock stopped in New York on his way back to Washington from his vacation in Southampton, Long Island and, while there, met with Warburg. Afterward, when Hitchcock was asked whether Warburg had agreed to appear before the committee, he said: "No, but he seemed to understand after our talk just how the Committee felt toward him, and that there had been no discrimination against him, and he indicated in every way that he would be willing to appear. I believe Mr. Warburg's attitude has been changed by the explanation I have been able to make to him."[96]

CONGRESS CLOSES RANKS

To help fight the financial panic, Wilson and McAdoo wanted "no further serious delay in getting the new reserve bank system fully organized." Wilson asked Attorney General McReynolds whether the board could be sworn in for duty with only five members, the three that had already been approved by the Senate—Miller, the economics professor from the University of California; Harding, the banker from Birmingham; and Hamlin, the former assistant treasury secretary—plus ex officio members McAdoo and Comptroller Williams. McReynolds ruled that the Federal Reserve Act required the confirmation of all seven members of the board before it could be organized.[97]

The legal setback forced Wilson's hand. He promised to nominate a replacement for the rejected Edward Jones and also to exert his influence on Warburg to reconsider his refusal to appear before the Senate committee.

Warburg cloaked his change of heart under the cover of patriotism. He cabled the Senate Banking Committee on July 31, the day that McAdoo shut the New York Stock Exchange: "In deference to the President's urgent request, and in view of the seriousness of the present emergency, which renders desirable the promptest possible organization of the Federal Reserve Board, I have decided to waive all personal considerations, and am prepared to appear before your committee at the earliest convenient date."[98]

Warburg's main antagonist on the Senate Banking Committee was Senator Joseph Bristow of Kansas, described by the *New York Times* as "a radical Republican" who has "on every occasion used his place in the Senate to play to the lowest prejudices."[99] Before the hearings began, Bristow had said: "If Mr. Warburg appears before the committee, any member has the right to ask him any question he pleases. Is this man to dictate what kind of hearing he shall have? I do not want him to come to Washington under any misapprehension. This is not going to be a pink tea affair and no one can make a pink tea affair of it."[100]

Bristow did not disappoint. He peppered Warburg with accusations that Warburg's firm, Kuhn, Loeb, gouged the public. His colleagues on the Banking Committee refused to participate in the inquisition. Republican Senator Knute Nelson of Minnesota, who had opposed Warburg only a few days earlier, reflected the changed sentiment in the following pronouncement: "In Europe they mobilize armies and navies. In America we mobilize bank reserves."[101] On August 4, a day after Bristow completed his cross-examination of Warburg, came the ultimate reprimand: the Kansas electorate refused to renominate Bristow for his Senate seat.[102]

Wilson kept his word and nominated Frederic Delano of Chicago to replace Edward Jones. The death of Edith Wilson on August 6 postponed all congressional deliberations. On August 7 the Senate confirmed both Warburg and Delano, completing the Federal Reserve Board a week after the crisis began.

On August 10 Treasury Secretary McAdoo administered the oath of office to the other members of the Federal Reserve Board, and concluded the ceremony by emphasizing the board's mission: "You gentlemen are to form the bulwark against financial disaster in this nation and the basis for financial development at home and expansion abroad."[103]

McAdoo believed the Federal Reserve System would help resolve the

Members of the Federal Reserve Board as they took office on August 10, 1914. *From left to right, standing*: Paul M. Warburg, John Skelton Williams (comptroller of the currency), W.P.G. Harding, Adolph C. Miller; *seated*: Charles S. Hamlin (governor), William G. McAdoo (chairman), and Frederic A. Delano. McAdoo is wearing a mourning armband to commemorate the death, four days earlier, of his mother-in-law, Ellen Axson Wilson.

crisis. The central bank could protect America's gold reserve the way central bankers around the world did—by raising the interest rate to attract deposits. But he also knew that establishing the Federal Reserve Board was only a first step. The Federal Reserve Act conferred direct control over interest rates with the individual Reserve Banks. Only the banks could establish the discount rate—the rate charged for extending credit to commercial banks. McAdoo's timetable for opening the banks would be derailed by fierce opposition within the emerging Federal Reserve System. At the same time, American obligations abroad would produce the largest gold outflow in a generation.

McAdoo had to improvise.

CHAPTER TWO

The European Gold Rush

MORE THAN fifty ships lined New York harbor during the week of July 27, 1914, destined for ports like Marseilles, Naples, Hamburg, Rotterdam, Havana, and Rio de Janeiro.[104] The local press focused on three departures: the German ship *Kronprinzessin Cecilie* leaving for Bremen on July 28; the Cunard liner *Carmania* scheduled to depart for Liverpool on July 29; and the French steamship *La Savoie* headed for Le Havre, also departing on July 29. These were not the largest or fastest ships in the merchant fleets of Germany, Britain, and France, but they carried record shattering cargo.

The *Wall Street Journal* wrote: "The most prominent development in financial circles [on June 28] was the engagement of $14,750,000 gold for export, principally to London. This sum, beyond a doubt, constitutes a new record for a single day's consignment."[105] The *Journal*'s single-day record referred to the exports scheduled for July 29 that were divided between the *Carmania* carrying $12,250,000 gold and *La Savoie* with $2,500,000 aboard. On July 28 the *Kronprinzessin Cecilie* left New York with $10,700,000 gold bars. The Austrian Ultimatum of July 23 provoked more than $25 million in gold exports in less than a week, about five times larger than the average exports for an entire month since 1900.*

With Europe spiraling into war, who arranged to ship the gold? The New York banking elite shared the business, as it often shared major bond offerings: $10 million came from the Guaranty Trust Company; $6.5 million from National City Bank; $2.5 million from Lazard Frères; and $1.75 million from Goldman Sachs.[106]

How did the price of gold respond to Europe's scramble for the yellow metal? Did it jump 15 percent over a few fitful hours as it did when Jay Gould manipulated prices on the Gold Exchange on Friday, September 24, 1869?[107] Did it quadruple in value in less than a year, like it did a

---

* The total from July 23, 1914, until July 29, 1914, was $27,850,000 (see the *Wall Street Journal*, July 29, 1914, 1). The U.S. Treasury provides monthly data on gold exports and imports in its annual reports. The data show that from the beginning of 1900 until the end of 1913 the United States exported an average of $5,338,784 gold per month, with a standard deviation of $6,556,493. The United States imported an average of $6,237,234 per month, with a standard deviation of $7,848,357.

century later when Nelson Bunker Hunt cornered silver on the Comex at the end of the 1970s?*

Those speculative frenzies, accompanied by wild gyrations in gold prices, occurred when commodities traders bought and sold gold, just like they did wheat or corn. The *New York Times* described the Gold Exchange on Black Friday, September 24, 1869, the day of Gould's manipulation: "Before the opening of the board, the room was packed with members and spectators, while the passageways and stairs were crowded with men trying to press in, and New Street was blocked up with masses which spread around Wall and Broad Streets. . . . The shouts and cries of the hundreds of active operators seemed more like the outpourings of maniacs, and for a short time a pallor seemed to overspread their faces . . . [as] they stood bewildered and perspiring."[108]

By 1914 gold no longer traded in frenzied public combat. The dollar price of gold had been fixed at par—$100 in paper currency per $100 in specie (gold coin) since January 1, 1879, when the U.S. Treasury resumed the free conversion of paper currency into gold as legislated by the Resumption Act of 1875.[109] The renewed convertibility ended fluctuations in the dollar price of gold that began with the suspension during the Civil War. The highest price gold reached in any year declined steadily, from $285 in 1864 to $107 in 1878, except for an upward spike to $162 in 1869, inspired by Jay Gould.[110]

On December 17, 1878, the Gold Department of the New York Stock Exchange (the old Gold Exchange) recorded a virtual requiem: "At 12:29 o'clock Mr. Gimbernat, of 60 Exchange Place, sold $10,000 gold to P. Gillet, of 16 New Street, at par. This is the first sale at par that has taken place in 16 years. The room was almost empty at the time the transaction was made, and so quietly was it accomplished that only three or four persons knew anything about it."[111] This is quite a letdown from the scene a decade earlier, on Black Friday, which more closely resembled a medieval square during a public hanging than a division of the New York Stock Exchange. It would take nearly a century before gold trading resumed on the nation's organized exchanges.[112] In January 1975 New York's Comex inaugurated futures trading in gold four years after President Nixon severed the official connection between the dollar and gold.[113]

What determined gold prices between 1879 and 1975? In 1914 the gold standard locked the price of the precious metal in a straightjacket. Each government adhering to the gold standard committed itself to maintain a fixed price of gold in terms of its own currency. For example,

---

* Gold rose from a low of $216 in 1979 to a high of $850 in 1980 on Comex, the Commodity Exchange located at the time in the World Trade Center in New York City. The corner in silver is discussed in *Committee on Government Operations* (1981).

the U.S. Treasury fixed the price of an ounce of gold at $20.6718 by buying gold at that price from anyone wishing to sell and selling gold at that price to anyone wishing to buy.* The Bank of England fixed the price of an ounce of gold at £4.247727 in a similar way.

The U.S. Treasury and the Bank of England not only prevented fluctuations in the price of gold under the gold standard but also established a fixed rate of exchange between the dollar and the pound. A tourist going to London who needed pounds (sterling) could take $20.6718, buy an ounce of gold at the U.S. Treasury, and turn it into £4.247727 at the Bank of England. Therefore, it would take $4.8665 (equal to $20.6718 divided by £4.247727) to buy one British pound.† This exchange rate is called the "mint parity exchange rate" because it comes from "minting" precious metal into legal tender by the government (the Bank of England or the U.S. Treasury).

The exchange rate of dollars for British pounds is nothing more than the price of pounds in terms of dollars. Just like $60.75 could buy one share of U.S. Steel on the New York Stock Exchange on July 1, 1914, $4.8665 could buy one British pound through the U.S. Treasury and the Bank of England on that same day. Most ordinary people, tourists included, did not exchange dollars for British pounds through official channels. Instead they would call a foreign exchange dealer, such as the Guaranty Trust Company, for an exchange rate. People relied on competition among foreign exchange dealers, combined with the option of gold shipments, to anchor the actual exchange rate close to mint parity.

Europe's demand for gold prior to the outbreak of the war left its price unchanged because of the shackles imposed by the gold standard. Instead, the demand provoked the major New York banks and trust companies into shipping gold to Europe during the week of July 27, 1914, including the massive $10 million shipment from the Guaranty Trust Company. Max May, the vice-president at the Guaranty Trust Company in charge of foreign exchange operations, arranged for the $10 million gold shipment aboard the *Carmania* on July 29. Recall that May had testified at Treasury Secretary McAdoo's Federal Reserve System hearings in January 1914 on the role of the central bank in controlling gold flows. He knew firsthand about exporting the precious metal.

Max May emigrated in 1883 from his native Germany to the United States at age twenty-two, after having spent five years learning the foreign

---

* Gold quotes are per troy ounce. A troy ounce is about 10 percent heavier than a standard ounce. I drop the word troy throughout the book.

† More precisely, $20.6718 buys one ounce of gold from the U.S. Treasury and one ounce of gold buys £4.247727 at the Bank of England. Hence, each pound costs $20.6718 divided by £4.247727, equaling $4.8665637, which is often designated $4.8665+. The plus is often ignored.

exchange business.[114] He worked at the First National Bank in Chicago and became an American citizen in 1888. In 1904 he moved to New York to work at the Guaranty Trust Company. By 1914 May had built the Guaranty Trust's franchise to the point that he was considered "one of the Big Three who practically controlled the New York foreign exchange business."[115]

What made Max May ship $10 million in gold on the *Carmania*? Max did it because he could make a profit when the British pound rose to "unprecedented levels that had not been witnessed before" during the week of July 27.[116] A close-up view of Max's business offers a peak into the very secretive and very profitable world of gold arbitrage.

FOREIGN EXCHANGE RATES

Financial markets anticipated extensive gold exports as early as July 23, the day of the Austrian Ultimatum to Serbia. This was not because the Ultimatum necessarily implied war, but because the exchange rate between sterling and the U.S dollar made it profitable to pack up the yellow metal and ship it off to England. As the *Wall Street Journal* observed, "The resumption on Thursday [July 23] of gold exports . . . draws attention to the spectacular advance of the [foreign] exchange market during the present week. [The market] advanced by leaps and bounds until the present level—$4.8815—causing the renewal of gold shipments."[117]

Why did the exchange rate of $4.8815 per British pound trigger gold exports? Suppose a U.S. clothing manufacturer owed a British exporter £42,477 for a shipment of Shetland wool. The U.S. manufacturer would turn to a foreign exchange dealer, like Max May, to buy British pounds. Where did Max get the pounds to sell? He usually bought them from an American exporter, like a farmer, who received pounds in payment for cotton shipped to Liverpool. A foreign exchange dealer like Max May is a middleman, buying British pounds from one customer, the cotton farmer, and reselling them quickly to another customer, the U.S. clothing manufacturer.

If Max May bought pounds at $4.8814 from a cotton farmer and resold them at $4.8815 to the clothing manufacturer, he would earn $0.0001 per pound. On this particular transaction his total profit would be $0.0001 times 42,477, or $4.25. Max could earn a nice living if he bought and sold enough pounds. But at the price of $4.8815 per pound he could make more than ten times that amount by shipping gold to London and creating British pounds. Max would become a gold arbitrageur.

Here is how Max May executed the arbitrage. He would sell 42,477 British pounds at $4.8815 to the U.S. clothing manufacturer for $207,351 (equal to $4.8815 times 42,477). He would then take $206,718 of that sum to the U. S. Treasury and buy 10,000 ounces of gold at the official price of $20.6718 per ounce ($206,718 is equal to $20.6718 times 10,000 ounces). Max would then ship the 10,000 ounces of gold to London and exchange them for pounds at the Bank of England at the official price of £4.247727 per ounce. He would then have the 42,477 British pounds (equal to £4.2477 times 10,000 ounces) that he just sold. Max would also have $633, the difference between $207,351 and $206,718. The $633 had to cover Max's cost of shipping gold from New York to London. Anything left over was his profit on the transaction, called an arbitrage because it was riskless.

Max spent a good part of his life, when he was not testifying at government hearings, worrying about shipping costs. The physical details required his attention. The *Wall Street Journal* described how it was done: "The gold is handed out [at the assay office] in slabs some six inches long, four inches wide and two thick. On each is stamped the exact weight, fineness, and the seal of the assay office. The bars are checked off by numbers and whisked away to the bank packing room. [There] they are checked again, placed in kegs, each bar in a sawdust bed to prevent loss by abrasion. It is aimed to have about $50,000 in each keg. When a keg is properly filled it is headed and nailed shut by a cooper, then passed to a sealer and marked respectively [until] the whole shipment is ready to be taken to the pier. . . . When the wagon reaches the pier the precious metal is immediately taken to the strongroom of the steamer under the charge of the purser."[118]

The *Journal* reported that the total cost of shipping gold before the war started, including insurance, foregone interest, handling, and freight charges, was .28 percent.[119] Therefore, Max's shipment of 10,000 ounces, valued at $206,718, cost a total of $578.81 (equal to .0028 times $206,718). Max realized a profit of $54 (equal to $633 minus $578.81) on the transaction, more than enough to buy a brand new set of golf clubs (about $25).*

After thirty-five years in the foreign exchange business, Max May could execute the gold arbitrage blindfolded. At an exchange rate of $4.8815 between the British pound and the U.S. dollar, he would crate the gold himself to accommodate the U. S. clothing manufacturer. Even small arbitrage transactions were irresistible because they added up to

---

* An advertisement (*New York Times*, July 28, 1914) reported that a golf club cost $2.50. Thus, nine irons plus a putter cost about $25. A driver and fairway woods would be extra.

big profits—without risk—in the Guaranty Trust Company's billion dollar foreign exchange operation.[120]

Max May wanted contented customers. The more he bought and sold, the more profitable his business. Max might have offered to sell pounds at $4.8814 (which left Max with a $50 profit—still enough to buy a set of golf clubs) to keep the U.S. clothing manufacturer from patronizing some other foreign exchange dealer, like National City Bank. Competition among foreign exchange dealers for arbitrage profits kept the foreign exchange rate from wandering too far above the mint parity of $4.8665 plus the cost of shipping gold. An exchange rate of $4.88 (which is .0028 above $4.8665) just covers shipping costs and is called the "gold export point." Gold exports by dealers occur when the exchange rate nudges above $4.88 because that is how they make their profit. A similar number below mint parity, called the "gold import point," triggers shipments of gold to the United States.[121]

The $4.8815 sterling exchange rate on July 23, the day of the Austrian Ultimatum, made it profitable for the Guaranty Trust Company, National City Bank, Lazard Frères, and Goldman Sachs to arrange gold shipments to Europe. But why did the exchange rate move up to that level in the first place? Why didn't the price of British pounds remain closer to the mint parity level of $4.8665?

The price of sterling increases when many American dollars chase a small supply of British pounds on the foreign exchange market, just like the price of U.S. Steel rises when investors spend more dollars on a limited supply of stock. No one knows for sure the identity of buyers and sellers in the stock market (or in the foreign exchange market) because brokers hide their customer lists as though they were state secrets. But the *Wall Street Journal* suggested on July 24 that "sales of American securities by European holders, who have been frightened by the strained relations obtaining between [Serbia] and Austria-Hungary . . . is the responsible cause for the exchange rate advancing to the export point."[122] In other words, the threat of war led British and French investors to transfer the dollar proceeds of their stock sales into pounds (and francs) at foreign exchange dealers. The price of pounds rose to $4.8815 because British investors wanted more pounds and fewer dollars.

But when the price of pounds hits the gold export point, foreign exchange dealers like Max May don their arbitrage hard hats and work twenty-four-hour shifts exporting gold to supply as many pounds as British investors, or anyone else, would want. In the process of supplying pounds, they accomplish two things: they earn riskless profits for their firms, and they impose a ceiling on the foreign exchange rate at the gold export point.

Max May and his fellow arbitrageurs shipped enough gold to keep a lid on the exchange rate from Thursday, July 23, through the end of the week. The British pound remained unchanged on Friday July 24, and it advanced ever so slightly to $4.8820 on Saturday.[123] But on Monday, July 27, sterling punched through the export barrier as though it were made of paper rather than gold.

Where was Max May?

THE FOREIGN EXCHANGE CRISIS

War had not yet been declared on July 27, but the *Wall Street Journal* described the mayhem: "Conditions which have not been witnessed before by some of the oldest operators prevailed in the foreign exchange market on Monday. A well-nigh complete state of demoralization characterized the market, and where rates were quoted they fluctuated with a violence that deterred operators from transacting in the majority of instances. . . . Sterling was driven to the unprecedented level of $4.92."*

How abnormal was an exchange rate of $4.92? Daily records collected by the U.S. National Monetary Commission in 1910 show that since 1889 the British pound never once rose above $4.90,[124] confirming the *Journal*'s description of $4.92 as "unprecedented." During the first half of 1914 sterling reached a peak of $4.8900, only to wither under the weight of gold exports.

The exchange rate of $4.92 turned Max May's arbitrage into a money machine. Instead of making $54 selling 42,477 British pounds to the clothing manufacturer, he would have made $1,690.[125] Max could have bought a deluxe Paige 36 automobile ($1,275 with electric lights and starting system) on that trade alone.[126] He would have made about $14 million on his London foreign exchange business during 1913 if the exchange rate had remained at $4.92 all year, producing a 43 percent return without risk on the Guaranty Trust Company's capital (and without using any of the firm's capital).† Max should have been selling pounds at $4.92 and shipping gold to London until they made him president of the

---

* Sterling refers to the exchange rate on a sight (or demand) bill of exchange. This foreign exchange instrument obligates the immediate payment in pounds when the bill is shipped across the Atlantic and presented in the United Kingdom. The exchange rate on a telegraphic transfer of funds is called "cable transfer" or "cable" (after the transatlantic cable that made telegraphic transfer possible). See *Wall Street Journal*, July 29, 1914, 8.

† The Guaranty Trust Company did about $1.8 billion in foreign exchange with London in 1913 (see *New York Times*, January 7, 1914, 7). A profit of .81 percent (= $.04 divided by $4.88) times $1.8 billion equals $14,580,000. The Guaranty Trust Company's balance sheet (JP Morgan Chase Archives, JP Morgan Chase, New York) on December 9, 1913, showed $34 million in capital plus surplus plus undivided profits. $14.58 million divided by $34 million equals .43, or 43 percent.

company. Was Max asleep at the wheel of his new car or did something, or someone, prevent him from locking in the arbitrage?

On Sunday, July 26, the day before sterling reached $4.92, the *New York Times* headline announced a break in diplomatic relations between Serbia and Austria-Hungary: "Austrian Minister Recalled as Reply to Ultimatum Rejected."[127] Emperor Franz Joseph also instituted martial law throughout Austria-Hungary. Austria's declaration of war on Tuesday, July 28, was almost a formality, but most people still did not expect the conflict to ensnare the Great Powers. The *New York Times* headline announcing Austria's rejection of the Serbian reply to the Ultimatum also included the following: "Britain to Work for Peace: Hope Entertained That Trouble Can Be Adjusted by Means of Mediation."[128]

Did the U.S. Treasury turn the diplomatic confrontation into an excuse to curtail the availability of gold at $20.6718 per ounce? Perhaps the Treasury adapted the advice that John Maynard Keynes would give the British government: "To maintain specie payments . . . while making it extremely difficult for the ordinary man to get gold. [For example] Gold should only be available at the head office of the Bank of England."[129] Cutting off the gold supply at the U.S. Treasury would kill Max May's arbitrage like a stake through the heart, allowing the price of sterling to rise unchecked.

The U.S. Treasury had changed the arbitrage game before. On March 18, 1891, Lazard Frères applied for $500,000 in gold bars for shipment to Germany. The Treasury Department forced the bankers to settle for gold coin at the subtreasury by ruling temporarily that "no more bars should be issued for export."[130] Bars dominate coin for shipments abroad because coins suffer from abrasion in everyday use and bars do not. In Europe, the U.S. coins were weighed for their precise gold content and exchanged for foreign currency accordingly, while normal wear and tear did not infringe on their domestic value. For similar reasons, exporters prefer high-denomination U.S. gold coins like double eagles ($20), to eagles ($10) and half eagles ($5).

When Lazard Frères came to collect the $500,000 gold coin, Assistant Treasurer Roberts added further insult by ruling that the coin "would be paid out in proportion to the amount of the various coins on hand . . . $285,000 in double eagles, $145,000 in eagles, and $70,000 in half eagles." Roberts assured the public: "There is no difficulty on the part of the Treasury in meeting any calls for gold coin that are likely to arise . . . [but] the fair and proper method is to pay all comers a fair share of all denominations of gold coin."[131]

During the entire week of July 27, 1914, the U.S. Treasury never wavered in its commitment to exchange gold for dollars at $20.6718. The Treasury cannot be blamed for preventing arbitrageurs from responding to the jump in the British pound to "unprecedented levels" on July 27. The *Wall Street Journal* noted: "In some quarters it has seemed somewhat anomalous that sterling should maintain its high level in the face of an unprecedented export of gold."[132] What deterred Max May's arbitrage?

The withdrawal of $2.5 million gold bars on July 27, for shipment to France two days later aboard *La Savoie*, depleted the New York subtreasury's inventory of gold bars. The last bars were withdrawn by Lazard Frères. Max May had to accept gold coin from the subtreasury for export on the *Carmania* on the July 29.[133] And Assistant Treasurer Roberts's 1891 decree regarding the distribution of coins remained in force in July 1914. But the presence of eagles and half eagles in Max's consignment of gold did not interfere with his arbitrage.

Coin abrasion added only about .07 percent to arbitrage costs, implying a gold export point of $4.8835 rather than $4.88.[134] According to Max May, "At the quoted [foreign exchange] figures gold could be exported to any part of the globe at a profit."[135] The exchange rate responded to the extensive gold shipments by declining from $4.92 on July 27 to $4.915 on both July 28 and July 29. But why didn't arbitrage activity drive the exchange rate all the way back to $4.8835?

Percy Chubb, of Chubb & Sons, marine underwriters, implicated wartime insurance in blunting the downward pressure of arbitrageurs on the exchange rate: "[I have] never known a time when the [insurance] rate on gold was as high as at present."[136] Gold sailing on July 28 aboard the *Kronprinzessin Cecilie* paid $600 per $1 million for insurance compared with the normal $500.[137] When the *Carmania* left port on July 29 insurance costs tripled to $1,500 per $1 million.[138] But those numbers merely rippled the surface compared with the tidal wave about to hit. On Thursday July 30, the *New York Times* reported that "marine underwriters were loath to assume new risks, but the rate was . . . $10,000 per million."[139]

Soaring insurance costs infringed on Max May's gold arbitrage. The 1 percent rate (equal to $10,000 divided by $1,000,000) pushed the gold export point up to nearly $4.93.[140] But within a day the price of sterling left even this bloated barrier behind.

On Thursday, July 30, sterling soared to $4.98, 5¢ above the new gold export point. The *Wall Street Journal* noted: "To describe the conditions in the foreign exchange market in the past few days as being unparalleled is portraying the truth, but hardly conveys a proper notion of the real state of affairs. As a matter of fact, the most experienced operator would never have dreamed that any combination of circumstances could have arisen to drive . . . sterling to $4.98."[141] The *Journal* explained the source of the spiraling demand for the British currency: "Huge amounts of American securities were sold here for foreign account by direct cable, which created an extra demand for [sterling] remittance just at the juncture when a supply was least to be had."[142] European investors wanted sterling rather than dollars and evidently were willing to sacrifice an extra nickel to get British pounds.

What was wrong with dollars?

Nothing under ordinary circumstances, but wartime uncertainties drove investors to safety. In 1914 the British pound was the safest currency in the world. Most countries held their international reserves in gold or sterling.[143] The dollar's credibility suffered from periodic bank suspensions in the United States, most recently in 1907. The Panic of 1907 had damaged the reputation of American finance.* Sterling rose relative to the dollar because it was a safe-haven currency.

None of this made Max May's arbitrage any less profitable, however. He could sell pounds to anyone wanting to pay $4.98, take the proceeds to buy gold from the U.S. Treasury, and ship the gold to the Bank of England, where he could get the pounds just sold. Max would earn $4.98 minus $4.93 (the mint parity exchange rate for pounds plus shipping costs at wartime insurance rates) per pound. The arbitrage was more profitable than ever and should have pushed the sterling exchange rate back toward the $4.93 gold export point—except for one detail.

Max needed ships to transfer the gold across the Atlantic. Although fifty ocean liners were scheduled to leave New York harbor during the week of July 27, not all ships were equally helpful for Max May. Less than twenty were destined for Europe, and fewer actually sailed as scheduled. A further reduction in available shipping space occurred because "no insurance could be obtained for German vessels"[144] and "underwriters were unwilling to insure more than about $10,000,000 going in one bottom."[145] As the *New York Times* observed, "With cancellations of sailings and the most prohibitive insurance rates on such ships as are still running it has become almost impossible to ship gold to Europe."[146]

A number of cautious arbitrageurs refused to ship gold with the merchant fleets of likely combatants. The *Wall Street Journal* said: "Some international houses, which have abstained from making shipments either because of their inability to secure insurance against war risks or their refusal to accept the prevailing rates of such insurance, may ship by the *St. Louis*, which is an American vessel and, therefore, not subject to seizure in the event of war between the [European] Powers."[147]

The caution made sense, especially after the German ship, *Kronprinzessin Cecilie*, which had sailed to Europe with part of the record-breaking gold exports that began on July 27, returned to American

* Chapter 3 discusses the Panic of 1907.

soil the following week, unable to deliver its cargo.* Foreign exchange dealers puzzled over what to do with the gold. According to the *Journal*, "The banks have already sold [foreign] exchange against the gold and unless the metal goes forward with another ship they will be that much 'short' of exchange."[148] Dealers needed their gold to reach England so they could purchase the sterling they had promised to their customers.

Turmoil in the foreign exchange market precipitated a meeting among the major dealers to confront the escalating crisis. The foreign exchange bankers created a committee to meet every day while the strain lasted "to enforce for all the brokers any regulations it may decide are necessary."[149] When the *Wall Street Journal* asked Max May, a member of the committee, about the gold that had been brought back to America by the *Kronprinzessin Cecilie*, his response was "that gold will stay here and will be deposited in the sub-Treasury to the credit of the banks that had made the shipment. Now that foreign exchange transactions are to be placed on a war basis the shipment of gold abroad is out of the question."[150]

To sum up: During the week of July 27, before Germany, Britain, Russia, and France declared war, Max May and other foreign exchange bankers took as much gold from the U.S. Treasury as they possibly could. But ships and insurance constrained Max and his fellow financiers as effectively as a longshoreman's wildcat strike. The price of sterling rose above even the bloated gold export point because Max & Company could not do the arbitrage as often as they wished. On Friday July 31, sterling reached one more unprecedented level—$6.00—causing an unnamed foreign exchange dealer to throw up his hands and scream: "It's just criminal, that's all."[151]

Figure 2.1, showing the exchange rate between the British pound and the U.S. dollar for 1914, illustrates the dimensions of the crisis.† The narrow movements in the price of sterling during the first half of the year reflect the arbitrage operations of foreign exchange dealers. The panic that erupted at the end of July drove the value of the British pound to levels

---

* The *New York Times* (August 5, 1914), reports that the *Kronprinzessin Cecilie* "had been turned back by wireless orders from the steamship company's offices in Bremen, Germany, when within two days steaming of her first port of call, Plymouth, England, for fear of capture by British or French warships."

† The exchange rates on the dollar versus the British pound used in all of the figures throughout this book are taken from daily issues of the *Wall Street Journal* during 1914 and 1915. They reflect the bid price, in dollars, on demand sterling bills of exchange. The demand or sight bill of exchange obligates the immediate payment in pounds when the bill is shipped across the Atlantic and presented in the United Kingdom. According to Sprague (1915, 500) the rate on *demand sterling* is "the most significant single exchange rate." Bid prices are used since they formed a continuous series for 1914 and 1915. Ask prices were frequently missing.

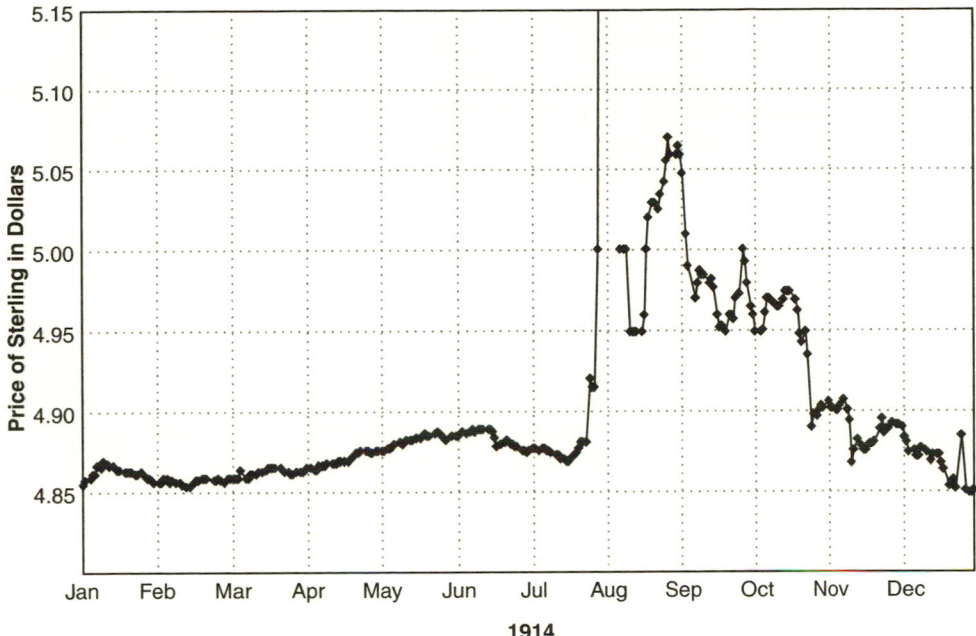

Figure 2.1. Sterling Exchange Rate, 1914.

Data Source: *Wall Street Journal.*

not witnessed in more than a generation. During the first week of August, foreign exchange prices literally disappeared from view, with only a few transactions taking place privately.* Quotations reappeared the following week but fluctuated with uncommon violence until the end of the year.

The declaration of war among the Great Powers during the week of August 2, 1914, turned thoughts of gold shipments into a fantasy from Oz. The dealers could not arrange exports until the Bank of England conspired to lend a helping hand. How much damage did the bankers do before the war temporarily halted exports?

THE GOLD SCORECARD

The *Wall Street Journal* reported on August 1: "Considerable takings in gold for local banks and by individuals from the sub-Treasury yesterday.

---

* The *Wall Street Journal* (August 3, 1914, 8), explained its failure to report prices: "Quotations are more difficult to be had than at any time since the present situation developed. Business is entirely a matter of private negotiation." The newspaper resumed regular quotations on August 8.

A line of about fifteen persons was seen at the hall of the sub-Treasury at the paying teller's window redeeming notes. Bank runners were frequently seen in the line and from time to time reports were spread that banks would continue taking gold to meet any possible emergency."[152]

Secretary of the Treasury William McAdoo assured the public that "there would be no gold stringency at the New York sub-Treasury,"[153] and backed that up with action. According to the *New York Times*, "The Treasury department is closely watching its diminishing supply of gold at New York, and strengthening it by shipments from other points. Another $10,000,000 came from Philadelphia yesterday by parcel post and was delivered at the sub-Treasury. More is on the way from more distant cities. . . . Chief Postal Inspector James T. Cortelyou . . . arranged the details of the shipment. A guard of ten postal inspectors, with magazine pistols, squatted on 400 canvas sacks containing the gold as the single mail car carrying it was drawn out of the Broad Street station."[154]

A day earlier the *Wall Street Journal* recorded the following scene: "Protected by a force of over twenty men, seven large United States mail auto trucks drove up to the sub-Treasury at three o'clock yesterday afternoon and proceeded to deposit there piles of mail pouches filled with gold. It is estimated that in all there was at least $50,000,000. No official statement could be secured, however, from either the post office or the treasury officials up to the time of going to press. . . . This is the first time that gold has been shipped by the mail service. It is believed that the gold was sent here from the Treasury at Washington."[155]

Delivering gold to the heart of Wall Street with military precision in the middle of a weekday afternoon obviated the need for a formal statement. Passersby would conclude that the U.S. Treasury had more than enough of the yellow metal to go around. Secretary McAdoo delivered a message along with the gold.

The threat of escalating war-related demands from Europe forced McAdoo to put on a show. The Treasury's obligations to pay gold exceeded its resources.* And the gold outflow that began with the Austrian Ultimatum on July 23 did not tell the whole story. The entire month of July witnessed more than $33 million gold exports and only $3 million gold imports.[156] Net imports (imports minus exports) track the amount of gold coming into the United States. For July 1914 net imports equaled *minus* $30 million—that is, the U.S. exported $30 million more gold than it imported. Minus $30 million for net gold imports was very unusual.

Figure 2.2 shows net gold imports on a monthly basis from 1900 through the end of 1914.[157] Before 1914 net gold imports averaged about

---

* Chapter 5 shows that the gold outflow threatened the U.S. Treasury's commitment to redeem all of its paper obligations in gold.

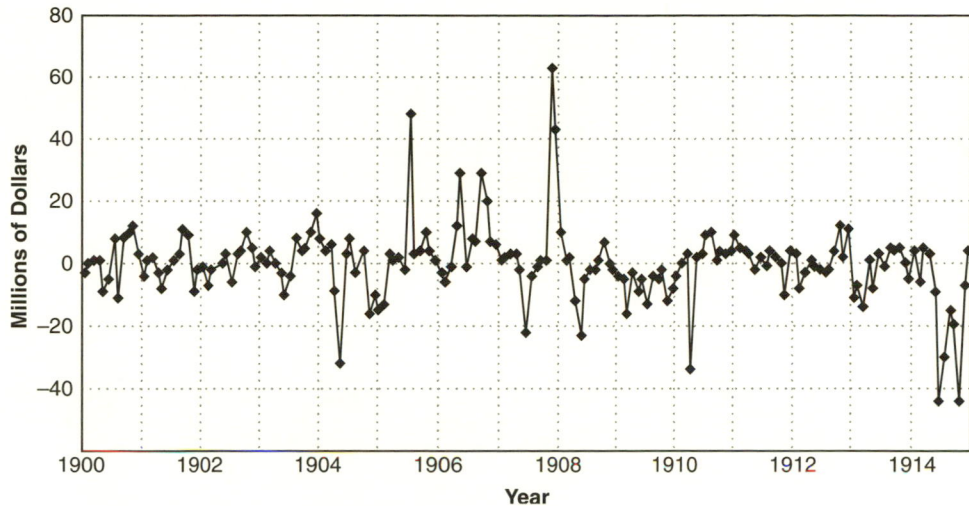

Figure 2.2. Net Gold Imports, 1900 to 1914.

Data Source: U.S. Treasury, *Annual Reports*.

$1 million per month. In other words, on average the United States imported about $1 million of gold more than it exported per month during the fourteen years between 1900 and 1913. During this period, only two months (May 1904 with minus $32.6 million and April 1910 with minus $34.2 million) showed a larger negative number for net imports than $30 million. The magnitude of the July outflow, by itself, would have been reason for concern.* But there was more to worry about.

Figure 2.3 allows a closer look at net gold imports for each month during 1914. The minus $30 million in net imports for July was not the largest of the year to date. It was preceded by a negative $44 million for June. The $44 million gold outflow in June was the single largest gold outflow of any month from 1900 until mid-1914. The combined outflow of June and July 1914 exceeds by $30 million any other two-consecutive-month period until that point. The gold outflow triggered by the Austrian Ultimatum on July 23 caused concern not only because the war would make further demands on the U.S. gold stock but because the gold outflow in July came on top of the largest monthly outflow in fifteen years.

* Monthly net gold imports between 1900 and 1913 averaged $898,000, with a standard deviation of $10.8 million. The observed negative $30 million net imports for July 1914 is significantly different from the mean at a confidence level of 1 percent. Also, recall that the *Wall Street Journal* (July 30, 1914), said: "The most prominent development in financial circles on Tuesday [July 28] was the engagement of $14,750,000 gold for export, principally to London. This sum, beyond a doubt, constitutes a new record for a single day's consignment."

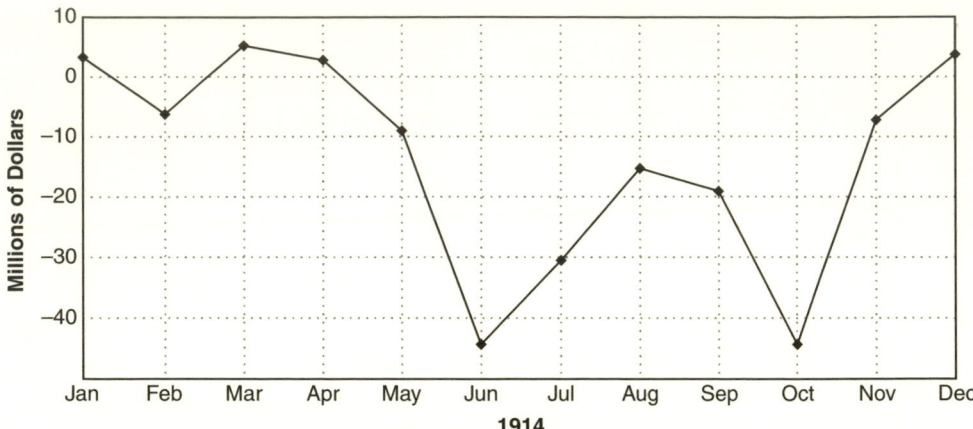

Figure 2.3. Net Gold Imports, 1914.

Data Source: U.S. Treasury, *Annual Reports*.

The public recognized the unprecedented outflow at an early stage, as a June 11 story in the *Wall Street Journal* indicated: "The gold export movement is now assuming proportions that attract general attention. For some time the approaching situation was only realized by a few far-sighted bankers who . . . were aware of the extent to which Europe had been quietly selling American securities and that during the process our balances abroad had been gradually reduced."[158] Why were Europeans selling American securities and accumulating gold even before the murder of Archduke Franz Ferdinand on June 28, 1914?

At first the *Wall Street Journal* explained the foreign sales of U.S. stocks and bonds as a response to the Wilson administration's unfriendly attitude toward business: "As long as the political conditions remain as they are there cannot be much change in sentiment on the part of foreigners regarding American securities. The present agitation against big business enterprises and the predicament of the railroads are a discouragement to Europeans. Probably in no other feature will the granting of the asked-for freight increase be more beneficial to the railroads in particular and the country in general than the changed attitude of the foreign investor."[159] The *Wall Street Journal* had taken the opportunity to lobby Washington for a freight rate increase to help American railroads.

On June 20, only two days after blaming domestic politics, the *Journal* focused on international intrigue: "Flow of Gold Abroad Analyzed, Russia's Mysterious Buying at High Rates Makes Foreign Situation Complex."[160] The *Journal* explained the ominous headline: "The position of England seems not to draw gold but to keep France and Russia from making inroads on the British supply. . . . Russia, however, has been the strongest bidder in the competition, and has paid unprecedented prices for its gold. Why Russia is doing so is something that is not known here. The thing that is causing this extraordinary movement is some strong current underneath the market that we cannot see or trace."[161]

The *Wall Street Journal* had reported the Russian accumulation of gold as far back as April 24, 1914: "Attention in international banking circles is being directed to Russia because of her heavy absorption of the new Cape [of South Africa] gold laid down in the London market. For some weeks past she has practically divided the weekly consignment with India."[162] The *Journal* added an explanation for Russia's accumulation: "The real reasons for the importation of the metal are said to be the flotation of the recent heavy issue of government bonds in Paris, and the desire to fortify the reserve position against possible political contingencies. In this respect Russia has emulated both Germany and Paris in their avidity for the metal."[163]

No one knows for sure why Russia started the scramble for gold more than two months before the murder of Archduke Franz Ferdinand in Sarajevo on June 28. The accumulation might have reflected an innocent, but well-timed, precaution against "political contingencies," as the *Wall Street Journal* suggested on April 24. Alternatively, there could have been a more sinister motive at work, as hinted by the *Journal's* June 20 suggestion of "some strong current underneath the market that we cannot see or trace."*

Figure 2.3 highlights the enigma. A total of $83 million gold exports—$9 million in May, $44 million in June, and $30 million in July—occurred *before* the war among the Great Powers began. This record setting three-month period of gold exports—twice as large as any other three-month period of gold exports between 1900 and mid-1914—spelled trouble for the Wilson administration.

---

* Speculation existed about a wide conspiracy in the archduke's assassination. Sidney Fay (1928, 62) quotes an article written by M. Ljuba Jovanovitch, the minister of education in the Serbian government of 1914 in which Jovanovitch says: "I do not remember whether it was the end of May or the beginning of June [1914] when one day M. Pashitch [the Serbian prime minister] said to us . . . that certain persons were making ready to go to Sarajevo to murder Franz Ferdinand who was to go there to be solemnly received on St. Vitus Day [June 28]." Did the Russians know about the plot as well? Charges of Russian complicity in the murders at Sarajevo focus on the relationship between Colonel Dmitriyevitch, of the Black Hand, a Serbian secret society, and a Russian military attaché in Belgrade named Artamonov (see Schmitt 1930, 237). Did the Russians know of the plot in time to accumulate a gold arsenal for a potential war? The press had publicized the archduke's upcoming visit to Sarajevo in mid-March 1914. Gavrilo Princip's preparations for the assassination began at the end of March. He left for Sarajevo on May 28, 1914. Of course, none of this proves that the Russians accumulated gold because they knew about the attempted assassination—only that the facts are consistent with that explanation.

CHAPTER THREE

The Nightmare of 1907

PRESIDENT WILSON sent Treasury Secretary McAdoo to New York City for an emergency meeting with leading bankers on Sunday, August 2, 1914.[164] McAdoo left Washington's Union Station Sunday afternoon and arrived in Manhattan at eight o'clock that evening. He was met at Penn Station by Francis L. Hine, president of the First National Bank and chairman of the New York Clearing House.[165] Max May arrived on the same train as McAdoo, having spent Saturday in Washington conferring with the treasury secretary about the foreign exchange crisis.[166] May and McAdoo parted ways without commenting to the press about their discussions. Hine escorted McAdoo to the Vanderbilt Hotel at Madison Avenue and Thirty-third Street to meet the assembled financiers, while May went to his office to catch up on cablegrams from Europe. Germany had declared war on Russia on Saturday, removing doubts about the scope of the European conflict.

More than twenty bankers waited for the treasury secretary in a conference room on the second floor of the Vanderbilt Hotel, including A. Barton Hepburn, chairman of the Chase National Bank (now J. P. Morgan Chase); Frank A. Vanderlip, president of the National City Bank (now Citibank); Benjamin Strong, at the time president of the Bankers Trust Company; and, representing the House of Morgan, Henry Davison and J. P. Morgan Jr.[167] Representatives of America's banking elite had come to a meeting on the first Sunday of August 1914 to discuss the problems of gold and foreign exchange; they were "unanimous that the banking situation would shortly develop along the lines similar to those experienced in the fall of 1907."* The bankers needed a plan to avoid a replay of the Panic.

The Panic of 1907 had started when banks were forced to suspend the convertibility of their deposits into currency and gold in October of that

---

* The consensus is recorded in a memo written by Benjamin Strong, Albert Wiggin (Chase National Bank), and James Brown (Brown Brothers): "At the conference of New York bankers held immediately prior to the declaration of war by England, opinions were unanimous that the banking position in this country would shortly develop along the lines similar to those experienced in the fall of 1907" (see Memo, November 2, 1914, Board of Governors of the Federal Reserve System, Central Subject File, 1913–1954, box 1470, National Archives II, College Park, Maryland).

year. Europe helped alleviate the crisis by shipping over $100 million gold to the United States during the last two months of 1907. On August 2, 1914, the bankers assembled at the Vanderbilt Hotel worried with good reason. This time Europe would exacerbate the problem rather than help rescue America from a panic. The bankers feared the threat of 1907 as though an epidemic were about to strike.

THE PANIC OF 1907

At age seventy J. P. Morgan Sr. hatched what would become known as his crowning public achievement. On Thursday, October 24, 1907, as depositors fought to withdraw cash from beleaguered trust companies, Morgan saved the stock market from a freefall. The next day the *New York Times* front-page headline read: "Millions Meet All Demands: Money Poured into Banks, Trust Companies and the Stock Exchange." The *Times* elaborated on the role of J. P. Morgan & Company: "It was only after money had reached 100 percent, with frantic and unavailing bidding by the brokers on the floor of the exchange [and] with Union Pacific dropping point by point . . . that Morgan & Co., uniting with them a group of the big banks, . . . threw $25,000,000 into the shouting throng, meeting every demand, rallying stocks and cheering sentiment."[168]

After conferring several times with Treasury Secretary George Cortelyou at the New York subtreasury, Morgan partner George Perkins sounded a hopeful note: "The situation is working itself out satisfactorily. Confidence is being restored and I can say that the financial institutions of the city are perfectly solvent. Today is better than yesterday, and tomorrow will be better than today."[169] In fact, the panic had scarcely begun, and neither J. P. Morgan nor Treasury Secretary Cortelyou could do anything to stop it from flattening the financial landscape.

The stock market had relatively little to do with the crisis that began during the week of October 21, 1907. Figure 3.1 shows prices on actively traded railroad and industrial securities on the New York Stock Exchange from the beginning of September 1907 through the end of December. The index of twenty railroad stocks dropped by 8 percent from the close on Monday, October 21, to the close on Thursday, October 24, and the index of twelve industrials declined by a little more than 4 percent over the same time interval. Earlier in the year, stocks declined by more than 8 percent in *one* day.[170] Investors were poorer at the end of that day—March 14—but the public did not panic. People who own stocks must accept violent price fluctuations, often for no apparent reason.

The fifty depositors standing outside the Knickerbocker Trust Company before it opened on the morning of October 22, 1907, did not care

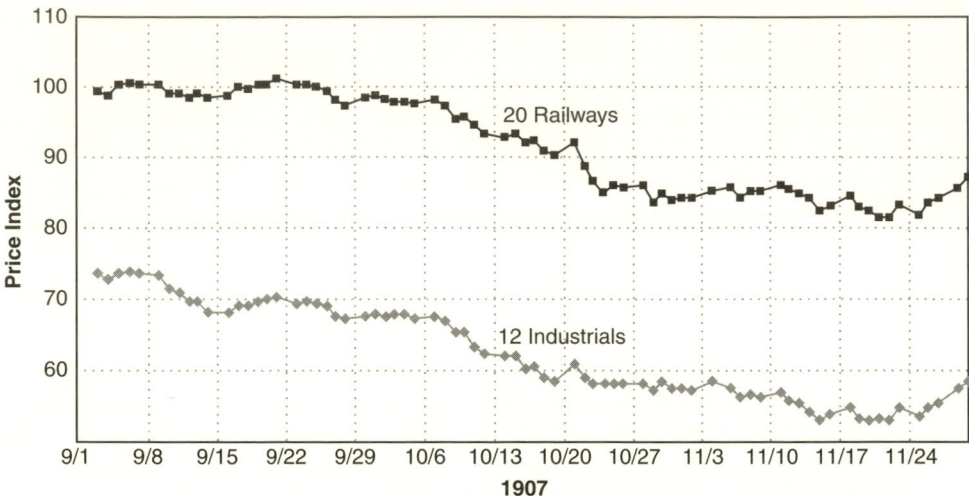

Figure 3.1. Stock Prices on the New York Stock Exchange, September 1, 1907, to December 31, 1907.

Data Source: *Wall Street Journal*.

about stocks; they worried about the safety of their checking and savings accounts. Deposit insurance did not arrive in the United States until 1933, when Congress established the Federal Deposit Insurance Corporation.[171] In 1907 depositors had nowhere to turn if their bank closed its doors. The *New York Times* reported that the demand for cash grew quickly after the Knickerbocker opened at ten o'clock until "the line doubled back on itself in a great S, and care was taken by the special officers to crowd everyone inside the building. . . . The first word the crowd in the lobby had from the company officially came when Vice President Benjamin Allen announced from the door: 'There is no cause for worry. There [are] plenty of funds on hand.'"[172]

Less than two hours later, after paying out a total of $8 million to hundreds of depositors, the Knickerbocker Trust Company, second largest trust company in New York, suspended cash withdrawals. Depositors remained in line for more than an hour after the doors closed. A man from Rahway, New Jersey, said to his neighbor, while they both continued to wait: "I know something about the bank in my town. I know the officers and I am going to take my money there."[173] He did not get the chance.

What caused the run on the Knickerbocker Trust Company on Tuesday, October 22, 1907? Charles T. Barney, the company's president had been forced to resign a day earlier because he had joint business ventures with Charles W. Morse, who had been forced out over the weekend as a director of the Mercantile National Bank and the National Bank of North America because of his losses in copper speculation. The *New York Times* tried to defuse the problem: "In view of the fact that the position of Mr. Barney has become greatly extended, and although he had no loans with the Knickerbocker Trust Company, because of his connection with Mr. Morse and the Morse companies, the Directors decided that the best interests of the company would be served by his withdrawal."[174]

Depositors obviously lost confidence in the Knickerbocker Trust Company but just a few days earlier they remained faithful to the two banks—the Mercantile National Bank and the National Bank of North America—that were more intimately connected with Charles Morse.[175] Why did depositors abandon the Knickerbocker Trust Company but remain loyal to the two banks?

No institution that accepts deposits payable on demand can survive *by itself* when depositors clamor for cash. Banks make money lending out depositor funds in the form of interest-earning loans. They retain only a fraction of their deposits—usually less than 25 percent—in ready cash and rely on the normal ebb and flow of deposits and withdrawals to balance each other. A bank's cash reserve can bridge a small excess of withdrawals over deposits, but large withdrawals can be met only by borrowing cash.* Without a central bank in the United States in 1907, the main source of immediate funds was other banks.

Both the Mercantile National Bank and the National Bank of North America belonged to the New York Clearing House, the association of local banks in New York City that arranged the transfer of funds to settle checks drawn on each other. A member in good standing of the Clearing House could count on borrowing from other banks to tide itself over a temporary flurry of withdrawals. In a meeting on Saturday night, October 19, 1907, which lasted well into Sunday morning, the New York Clearing House forced Charles Morse to resign as a director of the Mercantile National Bank and the National Bank of North America as a condition for arranging assistance.[176] Once Morse resigned, the Clearing House announced its support and avoided a run on the two troubled institutions.

The Knickerbocker Trust Company was not a member of the New York Clearing House. It was not even a bank, even though it had more deposits than the Chase National Bank and almost as many as the First National Bank.[177] It was a trust company, as its name clearly states. Many people

---

* Banks can also call in loans to meet withdrawals, but this is less desirable than borrowing for two reasons. First, the bank wants to maintain its reputation as a reliable source of credit because that is how it earns interest. Second, calling in loans sometimes triggers a default by the borrower. The collateral for the loan may decrease in value if it has to be liquidated on short notice.

overlooked the distinction between the two sets of institutions because the trust companies did everything that banks did except for issuing currency.* Depositors in trust companies sometimes paid dearly for the confusion, including the man from Rahway, New Jersey, who did not get to withdraw his funds on October 22.

Trust companies often cleared checks drawn on other local institutions through the good offices of a bank that was a member of the Clearing House. The Knickerbocker Trust Company cleared through the National Bank of Commerce, the second largest member of the New York Clearing House after the National City Bank. As with any clearing arrangement, the Bank of Commerce was exposed to losses if the Knickerbocker Trust Company failed to make good on balances that had already been paid for through the Clearing House by the Bank of Commerce.

Late in the afternoon on Monday, October 21, the National Bank of Commerce announced by messenger to other members of the Clearing House that it would no longer clear for the Knickerbocker Trust Company. Oliver J. Pilat, assistant cashier and director of the Bank of Commerce would only say: "I can make no explanation now. All that I will say is that I believe the notices have been sent."[178]

The abrupt termination dealt a critical blow to the Knickerbocker Trust Company's reputation, but the following morning's main headline on the front page of the *New York Times* offered a ray of hope: "Knickerbocker Will Be Aided; President Barney Quits and Financiers Promise to Support the Trust Company; J. P. Morgan & Co Help."[179]

J. P. Morgan Sr. and his partner George Perkins had met on October 21 with members of the Knickerbocker's board of directors until one o'clock in the morning at Louis Sherry's restaurant on Fifth Avenue. After the meeting a committee of the directors released the following statement: "The Knickerbocker Trust Company has in its vaults tonight $6,000,000 and more will be forthcoming immediately under the guarantees which have been given, if this becomes necessary." The *Times* story added: "These guarantees are understood to include aid which J. P. Morgan & Co. will furnish as the result of the conferences last night."[180]

Despite what the *Times* said, however, no agreement had been reached to help the beleaguered trust company. When it opened for business on October 22, the Knickerbocker Trust Company had to fight its own battle. The company ran through $8 million in cash by 12:30 that afternoon. When the tellers closed their windows the following announcement was

---

* Banks chartered by the comptroller of the currency (in the U.S. Department of Treasury) could issue national bank notes (authorized by the National Bank Act of 1863) by depositing U.S. government bonds as collateral with the U.S. Treasury. Banks that were chartered by the comptroller of the currency almost always had the word National as part of their name.

shouted through the doorway: "Payments will be temporarily suspended until more cash can be secured. We hope to resume in the afternoon."[181] No additional cash came forward that afternoon, nor in the days and weeks that followed. The Knickerbocker Trust Company remained shut until March 26, 1908, after much of the pain and damage of the Panic of 1907 had subsided.

Sparks from the Knickerbocker's suspension blackened the surrounding financial institutions. The interest rate on stock exchange call loans—overnight loans collateralized by securities—jumped to 70 percent on the afternoon of October 22, compared with an average of 5 percent during the first three weeks of October.* On the morning of October 23 more than 1,200 depositors rushed the Trust Company of America, the third largest trust company, to demand their cash. This time the front page of the *New York Times* correctly announced: "Aid Trust Company of America; J. P. Morgan Is to Help."[182]

J. P. Morgan Sr. and other leading bankers, including James Stillman, president of the largest bank, the National City Bank, and A. Barton Hepburn, president of the Chase National Bank, and formerly the New York State superintendent of banks, met at the Manhattan Hotel on Madison Avenue on the evening of October 22. They were joined by Treasury Secretary Cortelyou who had come up from Washington during the day. After the meeting they issued the following statement at one o'clock in the morning: "The chief sore point is the Trust Company of America. The conferees feel that the situation there is sound. Provision has been made to supply all the cash needed for this morning. The conferees feel sure that the company will pull through. . . . It is safe to assume that J. P. Morgan & Company will be the leaders in this movement to furnish funds."[183]

The Trust Company of America did, in fact, pull through without suspending payments, but not without a struggle. Depositors tested the company's resources until November 7, when the *New York Times* headlined victory: "Trust Company of America Wins Its Long Fight: Have Paid Out $34,000,000." During the two-week period beginning October 23, depositors drained the company of nearly three-quarters of its funds.[184] Some of the transactions were amusing, like the person who had successfully withdrawn his money from the Knickerbocker Trust Company on October 22, only to have redeposited the cash in the Trust Company of America that very same day. After withdrawing his money a second time he said: "Going forward I'll keep my money in a stocking."[185] This

---

* The 70 percent rate is per annum, of course. Call loans are considered among the most liquid loans since they are collateralized and can be terminated (called) on a day's notice. See *New York Times*, October 23, 1907, and Andrew 1910, 136.

twice-lucky depositor's cautionary attitude would cost the economy dearly. Money in a stocking cannot be lent to business firms needing working capital.

Why did it take two weeks to convince depositors to stop attacking the Trust Company of America? Depositors did not test the Mercantile National Bank and the National Bank of North America when the Clearing House announced support for those troubled institutions, even though the U.S. district attorney would subsequently bring criminal indictments against the former officers of those banks.[186] Was there something wrong with J. P. Morgan's guarantee?

Perhaps there was. Recall the *New York Times* front-page headline on the morning of October 22: "Knickerbocker Will Be Aided . . . J. P. Morgan & Co Help." No one knew that the *Times* headline was incorrect. Morgan had, in fact, tried to arrange assistance but failed. The average depositor, and there were many, could only conclude that J. P. Morgan could not always deliver on his promises. And they were right— Morgan was not a central bank that could lend without limit in times of crisis. Had J. P. Morgan's guarantee not been tarnished by the failure of the Knickerbocker Trust Company, the panic that began on October 22, 1907, might have ended before it started.

In a history of crises written for the National Monetary Commission in 1910, O.M.W. Sprague offers his assessment: "Had the Knickerbocker Trust Company been a bank and a member of the Clearing House it is highly probable that it would have been assisted."[187] New York State bank examiners declared the company solvent after examining the Knickerbocker's books on the morning of the October 22.* Deputy State Superintendent of Banking George Skinner said: "I have no reason yet to alter my opinion expressed earlier this morning as to the solvency of this corporation if it can be given time to secure money to make its payments."[188]

Why wasn't the Knickerbocker helped? Banks resented the trust companies because they operated with fewer regulatory restrictions and competed with the banks for business. Morgan partner George Perkins summed up the attitude best: "Indeed, we hadn't any use for their [trust company] management and knew that they ought to be closed, but we fought to keep them open in order not to have runs on other concerns."[189]

The banking community, led by J. P. Morgan, spent $24 million to protect the depositors of the Trust Company of America. None of the

---

* A company is solvent if the value of its assets exceeds its liabilities. If those assets cannot be quickly turned into cash to meet obligations, the company may suffer a liquidity crisis. A company is in default if it misses a scheduled payment on its debt.

Trust Company's depositors lost access to their money. But it was too late. The fallout from permitting the crisis to surface spawned an avalanche of bank suspensions and a sharp contraction in the economy.

THE CONSEQUENCES

Depositors wanted currency rather than checking and saving accounts after the Knickerbocker Trust Company closed its doors. Secretary of the Treasury George Cortelyou responded to the problem within a day by depositing $25 million of the Treasury's cash into New York banks. He said: "If the public, on its part, will reflect upon the real strength of our banking institutions, there will be a prompt return of the confidence which their condition warrants. As evidence of the Treasury's disposition, I have directed deposits in this city to the extent of $25,000,000."[190] Optimism prevailed when not all the cash was exhausted by the close of business on Friday, October 25. A banker who had met with Cortelyou said: "It shows that the banks of the city have enough money to meet the situation. [If] there were such a shortage of ready cash in banks all over the city as has been reported by some irresponsible newspapers, that $25,000,000 would not have lasted two hours."[191] Late Friday night Cortelyou also seemed confident that the worst of the crisis had passed: "There will be no statement tonight. I do not think the situation demands one. I am going to get a good long sleep tonight and I need it."[192]

A proper interpretation of why the Treasury's cash infusion remained underutilized would have shown little cause for optimism. Currency stayed inside banks because many of them refused to dispense it freely. Six banks and trust companies in Brooklyn, including the oldest financial institution in the borough, the Brooklyn Bank at Fulton and Clinton Streets, suspended all payments on October 25.[193] Three banks in Harlem closed their doors as well.[194] All were declared solvent by the state superintendent of banks but closed because they did not have sufficient cash to meet depositor demands. Many of the depositors accepted the developments stoically. Some did not. Gustave Oman, a brawny immigrant from Finland, tried to withdraw his $500 from the Harlem Savings Bank at 124th Street and Third Avenue.[195] The police arrested him for failing to follow the rules imposed on the crowd outside the building. The magistrate heard the case the same afternoon and suspended Oman's sentence on the condition that he not withdraw funds during the remainder of the run. The magistrate explained: "I have much more than you on deposit but I am leaving it in. The money is much safer in the bank than in your pocket, my man."[196] Oman turned to the judge as he left the court and replied: "Maybe you think that Judge but I don't."[197]

According to law, savings banks could require sixty days' notice for withdrawals of cash from savings accounts, but this regulation was ignored in the normal course of business. On Friday morning, October 25, the Franklyn Savings Bank at Eighth Avenue and Forty-second Street imposed a $100 limit per account on withdrawals. A mixed response greeted the restriction according to William G. Conklin, president of the bank: "Some [depositors] would not listen to reason but most of them went away with a realization that we are working for their own good. These are the times when people are ready to lose their heads at the slightest provocation and work against their own interests. They cannot be trusted to protect themselves. So it is up to us, as you might say, to look out for their interests."[198] Gustave Oman might have had a few choice words for Mr. Conklin's benevolence. Nevertheless, within a day *all* savings banks in New York City limited immediate withdrawals to a maximum of either $50 or $100 per account.[199]

Formal measures to conserve cash escalated on Saturday, October 26. The New York Clearing House declared that, until further notice, settlement in cash among member banks would not be necessary. Instead, banks could use Clearing House loan certificates to dispense their obligations.[200] The Clearing House issued these loan certificates to a member bank that posted acceptable securities as collateral with the Clearing House. The *New York Times* explained the Clearing House's objective: "Owing to the present scarcity of cash it has been found inconvenient by the banks to use their available funds for the purpose of effecting exchanges at the Clearing House. . . . These Clearing House certificates will circulate, of course, only among banks, leaving the banks' cash free for public use."[201]

Clearing House loan certificates helped to economize on local needs for currency, the same way they did during the Panics of 1873 and 1893. Clearing House Associations in thirty-nine large cities throughout the country, including, Chicago, Pittsburgh, Minneapolis, San Francisco, Philadelphia, and Omaha, authorized the issuance of loan certificates.[202] In some places, including, Atlanta, Peoria, Los Angeles, Spokane, and Wichita, small-denomination ($5, $10, $20) loan certificates circulated among the public.

As useful as these loan certificates were, they were not the equivalent of currency that was acceptable throughout the country to settle obligations. Currency in the United States in 1907 consisted primarily of gold and silver coins and certificates, national bank notes, and United States notes (greenbacks).[203] Under normal circumstances many people also accepted certified checks, or even personal checks, to consummate a business transaction. But the period beginning the last week of October 1907 was not normal. Currency was king. And it commanded a premium in the marketplace.

A. P. Andrew, a contemporary Harvard economist who specialized in statistical descriptions of economic and financial activity, captured the mood: "The closing months of 1907 were marked by an outburst of fright as widespread and unreasoning as that of fifty or seventy years before, by suspension of cash payments on the part of a very large proportion of our sixteen thousand banks, by the issue of private and unauthorized currency in multitudes of towns and cities and by the appearance and continuance during two months of a considerable premium upon legal money."[204]

The first recorded currency premium—3 percent—emerged on October 31. According to Andrew, "money brokers advertised regularly in the daily press the purchase and sale of currency."[205] A person wanting cash on October 31 had to present a certified check for $103 to acquire $100 in currency from a money broker. The premium reached a peak of 4 percent several times during the first two weeks of November, slid to 1 percent during the first half of December and then dwindled to less than 1 percent before disappearing on December 31, 1907.[206]

Most of the demand for cash came from out-of-town banks that normally held checking accounts, called correspondent balances, with New York City banks. These country banks used their New York City checking accounts like a clearing house—to settle balances with other banks. But suspension worried these country banks about the availability of cash when they would need it, even though New York banks introduced Clearing House loan certificates precisely so they could pay out currency on demand. From the last week of October until the end of the year, New York City banks shipped a total of $124 million in legal tender to country banks, compared with an average of $1.6 million over the same ten-week period during the previous five years.[207]

But it was not just country banks that hoarded cash. Real people stuffed currency into safe-deposit boxes. Rentals of safe-deposit boxes almost tripled in New York City during the five weeks from October 26 through the end of November compared with the previous five weeks.[208] In Chicago and Boston rentals doubled.[209] A letter written by the Mercantile Safe Deposit Company to Professor Andrew confirms that rentals did not come just from timid small depositors: "We think most of it among our customers was done by business men and manufacturers who drew the money for immediate use for payroll and wage disbursements."[210]

The real cost to the economy from the panic that began during the last week of October stemmed from the breakdown in the normal course of settling payments—as reflected in the currency premium. The use of checks and currency to complete transactions is taken for granted until it disappears, just like the presence of oxygen in the air. Comptroller of the Currency William Ridgely evaluated the impact of the panic: "The greatest hardship to business generally has been the derangement of the machinery for making collections and remittances. As can be readily seen, this has interfered with every kind and class of business and led to a curtailment of business operations of every kind. Factories have suspended, workmen have been thrown out of employment, orders have been cancelled, [and] the moving of crops has been greatly retarded."[211]

Interruptions afflicted businesses of every size and location. On October 23, companies controlled by the Westinghouse family in Pittsburgh were forced into receivership, leading George Westinghouse to issue a public statement: "When the Pittsburgh Clearing House Committee . . . concluded that, although the Westinghouse Electric and Manufacturing Company and the Westinghouse Machine Company were solvent, receiverships were advisable as the best means of protecting all concerned, it was clearly our duty to follow their friendly advice. The necessity of the receiverships is due solely to the financial stringency and the consequent inability to renew our maturing paper."[212]

On November 1, the following announcement appeared in the *New York Times*: "Five hundred of the 2,000 men in the various departments of the Kings County Light & Power Co., generally known as the Brooklyn Edison Co., are out of employment. Vice President Freeman said this step is taken owing to the condition of the money market."

Regional strife also surfaced over monetary conditions. On November 7 Senator Heyburn of Idaho protested to President Theodore Roosevelt against further deposits of the Treasury's cash in New York Banks until "those institutions pay the reserves of Western banks in cash instead of cashier's checks . . . crops could not be moved on checks."[213]

The Panic of 1907 turned a mild downturn in economic activity that began in May 1907 into a rout. Milton Friedman and Anna Schwartz, in their *Monetary History of the United States*, describe the situation: "From May to September the contraction showed no obvious signs of severity . . . production in various lines of activity flattened out but did not decline seriously and freight car loadings behaved similarly. . . . In October came the banking panic [and] the contraction simultaneously became much more severe. Production [and] freight car loadings and the like all declined sharply."[214]

Everyone at the time understood the problem—not enough currency. Why didn't Treasury Secretary George Cortelyou order the Treasury's Bureau of Engraving and Printing to produce more legal tender and then deposit crisp new dollar bills in banks for people to use? Cortelyou simply could not do that. Congress kept the license to print money under lock and key.

THE CURRENCY PROBLEM

According to Article I, Section 8, of the U.S. Constitution, Congress has the right to "coin money and regulate the value thereof." On April 2, 1792, Congress established the dollar as the monetary unit in the United States and created the Bureau of the Mint to coin gold and silver into dollars that would be acceptable as legal tender in payment of all obligations.* Thereafter, Congress guarded its right to control money like the Marine Corps protecting the American way of life. It established a central bank in 1791 with a twenty-year charter. When the bank's charter expired in 1811, it took four years for Congress to establish another bank. When the Second Bank's charter expired in 1836, Congress left America without a central bank until it passed the Federal Reserve Act in 1913.

Congress especially wanted to prevent the executive branch, by way of the Treasury Department, from financing government spending the easy way—by printing money. The experience of the Revolutionary War, when prices doubled because the Continental Congress flooded the country with paper currency, left an indelible impression.[215] After the Constitution was adopted, Congress linked the dollar to gold to anchor the amount of lawful money in circulation. The mint would create currency by purchasing precious metal from individuals and businesses. Anyone bringing 232.2 grains of fine gold to the mint could receive a ten-dollar gold coin—known as the eagle.† The Treasury could spend money only by collecting taxes and tariffs in gold. Fiat currency—established by government decree (fiat)—was the exception rather than the rule. But there were some exceptions.

At the end of 1906, currency outside the Treasury in the United States totaled $2,628 million.[216] Gold and silver coin and certificates amounted to $1,750 million.[217] Thus about two-thirds of all currency arose from

---

* The U.S. Mint was originally established as part of the State Department and then became an independent agency in 1799. The Coinage Act of 1873 placed the mint within the Treasury Department.

† Congress established one dollar equal to 24.6268 grains of fine gold in 1792. Congress changed the value of the dollar to 23.22 grains of fine gold on January 18, 1837. It remained at 23.22 grains until 1934 (see Officer 1996, 15). Because there are 480 grains of fine gold in an ounce, between 1837 and 1934 the dollar price of an ounce of gold was set at $20.6718 (equal to 480/23.22). The Currency Act of 1900, also known as the Gold Standard Act, directed the U.S. Treasury to maintain the convertibility of all forms of currency into gold at the rate of 23.22 fine grains per dollar.

the receipt of precious metals by the U.S. Mint. The remaining one-third, U.S. notes ($336 million) and national bank notes ($542 million), arose from efforts to finance the Civil War.[218]

U.S. notes were called greenbacks when they were authorized under the Legal Tender Act of 1862 as the government's first fiat currency.[219] The word greenbacks now refers euphemistically to all American currency, but that is a more recent development. Congress fixed the amount of greenbacks outstanding after the Civil War.[220]

National bank notes were first authorized under the National Bank Act of 1863. A bank chartered by the Treasury Department's comptroller of the currency could create this currency by depositing U.S. government bonds at the Treasury and requesting the Treasury's Bureau of Engraving and Printing to ship newly printed national bank notes in return. The notes circulated as currency and helped finance the Civil War by providing a ready market among banks for the Treasury's debt obligations. Banks could and did continue to create national bank notes under the 1863 legislation long after the Civil War ended whenever they acquired the requisite government bonds.[221]

National bank notes were technically obligations of the individual bank that issued them, but because they were backed by government bonds, the public treated them like government currency.* Before the Civil War, circulating notes issued by banks varied in quality, depending on the creditworthiness of the issuing bank. Under the National Bank Act, all national bank notes carried the identical imprimatur on the face of the bill: "Secured by United States Bonds Deposited with the Treasurer of the United States." Individual notes differed only in the name of the originating national bank engraved on the front. No one paid any attention to that distinction except for numismatists and the Bureau of Engraving and Printing (because it needed different printing plates for each national bank).

By congressional design, the executive branch of government could not increase currency in circulation at its discretion. Additional bank notes might result from a government deficit financed by selling bonds, but Congress restrained deficit spending (more or less) by the budget process. Gold production would generate additional currency, but this too was beyond government control.

How did businesses support additional transactions as America grew during the last half of the nineteenth century? Banks provided checking accounts to substitute for scarce cash. Businesses liked checks (especially

---

* According to Friedman and Schwartz (1963, 781): "National bank notes were accepted throughout as interchangeable with currency issued directly as an obligation of the U.S. Government." For an exception to this during the Panic of 1873, see Friedman and Schwartz (1963, 21).

when making payments) because they were less vulnerable to theft than currency, even if checks were less generally acceptable. Banks maintained the credibility of their checking deposits by holding cash reserves to convert deposits into currency whenever depositors wished. This arrangement worked well until everyone wanted to convert deposits into currency at the same time. There simply was not enough cash to go around, and no one could create more on short notice. Under such circumstances, panic withdrawals would force banks to suspend the convertibility of deposits into currency. This, of course, is what happened on October 22, 1907.

If Congress did not permit the Treasury to print money, where did Treasury Secretary George Cortelyou get the $25 million in currency he deposited in New York banks on October 24, 1907? Cortelyou deposited currency that the Treasury had already collected through taxes and tariffs. These funds were held in the various subtreasury offices throughout the country.* This transfer of Treasury funds increased the public's cash just as effectively as a central bank's printing new money. In fact, the Treasury had been conducting these quasi-central banking operations for quite a while.[222] But the budgetary balance between government receipts and expenditures constrained the Treasury's flexibility and limited the potential for assistance.

During the Panic of 1907 George Cortelyou ran out of cash before he quenched the public's thirst for currency. On November 14 the *New York Times* reported:[223] "To strengthen the working balance of the Treasury, [Secretary Cortelyou] had withdrawn a small percentage of the government deposits held by the New York banks. . . . The working balance yesterday stood at $9,000,000 and the Treasury department officials desired to increase this amount."[224] New York bankers claimed they were not alarmed by the Treasury's cash withdrawals because they had already tapped into another source of reserves: European gold.

The National City Bank, Chase National Bank, Lazard Frères, and other leading New York financial institutions had arranged to import more than $20 million gold on October 28.[225] The ten-day ocean journey prevented the precious metal from providing immediate relief, but by mid-November the gold flow had become a tidal wave of support for the currency shortage. Figure 3.2 shows that more than $60 million gold entered the United States in November, a sharp reversal of the $28.9 million gold outflow that had occurred between May and

* The Independent Treasury Act of 1840 provided that government funds be held in its own subtreasuries. The system was abolished in 1843, reestablished in 1846, and lasted until 1921 (see Studenski and Kroos 1963, 112–19).

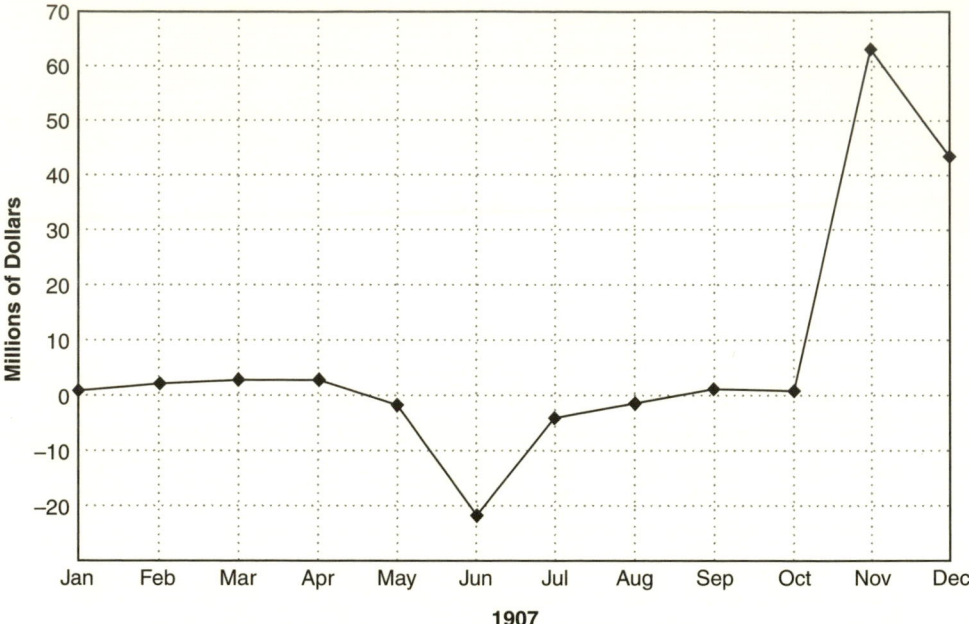

Figure 3.2. Net Gold Imports, 1907.

Data Source: U.S. Treasury, *Annual Reports*.

August.* In December more than $40 million worth of gold arrived, making the two-month total the largest gold imports of any two consecutive months between 1900 and 1914.

Why did gold flow into the United States in the middle of the financial crisis? Europeans wanted to buy U.S. securities that had declined since the beginning of the year. The *New York Times* reported: "Gold in the amount of nearly $20,000,000 was started on its way to the city; foreigners continued their purchases of our securities. . . . [They] were buying here in very large quantity and were profiting by an opportunity that

---

* The $28.9 million gold outflow has been blamed with setting the stage for the October panic. Friedman and Schwartz (1963, 158) maintain that the gold outflow contributed to a decline in the money stock that exacerbated the contraction: "The initial decline of about 2½ percent [in the money stock] from May to September 1907 reflected in part a decline in high powered money by about 1 percent, largely the result of the gold exports." Sobel (1968, 304) discusses the role of the gold outflow beginning May 1907 more casually: "All eyes turned towards Europe and New York to wait the next crisis. . . . wise money men began to hoard gold. . . . Paris began importing gold from America in May . . . more than 3.3 million in gold was taken . . . during the first week of June."

our own investors do not seem to realize."[226] British and French investors did not worry about a depreciation of the dollar relative to the pound or the franc.* The United States had formally adopted the gold standard guaranteeing the convertibility of all paper currency into gold in the Currency Act of 1900, also known as the Gold Standard Act. In October 1907 (unlike August 1914) no one questioned the U.S. Treasury's commitment to the gold standard.† The panic that began on October 22 caused banks to suspend the convertibility of deposits into paper currency but did not threaten the Treasury's commitment to convert U.S. paper currency into gold.

Did gold imports help to alleviate the crisis? Harvard economist O.M.W. Sprague belittled the importance of the gold inflow in his 1910 study of the crisis: "No reliance was placed on the prospective imports of gold, nor was the actual receipt of the gold made use of to cut short the period of suspension."[227] Most modern commentators, however, correctly recognize that gold imports were the only source of much needed flexibility in domestic U.S. currency during 1907. Friedman and Schwartz, in their *Monetary History of the United States*, point out that gold imports increased the monetary base and prevented bank deposits from declining more than they actually did.[228] Charles Goodhart, in his study of the New York money market, emphasizes how gold imports lessened the severity of the 1907 setback: "[Gold's] arrival was too late to stem the panic itself, though it aided substantially in shortening the period of suspension, in restoring the strength of the American banking system, and possibly in making the depression of 1907–1908, though it was extremely acute, one of the shortest on record."[229]

The Panic of 1907 served a higher purpose. Within six months Congress passed the Aldrich-Vreeland Act, creating emergency currency. No one liked the legislation, but McAdoo would not have succeeded in 1914 without it.

---

* According to Sprague (1910, 282ff.) even when the foreign exchange rate of the dollar moved away from the gold import point after October 29, 1907, the currency premium attracted gold imports. Suppose a British investor bought U.S. securities worth $486.65. If the exchange rate of the dollar were at the mint parity of $4.8665 per pound, the British investor could buy $486.65 dollars with 100 pounds from a foreign exchange dealer to complete the transaction. However, with a 4 percent currency premium the British investor would exchange 100 pounds at the Bank of England for gold and ship the gold to the United States at a cost of .28 percent (see chapter 2). The investor would then sell the gold for $506.12 ($486.65 times 1.04), pay $486.65 for the securities, pay $1.36 for shipping (.0028 times $486.65), and still have $18.11 left over.

† The Gold Standard Act of 1900 established a $150 million redemption fund to back the Treasury's guarantee to redeem all U.S. currency, not just gold certificates, in gold. For the first time greenbacks and silver certificates could be redeemed at the Treasury in gold.

ALDRICH-VREELAND EMERGENCY CURRENCY

The $100 million gold imports during the last two months of 1907 elim-
inated the currency premium by year's end. Throughout the country,
banks restored the convertibility of deposits into cash.[230] On January 7,
1908, Nelson W. Aldrich, the senior senator from Rhode Island and
chairman of the Senate Finance Committee (and grandfather of future
vice-president of the United States, Nelson Aldrich Rockefeller), introduced a bill to provide emergency currency to prevent future panics.
Aldrich's initiative drew inspiration from earlier proposals.

During the height of the panic, on November 12, 1907, ex–treasury
secretary Leslie Shaw offered a solution to America's banking problem:
"Our currency is non-elastic. Each and every distinct form of our money
is safe . . . and the parity of each with gold is assured. Its volume, however, does not respond to changing seasons. . . . This in my judgment is
the only weakness in our system. There were indications as early as August that people . . . were withdrawing money and locking it up. There
was no reason why they should do this but they did it. Had the National
banks been empowered to issue additional circulation equal to fifty percent of their capital without deposit [of government securities] to secure
its redemption, but subject to a tax of five percent, an aggregate increase
of $400,000,000 would have been possible. . . . The people would have
carried to their safe deposit vaults or taken home for concealment a National banknote as readily as a gold certificate, and they would have
been just as safe."[231]

Shaw, who had been succeeded by George Cortelyou in March 1907,
added a safeguard to his proposal for fiat currency: "Of course the
banks should not be permitted to issue this uncovered additional currency without the consent of the Comptroller of the Currency . . . [who
will if necessary] cause an examination to be made and grant or with-
hold consent in light of the record in his office."[232] The 5 percent tax on
the unsecured bank notes represented a premium paid to the government
for guaranteeing the redemption of the currency.

During his five-year tenure as treasury secretary, Leslie Shaw behaved
very much like a central banker, including using the Treasury's cash surplus to adjust bank reserves.[233] Shaw's activities as treasury secretary
had come under heavy attack from Professor A. P. Andrew: "If Congress will enact a law requiring the Secretary of the Treasury to deposit
with banks daily all receipts in excess of a fixed balance . . . the country
may again be freed from the spasmodic locking up and pouring out
of money at the Secretary's personal decree, from the incessant inter-
meddling of the government Treasury in speculative markets, from the

arbitrary manipulation of bank reserves, note circulation, and rates of foreign exchange, and from all the overnight changes of policy which the country has been afflicted with during the last five years. One cannot but hope that, with the reconvening of Congress, no time will be lost in annulling the dangerous and indefensible precedents left by Mr. Shaw."[234]

The distinguished Harvard professor's indictment of Shaw probably influenced the *New York Times* to balance its coverage of Shaw's proposal, to provide emergency relief within the existing monetary framework, with a headline on the same page calling for a completely new currency system: "Leading Financiers for a Central Bank; Special Committee's Report Says It Would Meet Emergency in Times of Stress." A Special Currency Committee of the New York Chamber of Commerce had issued a report proposing the establishment of a "central or national bank for this country along the lines of the Bank of England, the Bank of France, or the Imperial Bank of Germany."[235] The report said: "In our opinion the best method of providing an elastic currency, the volume of which would never be excessive, would be the creation of a central bank of issue under the control of the government."

The tension between these two solutions to America's currency panics, a complete monetary overhaul versus an emergency appendage to the existing system, colored congressional debate over Senator Aldrich's bill. The push for central banking nearly scuttled Aldrich's plan. Only a last-minute compromise saved the legislation from the scrap heap.

Senator Nelson W. Aldrich represented Rhode Island in the Senate since 1881. For about half his tenure he managed tariff and finance legislation as chairman of the Senate Finance Committee, earning a reputation as a staunch protectionist.[236] The marriage of his daughter Abby to John D. Rockefeller Jr. cemented his ties to Big Business. Aldrich also looked after Rhode Island's interests. When a visitor to the Capitol asked to see the other senator from Rhode Island—George Whetmore—he was told by an old timer: "My man, you know your own business best. Rhode Island has two votes in the Senate but only one Senator. He is Aldrich."[237]

The bill introduced by Nelson Aldrich on January 7, 1908, authorized $250 million of emergency currency secured by municipal and railroad bonds deposited with (and approved by) the secretary of the Treasury.[238] The authority to determine what constitutes an emergency rested with the comptroller of the currency. To encourage banks to provide currency in normal times, the bill restricted access to emergency currency to banks that already had national bank notes outstanding at least equal to 50 percent of their capital.* To encourage banks to withdraw the notes from circulation once the emergency had passed, the bill proposed to tax banks .5 percent per month (6 percent per annum) on the dollar amount of emergency currency outstanding.

Every appendage of this reasonable initiative met with a counterattack, as though it were a hydra-headed monster. Ex–treasury secretary Shaw, who should have been flattered by Aldrich's near copycat legislation, joined the critics: "The addition to the Government bond basis of banknote issues of municipal and railroad bonds as proposed by Aldrich was impractical. This emergency currency should be like any other money because if it was different from other money it would alarm the country."[239]

Professor J. Laurence Laughlin, a well-respected economist from the University of Chicago, complained: "The measure proposed in the Senate to remedy our monetary and financial ills furnishes another example of the deadening effect of politics, and a lack of expert knowledge in regard to banking, upon Congress. . . . If the right to issue these emergency notes is confined to banks already having outstanding notes . . . it should be noted that large banks in New York and elsewhere—which notoriously have not issued any notes to speak of—would be inhibited from resorting to any issues under the Aldrich bill."[240] Laughlin had identified a serious flaw.

Senator Knute Nelson, a Republican colleague of Aldrich's, splintered the party line with satire: "The Aldrich bill will not meet the exigencies of the case. It would issue currency, subject to a six per cent tax [per annum]. The banks will have to earn something on this currency, not less than six percent, and this will make the currency cost the borrower at least twelve percent. I should call this money 'stock exchange money' for it will be used only by those who could afford it—by those engaged in speculation. The relief held out by this bill is intended for the New York Stock Exchange. It is not intended for the people."[241]

Even Aldrich's arbiter of emergencies, Comptroller of the Currency William Ridgely, argued against the proposal. In his *Annual Report* of 1907, Ridgely said: "The high tax would prevent [its] use except when the situation became acute and the emergency very grave."[242] At an address to the School of Commerce at New York University, Ridgely sided with the central bank advocates: "It would be necessary to have a great central bank and the only proper currency must be a credit currency."[243]

---

* The *Washington Post* (January 8, 1908), reported: "The law will deprive banks of this privilege [to access emergency currency] which have not shown their willingness to do their share in maintaining a full volume of bank note circulation. Many banks have been derelict in this respect because of the fact that they could make more by speculating in stocks than by using it [their reserves] for the purchase of low-interest bonds to secure circulation."

Aldrich's Finance Committee amended the legislation several times to make it more acceptable.[244] To facilitate the immediate circulation of the emergency currency when a panic struck, the amended bill required the secretary of the Treasury to prepare bank notes in advance and deposit them in the subtreasury office nearest each bank. To guarantee that enough currency would be available to quell a panic the final bill raised the maximum that could be issued to $500 million. Finally, to avoid the criticism that emergency currency backed by railroad bonds catered to financiers and railroad tycoons, Aldrich reluctantly agreed to allow only municipal bonds to back the emergency currency.[245]

Preparing the bank notes in advance would prove to be a blessing.

Senator Robert La Follette of Wisconsin denounced even this democratized version of the bill as "legislation most desired by a comparatively small clique which has succeeded in dominating the finances of the country."[246] As he addressed the Senate, La Follette browbeat his colleagues with a sheet of paper in hand, a Wisconsin tradition that flourished nearly half a century later under Senator Joseph McCarthy: "I have here a list of about 100 men who control the industrial, financial and commercial life of the American people."* Despite the theatrics, the Senate passed Aldrich's bill on March 27, 1908, by an overwhelming majority of 42 to 16.[247] The opponents did not really care. A *New York Times* headline soon announced: "Aldrich Bill Seems Doomed; House Canvass Indicates That It Will Be Defeated There."[248]

Charles Fowler, chairman of the House Committee on Banking and Currency, had introduced a bill recommending a complete overhaul of the currency system a day after Senator Aldrich's January 7 initiative. The Fowler bill proposed replacing all bond-secured circulation with currency convertible into gold and promised to redeem the infamous greenbacks that had been issued during the Civil War.[249] When Congressman Underwood of Alabama asked Fowler what would be done in an emergency, Chairman Fowler said: "I don't admit that there will be any emergency."[250] It is not surprising that Fowler's bill garnered little support in the House. It is even less surprising that Fowler's Banking and Currency Committee voted unanimously on April 17 to table the Aldrich bill that had been passed by the Senate.

Congressman Edward Vreeland of New York introduced a bill in the House quite similar to Aldrich's except that his emergency currency would be backed by commercial paper rather than by bonds. Eligible commercial paper was defined as notes representing actual commercial

---

* La Follette's list included bankers and financiers, such as James Stillman, Edward H. Harriman, George W. Perkins, Jacob H. Schiff, John D. Rockefeller, and J. Pierpont Morgan, as well as politicians, such as former vice-president Levi P. Morton and former comptroller of the currency Charles D. Dawes. See *New York Times*, March 18, 1908.

transactions that bore the names of at least two responsible parties and had a maturity of less than four months.[251] To short-circuit the criticism that commercial paper varied too much in quality, Vreeland's bill required banks to form "national currency associations" that would approve the creditworthiness of the commercial paper. These currency associations, consisting of at least ten banks with aggregate capital of $5 million, would become jointly liable for the currency created by the commercial paper.[252] Stripped to the essentials, the national currency associations were like clearing houses that were authorized to issue loan certificates that could legally circulate as currency—Vreeland's emergency currency. To mollify Fowler, Vreeland proposed a national monetary commission to recommend permanent changes to the currency system.

The Panic of 1907 made it impossible for the Sixtieth Congress to adjourn without passing a currency bill. A. Barton Hepburn, president of the Chase National Bank, had lamented the pressure immediately after Aldrich first introduced his bill in the Senate: "One of the dangers of the present situation is that too much will be sacrificed of permanent value for something of immediate help, and unfortunately our Congress seems disposed always to give the half loaf."[253] Hepburn was right—the 1907 upheaval had been too harsh to ignore. President Theodore Roosevelt weighed in with an appeal to the Speaker of the House on May 6, 1908, to pass "a limited currency reform measure."[254]

The compromise legislation that passed on May 30, 1908, permitted both Aldrich and Vreeland methods for creating emergency currency. An individual bank could pledge municipal securities directly with the comptroller of the currency and receive emergency currency. Alternatively a bank could go through its national currency association and pledge commercial paper or other securities as collateral.[255] Emergency currency could be issued up to 90 percent of the value of the bonds but only up to 75 percent of the value of commercial paper or other securities.* The tax on both types of currency was identical: 5 percent per annum on the outstanding balance of emergency currency for the first month and an added 1 percent per annum for each additional month until a maximum of 10 percent.[256]

A number of features of Aldrich's Senate bill survived almost in tact. The bill restricted access to emergency currency to banks that already had national bank notes outstanding at least equal to 40 (rather than 50) percent of their capital.[257] The maximum amount of emergency currency

---

* In 1908 national banks held $105 million in municipal bonds, which could, therefore, support only $95 million of emergency currency. Commercial paper and other assets eligible to support emergency currency at the 75 percent level totaled $660 million. These other assets could, therefore, support $495 million in emergency currency (see Comptroller of the Currency, *Annual Report*, 1908, 11).

outstanding was fixed at $500 million.[258] The legislation directed the secretary of the Treasury "as soon as practicable to [prepare] circulating notes . . . as provided by law . . . to be deposited in the Treasury or sub-Treasury of the United States nearest the place of business of each [bank]."[259] To avoid potential alarm at the issuance of emergency currency, the bill included a clause requiring that emergency currency "be treated in the same way as circulating notes issued heretofore and secured by deposit of United States bonds."[260] All national bank notes issued after May 30, 1908, bore the inscription: "Secured by United States bonds or Other Securities."[261]

Vreeland's House bill contributed a clause establishing the "National Monetary Commission . . . to inquire into and report to Congress at the earliest date practicable, what changes are necessary or desirable in the monetary system of the United States or in the laws relating to banking or currency."[262] To prod Congressional action on monetary reform the final section of the legislation that passed on May 30, 1908, mandated: "That this Act shall expire by limitation on the thirtieth day of June, nineteen hundred fourteen."[263]

The compromise legislation, known as the Aldrich-Vreeland Act, satisfied no one. Congressman Carter Glass, who would shepherd the Federal Reserve Act through Congress in 1913, denounced the bill in predictable fashion: "The [Aldrich-Vreeland] bill is utterly wrong in principle, as any bill must be which merely provides emergency currency. What the country needs is not a makeshift legislative deformity, designed to help out a desperate situation, but a careful revision and a wise reformation of the entire banking and currency system of the United States."[264] Glass, a Democrat from Virginia, also attacked the nature of the compromises reached in the House and Senate conference report: "This [conference] report enjoys the unique distinction of having been signed by all of the Republican conferees, both of the Senate and the House, but not really approved by a single one of them. There is scarcely one important provision of this composite bill which has not been severely condemned by the Republican leaders of Congress. Those features which appeal to Members of this House have been mercilessly criticized in the other chamber, and those which suit the Republican managers of the Senate have been roundly denounced over here. Thus, upon high Republican authority, the conference report embodies a measure which is 50 percent House infamy and 50 percent Senate infamy, thereby making the whole of it utterly bad."[265]

Detractors also included those who thought the bill did too much, rather than too little. Senator Robert La Follette launched a futile filibuster, which included the following excerpt from a letter he received: "To enact the Aldrich-Vreeland currency bill would be to place machinery of inflation in the hands of the Secretary of the Treasury and the banks and would lead to the greatest political corruption since Rome. . . . The men who are urging this new bill might as well urge a currency issued by Standard Oil, redeemed by the steel trust, secured by the New York Stock Exchange and to bear on its face the picture of John D. Rockefeller."[266]

Professor J. Laurence Laughlin reviewed the Aldrich-Vreeland Act for the *Journal of Political Economy*. He described the bill as "a curious compound of conflicting views, compromise, haste and politics."[267] He admitted that the "purpose of the law, to remove in the future the inability of the banks to increase their note-issues in an emergency . . . has been accomplished."[268] But he concluded by saying: "We have in the Aldrich-Vreeland Act—the product of a few days struggle at the end of the [congressional] session—an unexpected freedom of issues based on banking assets, as well as a Pandora's box of unknown possibilities for evil. It is an amazing lesson on the folly of politics in banking."[269]

WOULD THE ALDRICH-VREELAND ACT WORK?

On June 10, 1908, in an obscure office in Washington, D.C., Joseph E. Ralph created $4 million.[270] As director of the Bureau of Engraving and Printing, Ralph had already launched an around-the-clock program to print the $500 million in emergency currency authorized under the Aldrich-Vreeland Act. The *New York Times* described some of the details: "Because of the desire to make ready for what promises to be a record breaking crop movement, the [printing] plates of the interior banks that are being prepared now are of the smaller denominations— fives and tens. The plates of the twenty, fifty, and 100 denominations will not be touched until there is a good supply of the others on hand."[271]

Despite the progress in creating the $500 million in new currency, fundamental questions about the Aldrich-Vreeland Act remained. Would the tax on the currency discourage banks from applying for relief even in a legitimate emergency? Would the power lodged within the Treasury Department lead to overissue and inflation? Would banks form the currency associations needed to create the full amount of emergency currency?

Time would answer all of these questions, but the early evidence on the formation of currency associations was not encouraging. Exactly one national currency association, in Washington, D.C., had been established by the end of 1908. More than a year later the total remained the same. In July 1910 Treasury Secretary MacVeagh urged banks to act before they had to: "Personally I do not expect that any national currency association will ever within the life of the law have to avail itself of the powers with respect to the issue of currency. Indeed I think that the very formation and existence of these associations would strongly tend to prevent the need to exercise their powers. I therefore minimize the use of these associations in emergencies and magnify the importance of their influence in preventing emergencies."[272]

MacVeigh's appeal bore fruit. Within a year banks in the major financial centers, including New York, Chicago, St. Louis, Boston, and Philadelphia, had formed national currency associations. A total of 284 banks, representing one-third of the capital and surplus of all banks in the United States, joined national currency associations.[273] But MacVeigh was wrong about never needing the emergency currency. The outbreak of the Great War created a crisis that, if unchecked, would have dwarfed the Panic of 1907. The existence of emergency currency, available immediately throughout the country by legislative design, brightened the prospects in August 1914.

Two fatal flaws in the Aldrich-Vreeland Act nearly destroyed the safety net. Congress had scheduled the Aldrich-Vreeland Act to expire on June 30, 1914, exactly one month before it would be needed, as a prod to total currency reform. In a stroke of luck the Federal Reserve Act, passed on December 23, 1913, extended the expiration date for one more year—until June 30, 1915. But the second fatal flaw remained on the books. Treasury Secretary McAdoo had to convince Congress to amend the law on August 3, 1914, to save the day.

CHAPTER FOUR

Unlocking Emergency Currency

THE BANKERS worried as they waited for Treasury Secretary McAdoo in Manhattan's Vanderbilt Hotel on Sunday night, August 2, 1914. They knew that the European war threatened America with a currency shortage. A day earlier the *Washington Post* had set the tone: "The disappearance of $45,000,000 of gold from the United States within the past week is responsible for a feeling that a situation might arise in which the United States as a whole would find itself short of circulating media."[274] The bankers feared the development of bank runs like "those experienced in the fall of 1907"—only worse.[275]

Recall that gold, such as the $20 double eagle coin, and paper money, such as greenbacks, served as bank reserves as well as circulating currency.[276] Gold withdrawals reduced reserves.[277] People knew that the banks had tried to conserve reserves in 1907 by suspending the convertibility of deposits into currency. In 1914 the bankers realized that the gold outflow to Europe could "inspire fear" and trigger an added rush into cash before suspensions took effect.[278] Precautionary withdrawals of currency from the banks would exacerbate the loss in reserves from the gold outflow.

The race for cash in August 1914 promised to make the October 1907 scramble seem like a leisurely stroll. As a *New York Times* editorial observed, "Probably never has the world witnessed a more general embarrassment of commercial relations. Its relation to our troubles in 1907 is about the same as a conflagration to a fire."[279] Gold movements confirm the contrast: the outflow during June and July 1914 was more than double the outflow experienced prior to the panic in October 1907.[280] And Europe was about to intensify the drain.

Many of the bankers assembled at the Vanderbilt Hotel had lived through the Panic of 1907. William Woodward, president of the Hanover National Bank and a recently elected director of the Federal Reserve Bank of New York, had been vice-president at the Hanover Bank in 1907. Woodward had called McAdoo in Washington on Sunday morning, August 2, 1914, requesting the meeting on behalf of the leading bankers of New York City.[281] A. Barton Hepburn, now chairman of the Chase National Bank, had been the president of Chase during 1907. Before that Hepburn had served as New York State's superintendent of banking. Frank A. Vanderlip, now the president of National City Bank, had been vice-president at that institution in 1907. National City Bank was the largest bank in the United States.

Both Hepburn and Vanderlip had emphasized the need for legislation establishing a central bank during the dark days of 1907; neither had much use for the Aldrich-Vreeland bill that had been passed instead in May 1908.[282] Hepburn had called the bill "communistic and socialistic" and said "no worse proposition had ever been moved in Congress."[283]

On August 2, 1914, Hepburn wished he had swallowed those words. Although Congress had authorized America's central bank in December 1913 by passing the Federal Reserve Act, the system remained inoperative on the eve of the world crisis. Two of Woodrow Wilson's nominations to the Federal Reserve Board had stalled in the Senate Banking Committee and preparations to open the individual Federal Reserve Banks were far from complete. The New York Bank welcomed William Woodward to its board of directors but had no office space, no staff, and no chief executive officer. Hepburn knew the Chase National Bank would need Aldrich-Vreeland emergency currency. As matters stood, however, his bank would not qualify under the law.

THE BANKERS PREPARE

The executive committee of the New York Clearing House had been in session since ten o'clock Sunday morning.[284] They had decided to issue Clearing House loan certificates and had scheduled a meeting of the entire Clearing House for the following day, Monday, August 3, 1914.[285] Clearing House loan certificates had been issued during the panics of 1873, 1884, 1893, and 1907 to allow banks to settle obligations among themselves with credits at the local clearing house. Clearing House loan certificates would conserve currency but would not provide a generally acceptable medium of exchange throughout the country. Cash commanded a premium during 1907 even after banks had resorted to the loan certificates.

New York State superintendent of banking, Eugene Richards, had been a guest for part of the day at the Clearing House Committee meeting. He advised the group that he would recommend imposing the "sixty-day clause" on savings deposits.[286] The clause had been last invoked in 1907 to allow savings banks to prevent cash withdrawals without sixty days' notice.

Richards also sought to control the behavior of private banks in New York that had operated beyond the pale of regulation. Most prominent among the private banks were the wholesale giants, J. P. Morgan & Company and Kuhn, Loeb & Company. These two banks accepted deposits primarily from wealthy individuals who craved anonymity. They remained private precisely so that they had no obligation to disclose their activities to regulators. Richards left the wealthy individuals and their bankers to their own devices. But he worried about the small private banks on the Lower East Side of Manhattan that competed for deposits from the local crop of immigrants.*

According to the *New York Times*, one of the first acts on August 2 was "a note sent out by Superintendent Richards to the private bankers requesting that no business be transacted [that day]."[287] The private banks amid the pushcarts on East Broadway and Delancey Street had been accustomed to remain open on Sunday, and in the evenings during the week, to accommodate their working-class depositors. The bankers had anticipated trouble and posted closing notices on their own. The *Times* reported that "large crowds gathered about the offices of the private banks in the congested districts, and discussed the brief notice on the door that no business would be handled on Sunday."[288]

With preparations under way to prevent a panic, why did the banking elite, including J. P. Morgan and his partner Henry Davison, and Benjamin Strong, who would soon be named governor of the Federal Reserve Bank of New York, gather at the Vanderbilt Hotel at 8:30 in the evening? They had already spent much of the day caucusing in executive session with the Clearing House Committee.

Reports from Britain stirred the bankers' nightmares. A *Wall Street Journal* article on August 1 carried the headline, "Run Started on the Bank of England and the Discount Rate Is Advanced to Eight Percent."[289] The *New York Times* highlighted London's distress: "The scene witnessed at the Bank [of England] yesterday [July 31] during the rush to obtain gold in exchange for banknotes was repeated this morning [August 1] but on a larger scale. A few persons who had been too late to get currency yesterday spent the night near the Bank, and reached the quadrangle at daybreak so as to be first in line today. . . . The crowd increased in the course of the morning and an hour after the opening about 500 persons were lined up. The bank porters had been sworn in as special policemen so that they could more easily handle the crowd and in case of necessity, arrest anybody causing a disturbance."[290]

The frenzy trapped thousands of Americans vacationing in Europe without resources. The *Washington Post* described the confusion: "Not even in the height of the tourist season are there more Americans in

---

* On April 16, 1914, New York State governor Glynn signed a law bringing private banks that dealt with the general public under the supervision of the New York State superintendent of banks (see *New York Times*, April 17, 1914).

London than tonight. In addition to those spending the holiday here . . . is another contingent . . . as a consequence of steamers from France and Belgium. Although the pockets of many of them are full of American and English bank notes and American express companies' bills, they might just as well have nothing, for only gold and silver is taken anywhere."[291]

The Bank of England had tried to deflect the demand for specie the way central bankers had been tutored—by raising the interest rate to discourage withdrawals. The bank doubled its rate of interest from 4 percent to 8 percent on Friday, July 31, 1914, and then raised it to 10 percent on Saturday, a level last witnessed in 1866, when the great private banking firm of Overend Gurney & Company failed.[292]

Londoners clamored for gold despite record-breaking interest rates. As a matter of law, local banks could exchange their customers' deposits either for Bank of England notes or gold; both were legal tender. On July 31 the local banks provided paper currency only and sent their customers who wanted gold to the Bank of England.[293] The lines at Britain's central bank on Threadneedle Street testified to the public's concern that the Bank of England might suspend convertibility of its notes into gold. People knew that war offered combatants a legitimate excuse to suspend the gold standard.* To buy time, the Bank of England, chartered in 1694, asked the British government to declare a bank holiday until Friday August 7.† The holiday closed all banks and King George V proclaimed a one-month moratorium on the payment of bills of exchange.[294]

New York bankers gathered at the Vanderbilt Hotel to avoid a similar fate. Without the Federal Reserve System, and without a king, only McAdoo could defend them.

McADOO'S PROBLEM

William G. McAdoo had unfinished business in the capital and wanted the bankers to come to Washington on Sunday, August 2. In a telephone conversation that morning, William Woodward, acting chairman of the executive committee of the New York Clearing House, told McAdoo that the bankers wanted to remain in New York to promote an air of "business as usual" on Monday morning.[295] McAdoo conferred with

---

* Britain suspended the convertibility of its currency into gold during the Napoleonic Wars, America suspended during the Civil War, and France suspended during the Franco-Prussian War (see Bordo and Rockoff 1996, 414–15).

† The holiday also gave the government time to print small denomination "emergency currency" needed by the public (see New York Times, August 4, 1914). Chancellor of the exchequer, Lloyd George, announced (Wall Street Journal, August 6, 1914) that one pound notes and 10 shilling notes would be available by Friday, August 7.

Woodrow Wilson over lunch at the White House. The president urged him to go to New York. McAdoo agreed, although he did not like changing plans on short notice.

Thin and angular, McAdoo prepared for every venture as though he were about to run a marathon. When he first came to New York in 1892 he formed a partnership with a friend he knew from Chattanooga, Francis Pemberton, to sell investment securities. Railroad bonds were the most popular corporate securities, and McAdoo realized that an intimate knowledge of railroad finances would help: "I became a walking encyclopedia of railroad statistics. . . . I could give the capitalization, earnings, and general characteristics of every well known railroad in the United States. . . . The drawers of my desk were crammed full of railroad maps. I studied them day and night. After a while I had a mental picture of every important railroad system; I could take a map of the United States and mark with a pencil the main line and principal branches of any railroad one might name."[296]

The securities venture succeeded, in part, because of McAdoo's preparation. His intimate knowledge of railroads contributed to his crowning triumph—tunneling under the Hudson River to create passenger rail service between Manhattan and Hoboken, New Jersey. "McAdoo's Tunnels," as they were called in the press, brought local fame to the lawyer-turned-entrepreneur and provided entry into the inner circles of the newly elected governor of New Jersey, Woodrow Wilson.*

On Friday, July 31, 1914, McAdoo had recognized the currency shortage confronting the American banking system. He invoked the Aldrich-Vreeland Act and invited banks to participate: "Currency may be issued under that Act . . . to meet any emergency. . . . There is in the Treasury, printed and ready for issue, $500,000,000 of currency, which the banks can get upon application under that law."[297]

Under the terms of the Aldrich-Vreeland Act, banks could bring their commercial paper and other securities to their local National Currency Association and receive in exchange currency in the form of emergency national bank notes. Depositors could not discriminate between emergency national bank notes and "normal" national bank notes, created by the deposit of government securities at the Treasury, because all national bank notes issued after 1908 looked the same. They all bore the inscription: "Secured by United States Bonds or Other Securities." Emergency currency would satisfy depositor demands for cash.

---

* On October 6, 1907, a *New York Times* headline announced "A McAdoo Terminal Finished," and on October 18, 1907, four days before the run on the Knickerbocker Trust Company, the *Times* headlined: "McAdoo Tubes from Christopher Street Nearly Completed." Also see McAdoo (1931, 113).

New York banks had plenty of commercial paper to use as collateral at the local National Currency Association, but most did not qualify for currency under the Aldrich-Vreeland Act. Recall that the original legislation contained two nearly fatal flaws. The first problem, the June 30, 1914, expiration date, disappeared in the Federal Reserve Act, which extended the emergency currency provisions for one year—through June 30, 1915.* The second defect prevented some of the largest banks from qualifying for Aldrich-Vreeland currency. The original legislation restricted emergency currency to those banks which had already issued national bank notes at least equal to 40 percent of their capital.

Most New York banks had a smaller amount of bank notes outstanding than required under the provisions of the Aldrich-Vreeland Act. Frank Vanderlip's National City Bank, the largest bank in the United States, had deposits of $196 million, capital of $25 million, and bank notes outstanding of only $3.6 million.[298] National City Bank would have had to triple its bank note issue to qualify for emergency currency under the Aldrich-Vreeland Act. A. Barton's Hepburn's Chase National Bank had $115 million in deposits, $5 million in capital, and less than one-half million in national bank note liabilities.[299] Chase would have had to quadruple its bank notes outstanding to qualify. These banks did not own the government bonds needed to pledge as collateral to create additional national bank notes.

When McAdoo arrived at the Vanderbilt Hotel at 9:30 p.m. on August 2, he asked the assembled bankers whether they really needed emergency currency. Frank Vanderlip jumped to the head of the line: "We certainly do. . . . Probably more than anybody else. We have more country correspondents than any other New York Bank."[300] McAdoo felt a sense of urgency from everyone in the room. Edward Shelton, president of the U.S. Trust Company, and a former classmate of Woodrow Wilson at Princeton, emphasized that "his colleagues had not exaggerated the condition of affairs."[301] Before McAdoo left the meeting, he promised the New York bankers that he would do his best.

McAdoo had, in fact, started to resolve the problem confronting New York banks but had been interrupted. On Friday afternoon, July 31, after declaring the emergency, McAdoo had visited the Senate and lobbied Robert Owen, chairman of the Senate Banking Committee, to suspend the 40 percent requirement by amending the Aldrich-Vreeland Act.[302]

Senator Owen addressed the full Senate after his conference with McAdoo and left no doubt about the origin of his initiative: "I will read

* Broesamle (1973, 112) credits McAdoo with the suggestion to extend the Aldrich-Vreeland Act through June 30, 1915. Broesamle provides no reference for his assertion, and I have been unable to verify his claim.

what has been prepared by the officers of the Treasury department bearing on this subject. It is a proposed amendment of section 27 of the Federal Reserve Act . . . [which] amended the Aldrich Vreeland Act and continued it until June 30, 1915. . . . The proposed amendment is: Whenever in his judgment he may deem it desirable, the Secretary of the Treasury may suspend the limitations [relating to] . . . banks having circulating notes outstanding not less than 40 percent of their capital stock."[303]

The Senate passed McAdoo's amendment after a ten-minute debate.[304] Minnesota Senator Knute Nelson tried to explain the Senate's haste without triggering undue alarm: "We passed [this bill] not because there is any immediate danger but as a precautionary measure. The difference between us and Europe is this: Europe is engaged in mobilizing its armies and navies, while we are simply engaged in mobilizing our bank reserves."[305]

The next day's newspapers trumpeted McAdoo's victory: "Responsive to the urgent request of Secretary of the Treasury McAdoo, the Senate at once passed a precautionary measure against financial disturbance in the United States in the form of an Amendment to the Aldrich-Vreeland emergency currency act permitting banks to avail themselves of the benefits of the act."[306]

McAdoo did not join the celebration. The House of Representatives had already adjourned on Friday afternoon, July 31, after the Senate had passed his amendment. A comment in the *Washington Post* set an ominous tone: "The sudden action of the Senate will meet with some disfavor in the House."[307] Congressman Hayes of California reflected the discontent: "It seems to me it is proper that I should call to your attention the fact that the Federal Reserve Act was passed eight months ago by this Congress, and I believe that the party in power has been almost criminally negligent in that at this time the federal reserve board is not even appointed. . . . It seems to me that the exercise of ordinary diligence would have had the system in full operation long before this, which would have provided, I hope, for all emergencies at this time without the necessity of this piecework legislation."[308]

Hayes's complaint about piecework legislation sounded as though it had been launched like a missile directly from Carter Glass's 1908 speech to the House savaging the Aldrich-Vreeland bill. Glass had referred to the original act as "a makeshift legislative deformity."[309]

When McAdoo left the Vanderbilt Hotel at midnight on August 2, 1914, he did not know whether his amendment would survive Carter Glass's House Banking and Currency Committee. That was why he had been reluctant to leave Washington on Sunday. He returned to the capital on Monday morning anxious to complete his job of protecting the American banking system.

DISPENSING ALDRICH-VREELAND CURRENCY

McAdoo's amendment stirred the anti–New York sentiment among mid-westerners in the House of Representatives. Congressman Victor Murdock of Kansas derided the legislation: "As the bill passed the Senate . . . it was unmistakably giving aid to the investment bankers, principally in New York City, at the expense of the discount bankers over the country. . . . Ordinarily [it] would not pass Congress without days of debate, if it could pass at all."[310] Representative Charles A. Lindbergh of Minnesota, father of the famed aviator and creator of the family isolationist philosophy, added: "It is rather strange that Congress acts so quickly to help out the speculators in emergencies, when neither the farmers nor the wage earners can secure legislation, however urgent it may be. We probably have an emergency . . . but it is one created by the speculators having put themselves in a position to be affected by a foreign war; and if they can get this act passed they will dare to speculate more on the results of the war."[311]

Carter Glass's Banking and Currency Committee reported the Senate bill to the House floor at noon on Monday, August 3. Glass worried that the emergency measure might delay his main priority, the birth of the Federal Reserve System. His committee added a provision "to extend the benefits of this Act to all qualified state banks and trust companies which have joined the Federal Reserve System or which may contract to join within 15 days after the passage of this act."[312] Thus Carter Glass transformed McAdoo's amendment into a vehicle for promoting system membership.

Congressman Murdock refused to support even Glass's more inclusive version of the amendment but still predicted that "this bill will pass against an unavailing protest here, as it passed one time previously when the camel was getting his nose in the flap of the tent. . . . It will be only a few months until the camel will be entirely in the tent."[313]

Murdock was right about the passage of the bill. The *Congressional Record* reported a vote of 231 in favor and 6 against in the House of Representatives on the evening of August 3.[314] Both Murdock and Lindbergh voted against. The *Congressional Record* remained silent, however, about the camel.

The final bill that passed on August 4, after a conference between the House and the Senate, suspended the 40 percent requirement, extended emergency currency to state-charted banks and trust companies, and eliminated the $500 million ceiling on the total amount of emergency currency contained in the original legislation. Under the amended bill, each bank could issue emergency currency up to 125 percent of its capital.

In the end, Carter Glass had joined forces with Treasury Secretary McAdoo to push the legislation amending the Aldrich-Vreeland Act through Congress. He had emphasized the sense of urgency before the House: "I too could wish that we had more time for consideration of so grave a subject as amendment of this Federal statute. . . . But we have not the time. . . . This [circumstance] is more than an emergency. It is a difficulty of such stupendous nature . . . the like never before confronted the world. . . . Congress should not hesitate one moment." He then drew on the support he had garnered for the Federal Reserve Act by explaining: "There is nothing extraordinary about the legislation aside from the fact that we are proposing to lodge with one public official—the Secretary of the Treasury—discretionary power, such as under the Federal Reserve Act we have lodged with the Federal Reserve Board."[315]

Carter Glass did not want to put everything under McAdoo's control. He said: "If the Federal Reserve System were fully organized there would be no earthly necessity for the action proposed here today."[316] Glass backed McAdoo's amended version of the Aldrich-Vreeland Act because he had no choice.

Carter Glass thought that the Federal Reserve would have been best equipped to combat the crisis because he had watched Treasury Secretary Cortelyou try and fail to defeat the Panic of 1907. Glass had no way of knowing that America's central bank would fail to prevent a banking crisis in the 1930s. He did not recognize that America was probably better off in August 1914 with McAdoo dispensing Aldrich-Vreeland emergency currency than it would have been with a fully organized Federal Reserve.* And neither did anyone else, except perhaps for William Gibbs McAdoo.

McAdoo had already mobilized emergency currency on Monday, August 3, 1914, the day before Congress passed the amendment. The *New York Times* described the arrival of the currency as though the cavalry had come to the rescue: "The new currency arrived at [New York's] sub-Treasury in twenty big mail trucks. . . . it attracted a great deal of attention from the crowds which quickly gathered." The *Times* added a sobering note: "John Skelton Williams, Comptroller of the Currency, spent the day at the sub-Treasury . . . to facilitate the delivery of Aldrich-Vreeland notes, of which $46,000,000 arrived here, but the banks were unable to complete their end of the arrangements. . . . They expected to call for a large amount of the notes today [August 4]."[317]

---

* Under the Aldrich-Vreeland Act the initiative for issuing emergency currency came from individual banks. Thus high-powered money (currency plus bank reserves) could expand endogenously to meet a shortage of liquidity. During the Great Depression the Federal Reserve knew Walter Bagehot's principle of lending freely but did not implement it consistently and automatically (see Silber 2006).

The original Aldrich-Vreeland Act, passed in May 1908 to guard against a replay of the previous year's panic, anticipated the importance of speed in containing a crisis. It had stipulated that the $500 million emergency currency that had been authorized be printed immediately after the passage of the act. Each national bank's allotment of notes, embossed with the bank's name and decorative logo, had been prepared for distribution by the end of 1908. The entire supply, including the $46 million delivered to New York on August 3, 1914, had been stored in an underground vault especially constructed for this purpose in Washington, D.C., under the supervision of Watson Eldridge, chief of the division of issues in the Currency Bureau.[318] But the congressional amendment suspending the 40 percent requirement, passed to accommodate the large New York City banks in August 1914, created a bottleneck. It altered the amount of emergency national bank notes that could be issued by each institution.

McAdoo's public display in delivering emergency currency to the New York subtreasury on August 3, 1914, similar to his armed escort for gold delivered to the same place four days earlier, was designed to reassure the public that each bank would get all the currency it needed.* Meanwhile Joseph E. Ralph, director of the Bureau of Engraving and Printing, hired one hundred extra men and women and ran the printing presses around the clock to meet the anticipated demand.[319] District of Columbia municipal commissioner, Oliver P. Newman, ruled that Ralph's twelve-hour shifts for treasury employees did not violate the "eight hour maximum law for women."[320] President Wilson suspended the Saturday half-holiday normally granted to bureau employees during the summer.[321]

During the first week of August 1914, the Treasury Department shipped $140,697,230 in Aldrich-Vreeland notes to the subtreasuries in New York, Chicago, St. Louis, Boston, Baltimore, Philadelphia, Cincinnati, New Orleans, and San Francisco.[322] As of Saturday, August 8, individual banks had drawn more than $100 million of that currency by depositing commercial paper and other securities with their national currency associations.[323] By the middle of August the comptroller began delivering the emergency currency directly to the issuing banks, and by month's end the total exceeded $200 million. The $200 million in emergency currency represented an increase of more than 25 percent in national bank notes outstanding during the month. National bank notes had been virtually unchanged during the previous year and had increased by an average of $15 million *per year* since 1910.[324]

* On July 31, 1914, the *Wall Street Journal* (p. 7) reported: "Protected by a force of over twenty men, seven large United States mail auto trucks drove up to the sub-Treasury at three o'clock yesterday afternoon and proceeded to deposit there piles of mail pouches filled with gold."

McAdoo had clearly anticipated the need to amend the Aldrich-Vreeland Act. He had also started the distribution process before formal congressional approval. Yet McAdoo had not thought about the Aldrich-Vreeland Act since it had been superseded by the Federal Reserve Act, passed on December 23, 1913. Since then, as chairman of the Federal Reserve Organizing Committee, McAdoo had been preoccupied with getting the Federal Reserve System up and running. He had presided over hearings throughout the country to determine the precise number of Federal Reserve districts. After the Organizing Committee had divided the country into twelve regions, McAdoo had been lobbied by cities within those districts for the right to house a regional Federal Reserve Bank. And since the middle of June 1914 McAdoo himself had to lobby members of Congress on behalf of Woodrow Wilson's nominations to the Federal Reserve Board. When did he learn the details of the emergency currency legislation that, absent an eleventh-hour amendment to the Federal Reserve Act, would have expired on June 30, 1914?[325]

A TEST RUN

McAdoo flirted with Aldrich-Vreeland currency during the spring of 1913, a year before the European war. The newly elected president, Woodrow Wilson, had proposed tariff reduction legislation that provoked considerable opposition in the business community. Wilson pushed simultaneously for prompt passage of Carter Glass's Federal Reserve Act, in part, because he expected that the new currency system could supply easy money during the first few months of reduced protection from foreign competition. When Wilson suspected that Republican senators wanted to block currency revision for the simple purpose of precipitating a financial panic and blaming the administration's new tariff policies, he turned to McAdoo for help.[326]

In the evening of June 11, 1913, McAdoo announced that "he would not hesitate to issue emergency currency to any banks making application and qualifying under the [Aldrich-Vreeland] Act."[327] When McAdoo was asked whether any applications had been made he simply said: "No." The press noted that: "The only explanation obtainable as to Mr. McAdoo's purpose . . . is that it is intended to give assurance . . . that the Wilson Administration will do its utmost to overcome any financial embarrassment that may come."[328]

Would Aldrich-Vreeland currency succeed in calming the business community? Opponents of the original legislation had argued that, instead of preventing a panic, the provision of emergency currency might backfire and provoke one. As the then comptroller of the currency,

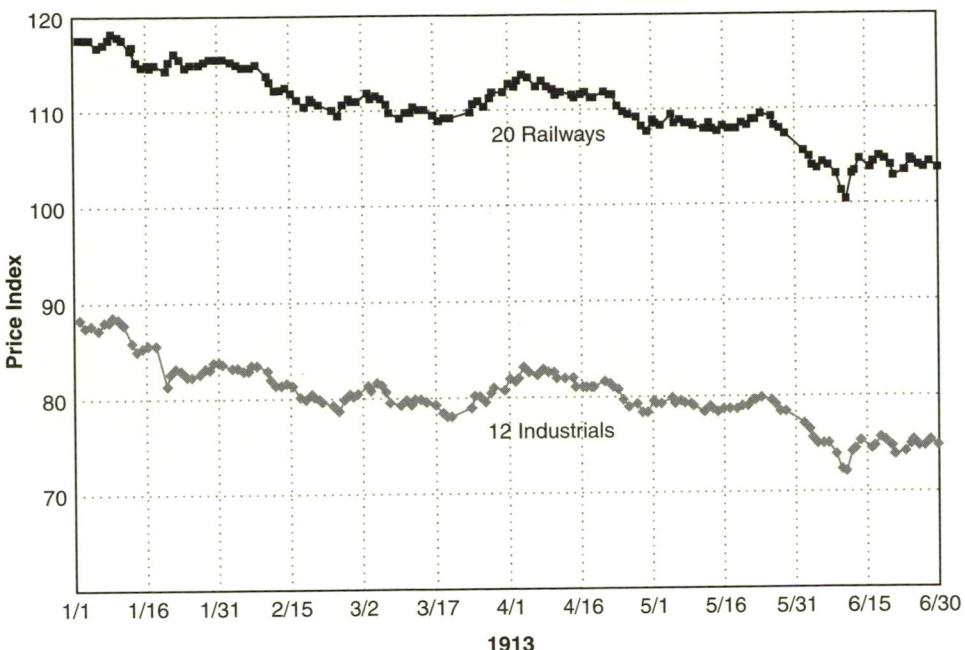

Figure 4.1. Stock Prices on the New York Stock Exchange, January 1, 1913, to June 30, 1913.

Data Source: *Wall Street Journal.*

William Ridgely, warned, "The issue of so-called emergency notes . . . would at once be a confession of weakness and a danger signal that no bank would dare make until in desperate condition."[329] Princeton professor Edwin Kemmerer echoed that sentiment years later: "Bankers generally expressed their unwillingness to issue currency under the Act, except in case of an extreme emergency, because to do so would be to advertise to the world that they were in a precarious financial condition, which would itself aggravate the evil to be remedied."[330] Perhaps that is why no emergency currency had ever been requested since the Aldrich-Vreeland Act had been passed in May 1908. How did the business world respond to McAdoo's June 11, 1913, invitation to taste the forbidden fruit?

Figure 4.1 shows the price levels of twenty railroad stocks and twelve industrials for each day during the first six months of 1913. Prices in both sectors trended down from the beginning of the year, interrupted by minor upturns, until registering a low point on June 11—the day of McAdoo's announcement. McAdoo released his statement invoking the

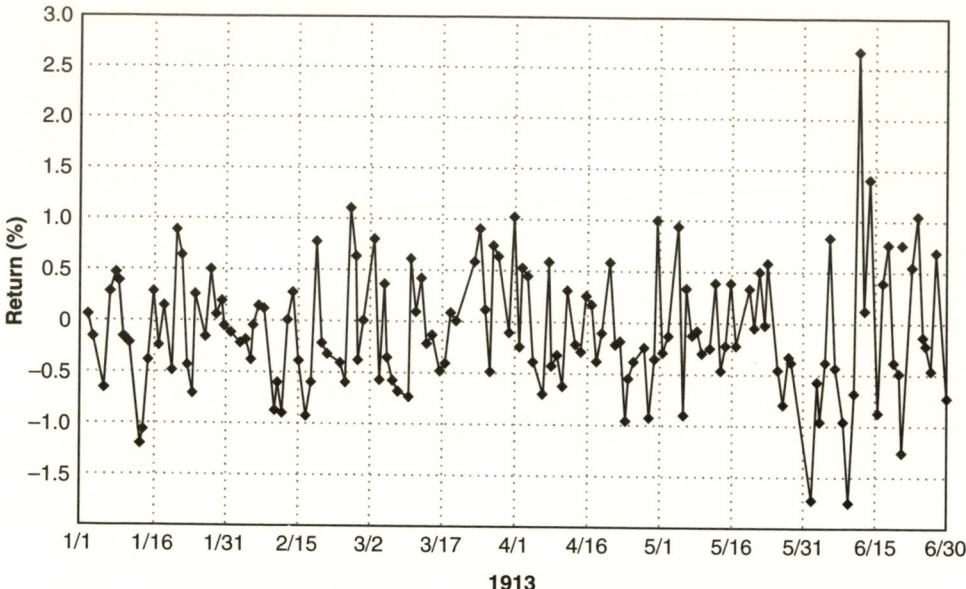

Figure 4.2. Daily Returns for Railroad Stocks, January 1, 1913, to June 30, 1913.

Data Source: Figure 4.1.

Aldrich-Vreeland Act on the evening of June 11, after the market had closed. Thus, if McAdoo's announcement had a material impact, for better or worse, it should have been reflected in stock price movements on June 12. Figure 4.2 transforms the price levels for railroad stocks in Figure 4.1 into daily returns—the percentage price change from one day to the next. The return of more than 2.5 percent on June 12 stands out as the largest significant positive return during the first six months of 1913. Industrial stocks recorded a similar outsized positive return of more than 3 percent on June 12.*

The *Wall Street Journal* highlighted McAdoo's announcement in explaining the June 12 stock market performance:[331] "The market was strong, active, and broad, rising with a resiliency exceeding anything seen previously this year, if indeed there was anything like it in the previous three or four years. The most potent cause of the improvement was the announcement of the Treasury Secretary in regard to emergency currency, which was tantamount to an invitation to the banks to avail themselves

---

* The price movements in both indexes on June 12, 1913, are statistically significant. During the first half of 1913 the daily standard deviation of returns equaled .61 percent for railroad stocks and .78 percent for the industrials.

of the provisions of the Aldrich-Vreeland law to provide against a possible severe stringency of money in the fall."*

McAdoo's offer of emergency currency during 1913 found no takers. Perhaps Comptroller of the Currency Ridgley and Professor Kemmerer were right—accepting the offer would shatter a bank's reputation. But Wall Street's vote of confidence on June 12, 1913, showed McAdoo the potential power of the Aldrich-Vreeland Act. He felt as though he had a loaded gun in his pocket.

TRIAL UNDER FIRE

On July 31, 1914, American markets ran into a roadblock, bringing financial traffic to a standstill. At 9:45 on the morning of the July 31 the governing board of the New York Stock Exchange voted to suspend all trading in stocks and bonds. Investors could no longer raise cash by selling securities on the New York Stock Exchange. On the international front, the foreign exchange market ground to a halt. As the *Wall Street Journal* reported, "Business on the foreign exchange market is completely suspended. No rates are quoted, though in some quarters . . . sterling is nominally given at 5.20 [dollars per pound]."[332] Importers and exporters could not convert dollars into British pounds, the generally accepted international medium of exchange.

Nothing darkens a crisis like the disappearance of a market. Routine transactions that barely merit a second thought become impossible, and business relationships, normally taken for granted, disappear. The double-barreled closures on July 31, 1914, disrupted the financial linkages that greased the wheels of American commerce.

The shutdown of the New York Stock Exchange, designed to short-circuit European access to American gold, simultaneously deprived U.S. investors of liquidity—the ability to turn assets into cash on short notice. Investors value liquidity and will pay a higher price for assets that are readily marketable.[333] In 1913 investors bought and sold more than 83 million shares, $502 million corporate bonds, and $29 million municipal bonds on the New York Stock Exchange.[334] Now they were stuck without a market.

The inability to purchase sterling on the foreign exchange market meant that American companies and municipalities that had borrowed

---

* The *Journal* noted that stock prices increased at the opening bell on June 12 and continued strong throughout the day. The *Journal* also cited the failure of the U.S. attorney general to oppose a plan for an exchange of stock by Union Pacific Railroad as another favorable factor. Despite this favorable industry event, the railroad index rose by 2.7 percent on June 12 compared with an increase of 3 percent by the industrials.

abroad might not meet their obligations. Most prominent among the debtors was New York City. America's largest city owed European investors $80 million in sterling denominated bonds that were due before the end of the year. Foreign banks offered to accept a "heavy discount" if New York City would have repaid those loans on August 1.[335] They were willing to accept a discount because New York City's credit had come under the cloud of war. City Controller Prendergast said he refused the offer because "he did not consider it a good bargain."[336] Prendergast refused the offer because he could not make the payment in pounds. He also could not send gold. The rumblings of war had shut the foreign exchange market and left the Atlantic too treacherous for the precious metal.

The run on the Bank of England showed that no institution, no matter how reputable, was immune from the scramble that began on July 31, 1914. The British government declared a bank holiday until Friday, August 7, to stem the assault.[337] American institutions, without a central bank and still tarnished by the suspensions of 1907, seemed even more vulnerable. Moreover, the loss of liquidity from the shutdown of the New York Stock Exchange should have exacerbated the problem. Investors would need larger cash balances to manage their affairs.[338] Yet banks in New York, Chicago, St. Louis, and every other American city remained open for business without a replay of 1907. Where did the unruly crowds go?

In August 1914 American bankers met the crisis like generals backed with heavy artillery. When depositors asked for their money, the financiers could answer with confidence: "How would you like it, small bills or large?" They knew that McAdoo had dispatched crisp new national bank notes to the rescue. And once depositors knew they could get their money they were less insistent about taking it home. Dollar bills were much safer in the bank than under the mattress, as long as they were equally accessible. In 1907 the bankers ran out of "fives" and "tens" before they ran out of customers—and depositors panicked.

The demand for cash did not simply melt away under banker swagger in 1914. The financiers appeased the public by dispensing emergency currency like a tranquilizer. Figure 4.3 shows that by Saturday, August 8, less than a week after Congress had passed McAdoo's amendment, $100 million in Aldrich-Vreeland currency entered circulation. Two weeks later the amount outstanding nearly doubled. By the first week in September the total outstanding had reached about $250 million.

Who took all this new currency?

New York's biggest banks applied for Aldrich-Vreeland notes a day after Congress passed the amended legislation. National City Bank, with $196 million in deposits, requested $15 million of emergency currency.[339]

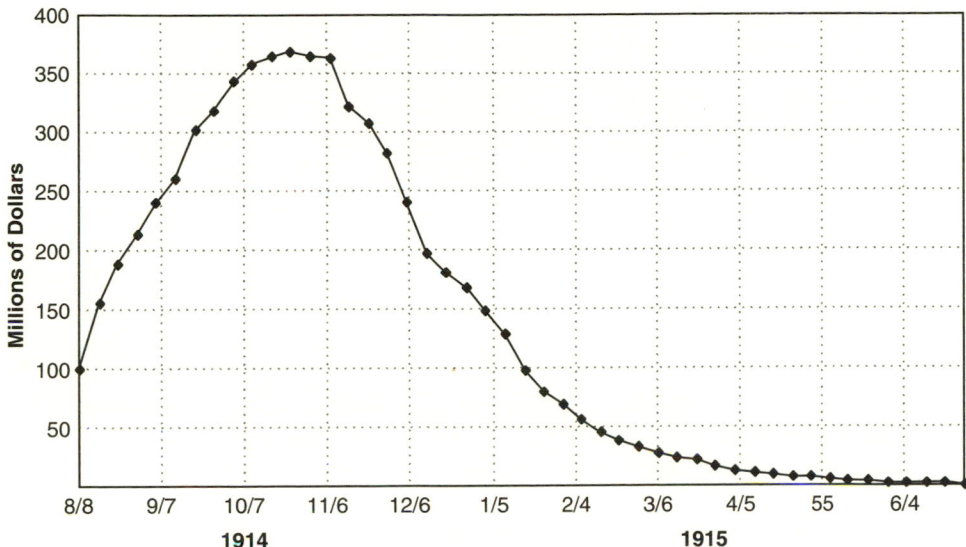

Figure 4.3. Aldrich-Vreeland Currency in Circulation.

Data Source: Comptroller of the Currency, *Annual Report*, December 6, 1915.

The second largest, the National Bank of Commerce, took $9 million.[340] And A. Barton Hepburn, chairman of the third largest bank, Chase National, drowned his distaste for the Aldrich-Vreeland Act with $9,550,000.[341]

Emergency currency lost its stigma during the first week of August as the Great War threatened major banks throughout the country. In Chicago, the Continental and Commercial National Bank applied for $21,000,000 and the First National Bank requested $17,000,000.[342] In Philadelphia, the Girard National Bank asked for $1,140,000.[343] And within days, the Wells Fargo Express Company delivered emergency currency to Minneapolis: $1,160,000 to Northwest National Bank and $1,000,000 to First National.[344]

TOO MUCH OR TOO LITTLE?

Figure 4.3 shows that Aldrich-Vreeland currency outstanding peaked during the last week of October with $368.6 million in circulation, representing a 50 percent increase in national bank notes since the war began. Banks could have issued more than four times that amount without violating the statutory maximum.[345] Institutions in thirty-nine different states of the Union provided currency to their depositors, with banks in New York, Massachusetts, Illinois, Pennsylvania, and Texas leading the pack.[346]

At this time nearly 50 percent of currency outstanding consisted of gold certificates and gold coin.[347] National bank notes and silver currency each contributed about 20 percent to currency in circulation. The final 10 percent consisted of greenbacks—the paper currency first issued by the federal government during the Civil War. The jump in emergency currency between August 1 and October 31 made national bank notes the second most important component of currency in the United States.

Although each form of currency had a unique appearance, they were perfectly interchangeable with one another as far as the public was concerned,[348] just like Federal Reserve notes with large images of great americans issued since 1996 and the older notes with smaller portraits.* Banks chartered by the comptroller of the currency could not use national bank notes as reserves—they were bank liabilities, not assets. But banks pursued a policy of paying out national bank notes over the counter to satisfy customer demands for cash while retaining gold and silver certificates and greenbacks—called legal tender—as reserves.[349] The New York Clearing House pitched in by permitting banks, for the first time, to settle balances with national bank notes rather than legal tender.[350]

The growth in emergency currency produced a 7 percent increase in the monetary base—currency held by the public plus bank reserves—from the onset of the crisis on August 1 through October 31.[351] The money supply, consisting of currency held by the public plus total bank deposits, grew at an annual rate of 9.8 percent over the same period.[352] By way of contrast, in 1907 the public's obsession with currency in October triggered a decline in the money supply at an annual rate of 11.6 percent during the last three months of the year.[353] According to Milton Friedman and Anna Schwartz's *Monetary History of the United States*, "the contraction became much more severe" as the money stock collapsed in 1907.[354]

Flooding the country with paper currency in 1914 met with mixed emotions. A *New York Times* editorial began with great praise: "The existence of these [emergency] notes is the only reason why the currency conditions are now so much better than in 1907." The *Times* concluded with a warning worthy of Jeremiah's Lamentations: "Already it is congesting in the banks, and there is temptation for setting it to work in un-

---

* The U.S. Bureau of Engraving and Printing began a newer series of Federal Reserve notes on October 9, 2003. The most recent redesign included the use of background color—a subtle peach surrounding the portrait of Andrew Jackson on the twenty dollar bill. Color appeared last on the twenty dollar gold certificate printed in 1905 (see Federal Reserve Bank of Minneapolis web site at www.minneapolisfed.org/consumer/money).

desirable ways. Business will take up currency just as a sponge will absorb water. . . . It would be well for bankers not to take more than is necessary."[355]

Concern with papering America with worthless currency haunted those who knew their history. McAdoo beat back an attempt by Congressman Sisson of Mississippi to supplement Aldrich-Vreeland notes with currency issued by state-chartered banks.[356] He reminded everyone of the monetary chaos that reigned when state-chartered bank currency smothered the country: "I am not old enough to know personally what happened prior to the Civil War. But I do know this from history . . . that before the National Bank Act was passed every man to whom a circulating note was offered in payment for anything had to get the Secret Service or detective agency . . . to trace that issue to see if it was worth anything."[357] McAdoo satisfied the South by allowing "notes and obligations based on and secured by cotton warehouse receipts" to back Aldrich-Vreeland currency, as long as a National Currency Association accepted the collateral.* McAdoo conferred credibility on the preachers at the *New York Times* by joking: "There is enough emergency currency authorized by law today to wreck the United States of America."[358]

The framers of the Aldrich-Vreeland Act had, in fact, worried about emergency currency overstaying its welcome. To encourage banks to use the currency only as a temporary stopgap, the original legislation levied a graduated tax on each issuing bank's outstanding notes that began at 5 percent during the first month and increased to a maximum of 10 percent after six months. Congress reduced the starting level of the tax to 3 percent, and the maximum to 6 percent, when it extended the Aldrich-Vreeland measure through June 30, 1915, as part of the Federal Reserve Act.[359] After the spurt in emergency currency during the first two weeks of August 1914 the *Wall Street Journal* complained that "emergency currency at 3 percent [was] unsound" and that Congress had lowered the rate in "its craze for easy money that permeated the currency legislation [the Federal Reserve Act] last year."[360] Did Congress turn emergency currency into a permanent honey pot of cheap credit?

Figure 4.3 shows that by the end of 1914 the amount of emergency currency outstanding had been cut in half. Money supply grew at a rate of 2.7 percent per annum from July 31 through December 31, less than half the annual growth rate recorded over the previous five years.[361] The

---

* The *Commercial and Financial Chronicle* (August 29, 1914), implied that McAdoo may have exceeded his powers: "It is open to question whether there is any warrant in the law for the use of such warehouse receipts as a basis for emergency issues." Laughlin (1908b, 504–5) pointed out that the Aldrich-Vreeland Act permitted "any security" to serve as collateral as long as it was acceptable to the secretary of the Treasury.

congressional blueprint for emergency currency as a temporary safety net could not have been implemented more faithfully.[362]

DID IT MAKE A DIFFERENCE?

No signs of excess liquidity emerged while emergency currency fueled the August through October jump in money supply. Interest rates on "choice" commercial paper actually rose to an average of more than 6.40 percent during this three month period, compared with an average of less than 4.10 percent during the previous three months.[363]

The failure of the spurt in money supply to drive down interest rates during August, September, and October implies that the emergency currency met a precautionary demand for cash triggered by the European conflict. Bankers drew on their allotment of emergency notes to short-circuit a replay of 1907. And they succeeded. Banks in the United States remained open without suspending convertibility of deposits into cash. Comptroller of the Currency John Skelton Williams had warned bankers during the first week of August, after the first delivery of Aldrich-Vreeland notes: "I see no reason why there should be any suspension of currency payments anywhere in this country and if this department hears of any national banks refusing to honor legitimate demands of its customers . . . [the] delinquent bank will be promptly investigated."[364]

The comptroller's *Annual Report* claims: "As a result of the instant and energetic action of the Secretary of the Treasury, August 2, 1914, authorizing and directing the issue of several hundred million dollars of 'emergency currency' . . . the banks in all parts of this country . . . were supplied promptly with all the currency they needed, which enabled them to maintain currency payments throughout the entire country, a record they were unable to make in 1893 and 1907, and in previous crises infinitely less far reaching than that which confronted us."[365]

The comptroller's self-serving evaluation gains credibility from the contemporaneous analysis of Professor O.M.W. Sprague, the crisis expert at Harvard: "For the first time since the establishment of the national banking system the banks exercising the powers conferred upon them by the Aldrich Vreeland Act of 1908 were able to issue bank notes freely in coping with a crisis. . . . Thanks to the emergency notes, the banks were able to maintain payments without difficulty, both over the counter and between themselves . . . and in striking contrast with experience in former crises, the banks were able to meet requirements for additional loans occasioned by the crisis. . . . In no former crisis was the aid rendered by the government so immediate and effective."[366]

On August 1, the *Commercial and Financial Chronicle* had satirized

McAdoo's efforts: "We see the Secretary of the Treasury is again referring to the fact that he has $500,000,000 of crisp new notes that can be put into circulation. . . . We hope the Secretary does not entertain the notion that what is wanted at this critical juncture is easy money."[367] Two weeks later the *Chronicle* sang a different tune: "It is to the credit of the authorities at Washington that in the present grave crisis in the world's history they have acted with commendable energy for the relief and protection of the country's monetary affairs. The vigor and promptness with which they set the machinery in motion for supplying emergency currency under the Aldrich-Vreeland law deserves all praise. . . . Quick action and quick comprehension were imperative, and Messrs. McAdoo and Williams, by their skillful handling of affairs, proved that they were equal to the task."[368]

A SECOND BATTLEFRONT

Most Americans did not care whether they received national bank notes, greenbacks, or gold when they cashed a check at their local bank. Department stores and saloonkeepers did not discriminate among the varieties of circulating currency. This indifference accounts for the success of emergency national bank notes issued under the Aldrich-Vreeland Act. But gold, not national bank notes, served as the only perfectly acceptable international medium of exchange. Companies needed gold or British pounds to make payments abroad, whether for English manufactured goods or to repay a loan denominated in sterling.

The collapse in the foreign exchange market made it impossible to turn U.S. dollars into British pounds. As the *Wall Street Journal* reported on August 1, "Business on the foreign exchange market is completely suspended."[369] Thus, Aldrich-Vreeland emergency currency could not resolve the crisis on its own. Europeans wanted gold, not American paper. Sprague summarized the problem: "The Aldrich-Vreeland notes provided an adequate means of meeting purely domestic requirements, but quite as clearly the course of the crisis indicated that something more was needed to enable the banks to cope with a crisis in which financial relations with foreign markets are disturbed."[370]

McAdoo's amendment to the Aldrich-Vreeland Act, and the prompt delivery of emergency currency, prevented bank suspensions, but they did not curtail the outflow of gold that threatened to overwhelm America's resources, especially after the British found an easy way to pry loose the precious metal.

CHAPTER FIVE

Sterling Steals the Spotlight

A PERSONAL TRAGEDY soon magnified McAdoo's public role. Ellen Axson Wilson, wife of the president and mother-in-law of the treasury secretary, died of Bright's disease, a kidney ailment, on August 6, 1914. According to McAdoo, "For the President her death was a genuine disaster. She supplied a calm excellence of judgment which had contributed uniformly to his happiness and success in life. . . . Her knowledge of human nature was remarkable. The President had an enduring confidence in her estimates of men and their ideas. She proved to be one of the soundest and most influential advisers."[371]

Wilson hid behind the oval office door after burying his wife. He resumed the business of state but retreated from unnecessary engagements. The president avoided a meeting with J. P. Morgan during the second week of August by sending the following note: "I find myself so out of spirits that I have for the moment only strength and initiative enough for the absolutely necessary duties of my official day."[372]

McAdoo had to pick up the slack. On August 8 he scheduled a conference of leading financiers and businessmen for Friday, August 14, to discuss foreign exchange.[373] The *Wall Street Journal* confirmed the scope of the problem by quoting an international banker: "It may seem absurd for Americans to pay $7 for a pound sterling but this price has been paid here for cable transfers. Of course, this is not a commercial transaction or for the movement of goods, but when a man finds his wife and children stranded abroad he will pay a premium of 50 percent or more to put gold in their hands by cable. You cannot, however carry on commerce on any such basis."[374]

The evening before McAdoo announced his foreign exchange meeting, America's largest bank unveiled its own initiative to relieve the problem: "The National City Bank is taking measures to assist exporters and importers in their trade operations which have been impeded owing to the serious derangement of the foreign exchange mechanism. It has conceived a plan of acting as clearing house for . . . those doing business in South America and in other such parts of the world as developments may make it appear necessary and feasible."[375] Frank Vanderlip, president of National City Bank, explained his bank's press release in layman's terms: "The new undertaking was a bartering of credits; in effect, articles purchased in other countries are to be traded for those produced here."[376]

Barter spelled disaster for McAdoo. The crisis had posed a double-barreled threat to American finance: an internal drain of currency from the banking system and an external drain of gold to Europe. McAdoo had neutralized the internal drain by distributing Aldrich-Vreeland emergency currency and had temporarily stemmed the external drain of gold by closing the New York Stock Exchange. McAdoo knew, however, that Americans would need gold, or British pounds, to settle maturing debts that were payable in sterling. His plan to end the crisis, therefore, focused on promoting exports of cotton and wheat to Europe. Exports would generate gold inflows in payment for American goods which could then be used to settle foreign obligations. McAdoo set the agenda for August 14 as follows: "First, providing sufficient ships to move our grain and cotton crops to European markets; and second, restoring through the bankers the market for foreign bills of exchange."[377]

Failure would push America off the gold standard.

TRUE TO GOLD

Alexander Noyes, financial editor of the *New York Evening Post* and author of a 1910 study on national bank notes for the National Monetary Commission, argued that the record-breaking gold shipments during the last week of July undermined the U.S. Treasury's commitment to gold:[378] "If, in response to London calling in its credits, the shipment of gold had continued at that weekly rate, the $308,000,000 gold in the vaults of New York banks . . . would have been exhausted in less than two months. A run on the Treasury reserve to get gold in exchange for government legal tender would have apparently followed."[379]

Noyes became financial editor of the *New York Times* in 1920 and would be referred to as the "dean of American financial journalists" during his twenty-five year tenure at the *Times*.[380] He would warn his readers before the 1929 crash of "the unsoundness of the situation."[381] Was Noyes also right nearly a generation earlier? Could the U.S. Treasury have withstood a widespread rush to turn currency into gold in 1914?

The government's promise to convert its paper currency into specie—gold—lay at the heart of the gold standard. The Gold Standard Act of 1900 established a $150 million gold reserve fund to insure that the Treasury's paper money—primarily greenbacks and silver certificates—could be redeemed at par in terms of gold. As of June 30, 1914, in addition to this $150 million reserve, the Treasury had $252 million in gold over and above what it needed to cover its direct gold liabilities.*

The Gold Standard Act of 1900 solidified America's pledge to gold. That commitment had come under assault in the mid-1890s from massive gold exports combined with political agitation to supplement gold with silver as backing for the dollar.[382] The Democratic Party adopted a pro-silver platform at its 1896 convention and nominated William Jennings Bryan as candidate for president. Bryan electrified the convention with a speech that included his now-famous indictment of gold: "We will answer their demand for a gold standard by saying to them: You shall not press down upon the brow of labor this crown of thorns, you shall not crucify mankind on a cross of gold."[383]

William McKinley defeated Bryan in 1896 and installed gold as king by signing the Gold Standard Act four years later. The total gold stock in the U.S. Treasury more than doubled over the ensuing decade and pro-silver agitation receded. But Bryan did not give up. He ran unsuccessfully for president in 1900 and 1908.

Were the Treasury's gold reserves in 1914 enough? Anything less than one-to-one gold backing against paper is not enough once a run turns into a panic. The U.S. Treasury had fewer gold reserves than potential paper obligations.[†] Nevertheless, Charles A. Conant, a financial author and banker, discounted Alexander Noyes's warning about a run: "The condition of the Treasury was vastly different from that of 1895 when it was necessary to make a contract with the Morgans and Rothchilds to obtain gold abroad to replenish the legal tender reserve and prevent the suspension of specie payments. . . . Under these [August 1914] conditions the Treasury was practically immune from any run on its own gold."[384]

Conant's views carried some weight. In 1901 Secretary of War Elihu Root asked him to analyze Philippine financial institutions and offer rec-

---

* The $252 million excess on June 30, 1914, is the difference between $1,254 million gold coin and bullion held in the U.S. Treasury and $1,026 gold certificates outstanding (see U.S. Treasury, *Annual Report*, 1914).

† Here are the numbers. The $252 million excess gold on June 30, 1914, plus the $150 million in the gold reserve fund could be used to redeem the non-gold paper liabilities of the U.S. Treasury. Direct paper liabilities of the U.S. Treasury on June 30, 1914, included silver certificates totaling $478 million and greenbacks (U.S. notes) totaling $337 million. Silver certificates were also backed by silver bullion so that the gold reserve would only have to cover the potential shortfall in the value of the silver bullion. In addition to these direct paper liabilities of the Treasury, Friedman and Schwartz (1963, 21) explain that, although national bank notes were liabilities of national banks, they were also "indirect liabilities of the federal government." National bank notes totaled $715 million on June 30, 1914. Government bonds secured these national bank notes so the gold reserve would only have to cover any shortfall in the proceeds of the sales of government bonds used to pay off the notes. If there were a run on the Treasury, the price impacts of the sale of bonds and silver would reduce the proceeds and increase the drain on the Treasury's gold reserve.

ommendations for remodeling their system. His suggestions were so successful that the new standard coins in the Philippines were known as Conants to distinguish them from the old Spanish currency.[385]

Charles Conant was probably right. The U.S. Treasury could survive a run at the outbreak of the Great War. But McAdoo could not take the chance. According to Professor J. Laurence Laughlin of the University of Chicago, "For many decades our flirtation with silver caused a loss of confidence among foreign countries in the stability of our standard."[386] William Jennings Bryan's position as secretary of state triggered special scrutiny of American credibility in August 1914. Bryan stood second in line for succession to the presidency, right after the vice-president.* He shared a rigid commitment to American neutrality with Woodrow Wilson at the outbreak of the war. And Bryan meddled in finance. When J. P. Morgan & Company proposed a loan to the French government, Bryan shot the following missive to Wilson: "Money is the worst of all contrabands because it commands everything else."[387] Wilson squashed Morgan's proposal.[388]

The *New York Times* also questioned America's commitment to gold: "Officials have not failed to observe the protective measures taken by European countries to keep intact their stores of gold. . . . The United States may find itself in a position where the administration will be called upon to keep American gold here and give out American paper in exchange."[389]

War offered the moral expedient to abandon the gold standard.[390] Few questioned the Bank of England's right to suspend convertibility of the pound into gold in 1797 during Britain's war with France. The British preserved their credibility by restoring convertibility at the prewar rate in 1821.[391] American neutrality at the outbreak of the Great War foreclosed that approach to McAdoo. France, Germany, and Russia, on the other hand, had good reason to abandon gold during the first week of August. And they did.[392] So would every warring country, save for Britain.

According to John Maynard Keynes, the United Kingdom had more at stake than everyone else.[393] World commerce revolved around London, with Paris and Berlin as junior partners.[394] Sterling served as international currency. Brazilian farmers shipped coffee to Spanish innkeepers and received payment in British pounds at the London office of their bankers, N. M. Rothschild. Brazil also raised capital by selling bonds denominated in pounds in the City of London. Sterling reigned supreme, in part, because London never waffled when asked to exchange pounds for

---

* The Presidential Succession Act of 1947, signed by President Harry Truman, changed the order to what it is today: vice-president, Speaker of the House, president pro tempore of the Senate, and then secretary of state.

gold. Keynes convinced the chancellor of the exchequer that the British government must preserve "the future position of the City of London as a free gold market."[395] Keynes advised the U.K. Treasury "to maintain specie payments so as to meet foreign demands, while making it extremely difficult and inconvenient for the ordinary man to get gold."[396]

McAdoo did not have London to protect. New York barely qualified as an entrant in the global financial race. But McAdoo knew that sustained credibility could help the dollar break into the upper echelon of world finance and behaved as though he had trained with Keynes. On July 31, 1914, McAdoo assured the public that "there would be no gold stringency at the New York sub-Treasury."[397] He backed his promise by delivering "nearly sixty tons of the precious metal . . . in twenty big auto trucks . . . to the back entrance of the sub-Treasury."[398] At the same time, McAdoo shielded America's dwindling supplies of gold. He shut the New York Stock Exchange to hamper Europe's ability to lay claim to American gold.* He invoked the Aldrich-Vreeland Act so banks could retain gold as reserves.[399] Even Conant complimented McAdoo's actions: "The fact that Europe had been dipping her arm up to her elbow in the only stock of free gold left in the world . . . [justified] some defensive measures."[400]

McAdoo understood the limitations of these initiatives. Europeans held U.S. securities that would mature in coming months. They could demand American gold in payment for maturing obligations even with the New York Stock Exchange shut by a wartime curfew. Aldrich-Vreeland currency helped bankers preserve their reserves of legal tender, but the U.S. Treasury would have to convert legal tender into gold to meet legitimate demands. Moreover, McAdoo knew that his emergency measures would damage the American economy if they remained in place. Shutting the stock exchange left the capital market without a compass and the flood of emergency currency risked inflation.

McAdoo needed an exit plan so he could safely remove the temporary stopgaps. He recognized that the gold outflows could be offset by promoting American agricultural exports, so that Europe would have to return the gold in payment. McAdoo focused his August 14 agenda on "providing sufficient ships to move our grain and cotton crops . . . and restoring through the bankers the market for foreign bills of exchange."

---

* Henry Noble, president of the New York Stock Exchange, summarized the argument from Wall Street's perspective: "The fundamental reason for closing the Exchange was that America, when the war broke out, was in debt to Europe, and Europe was sure to enforce the immediate repayment of that debt . . . to prosecute the greatest of all wars. . . . There was to be an unexpected run on Uncle Sam's bank and the stock exchange was the paying teller's window through which the money was to be drawn out, so the window was closed to gain time" (Noble 1915, 65).

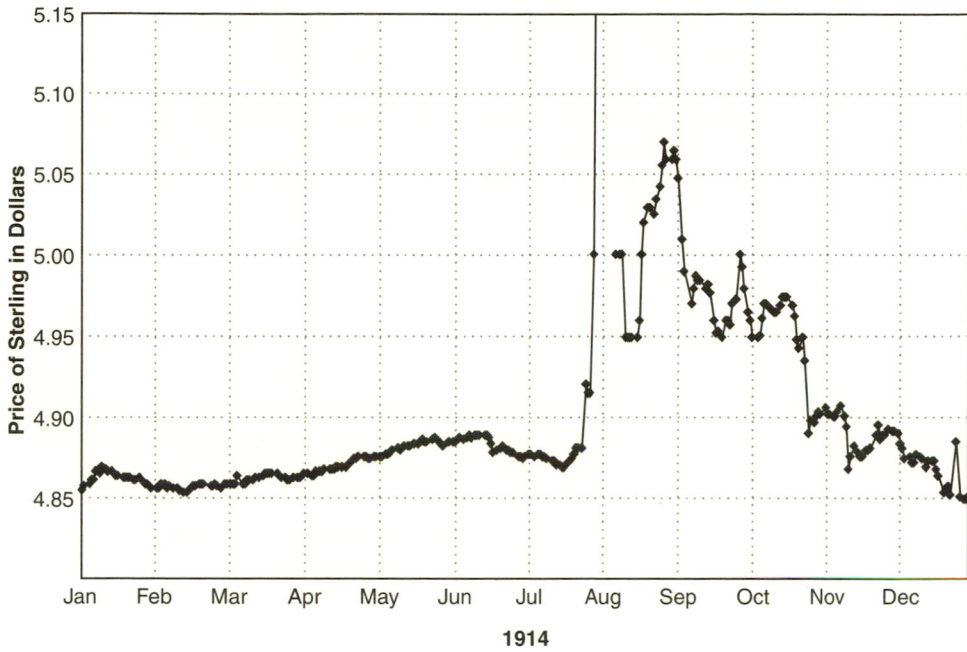

Figure 5.1. Sterling Exchange Rate, 1914.

Data Source: *Wall Street Journal*.

UNDERSTANDING THE FOREIGN EXCHANGE PROBLEM

Figure 5.1, reproduced from chapter 2, recalls the seismic shift in the exchange rate between the U.S. dollar and the British pound triggered by the war. During the first half of 1914 sterling varied narrowly around the mint parity of $4.8665—the rate never fell below $4.85 per pound and never rose above $4.89. Gold arbitrage restrained the exchange rate.* When mobilization for war impeded gold shipments across the Atlantic the pound broke through the old barrier and left all memory behind. After July the dollar price of sterling fluctuated like an internet stock.

The figure also shows that the price of sterling disappeared from view between August 1 and August 7. On August 3 the *Wall Street Journal* explained its failure to report prices: "Quotations are more difficult to be had than at any time since the present situation developed. Business is entirely a matter of private negotiation."[401] The newspaper resumed regular

---

* See chapter 2 for the arbitrage that held the exchange rate within one-half of 1 percent of its $4.8665 mint parity.

quotations with a price of $5 for August 8.[402] Trades in foreign exchange were still done for small amounts, but dealers had already labeled $5 as a commercially viable price for sterling.* The *Journal* noted: "The recent feverish state of the foreign exchange market has been succeeded by one of comparative calm."[403]

A number of news items on August 8 contributed to the improved conditions. McAdoo scheduled his August 14 conference and released his agenda of "providing sufficient ships to move our grain and cotton crops." Comptroller of the Currency Williams announced that banks had more than enough emergency currency to meet all depositor demands, freeing up gold for export.[404] National City Bank announced its barter initiative, offering a vehicle for agricultural exports should the foreign exchange market fail to revive. And a day earlier, J. P. Morgan arranged for a limited credit facility with its French affiliate, Morgan Harjes & Company, restoring a semblance of commercial relations with Europe.[405]

Figure 5.2 focuses on foreign exchange in August. The value of the dollar increased as the price of sterling dropped to $4.95 two days before McAdoo's conference of August 14. During the second half of the month the dollar gave up all of its gains: sterling rose above $5.05.

Why was the value of the American dollar so fickle?

McAdoo had analyzed the initial disruption in foreign exchange, and the resulting premium in the dollar price of sterling, with Max May, the Guaranty Trust Company's foreign exchange expert. May had come to the capital to represent the views of New York foreign exchange dealers to McAdoo.[406] May returned to New York on Sunday afternoon, accompanying McAdoo on his way to meet the bankers at the Vanderbilt Hotel.[407] Although there is no record of their conversation, it might have gone something like this:

> MCADOO: Why is the pound selling at such a ridiculously high price? Doesn't everyone know that Europe will need dollars to pay for the war?
>
> MAY: Supply and demand determine price, Mr. Secretary.
>
> MCADOO: I've heard that before . . . tell me in your own words what it means.
>
> MAY: Do you want me to go through the unpleasant details?
>
> MCADOO: I've spent my life learning from the details.

---

* On August 4, 1914, the *Wall Street Journal* reported (p. 1): "Pending today's meeting of foreign exchange bankers, it is understood that some sort of concerted action has been arrived at to carry on whatever exchange business is absolutely necessary at the present time. According to this tentative arrangement, transactions will be negotiated on the basis of $5 for the pound sterling."

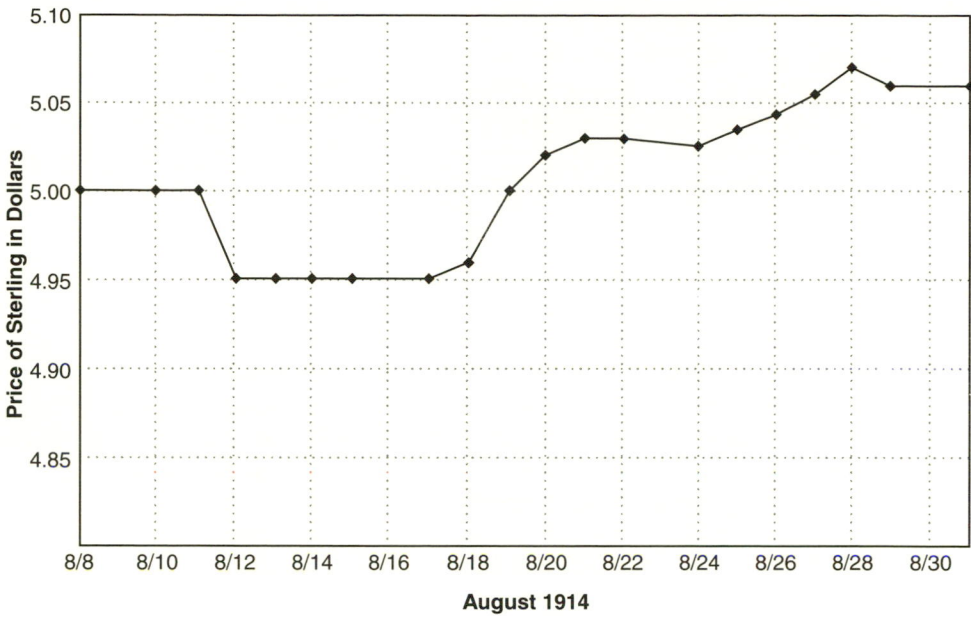

Figure 5.2. Sterling Exchange Rate, August 1914.

Data Source: *Wall Street Journal*.

MAY: Okay, here goes. The supply of sterling in America comes primarily from exporters who receive British pounds, or, more precisely, claims to pounds in the form of a bill of exchange, in payment for goods shipped abroad. For example, an Arkansas farmer will draw a bill of exchange that obligates a London importer, actually the importer's bank, to pay pounds for cotton.* Since American farmers want dollars to spend for more seed or for a night on the town, they sell those bills of exchange to a foreign exchange dealer like me. I pay the farmer in dollars for the bill of exchange at the going dollar price of pounds—and that, of course, is the exchange rate. I buy bills of exchange representing a claim on pounds because, just like any other merchant, I expect to quickly resell them at a small profit. But if farmers can't

* Bills of exchange come in a number of varieties (see Officer 1996, 61–63). The demand or sight bill obligates the immediate payment in pounds when the bill is shipped across the Atlantic and presented in the United Kingdom. A time bill of exchange is payable after an agreed upon delay. The rate on sterling that is transferred by telegraphic instruction over the transatlantic cable is called the cable exchange rate. When a bill of exchange is accepted by a bank for payment in the future it is called a bankers' acceptance.

export their products to Britain I have no pounds to sell. Price
jumps when supply dries up.

McADOO: But we both know that's only half the story. I thought
by closing the stock exchange I reduced the demand for pounds
by British investors. They can no longer sell their U.S. securities
on the New York Stock Exchange to get dollars and then demand pounds in exchange. And without any demand for pounds
by British investors, why should the price of sterling be so high?

MAY: Ah, but many British investors already liquidated their stocks
and bonds before the exchange closed. British investors who sold
on Thursday, July 30—and there were quite a few—had dollars
and wanted pounds. Some foreign exchange dealers accommodated these customers by selling pounds to them without having
first purchased bills of exchange.* They were then short pounds.

McADOO: Sounds like they were speculating—just like the accusations of some midwestern congressmen.

MAY: Only a little. Remember foreign exchange dealers can normally generate pounds even without bills of exchange. They could
always take the dollars they received from British investors to the
subtreasury, exchange them for gold and then ship the gold to
England where they would be credited with pounds. And that,
you recall, is how gold shipments constrain the volatility of the exchange rate—by creating a supply of pounds to meet the demand. But dealers had no way to cover their obligations in sterling
when it became impossible to transport gold across the Atlantic.
And that is why the price of pounds exploded.†

McADOO: Ships.

MAY: Excuse me?

McADOO: No one cares about ships but that's what we need—
ships to carry our exports .

MAY: You couldn't be more right, Mr. Secretary, especially since
America will need more pounds over the next few weeks and
months to pay maturing corporate and municipal bonds that are
still held in Britain and France.

---

* The *Wall Street Journal* (August 6, 1914, 8), observed: "It is estimated that 75% of
the large short interest outstanding represents recent sales [by foreign exchange dealers] of
finance bills in anticipation of the fall exports of cotton and the other commodities. . . .
The sudden outbreak of the European war has upset their calculations."

† The *Wall Street Journal* (August 5, 1914, 1), reported the return to New York of the
Kronprinzessin Cecilie with a $10 million shipment of gold and noted: "The banks have al-
ready sold exchange against the gold and unless the metal goes forward by another ship
they will be that much short of exchange. How to purchase this exchange in the present
state of the market appears a hopeless question at the moment."

MCADOO: It's seems like such a waste. Sending gold abroad to pay our debts knowing the British and French will just have to send it back to pay for our cotton. Why don't they just hold on to dollars?

MAY: Gold and sterling rule the world. Dollars just don't measure up as a means of international payment.

MCADOO: Perhaps we can do something about that.

• • •

Many people knew that American exports would force down the price of sterling and push up the value of the dollar as the war progressed. Sir George Paish, editor of the British financial weekly, the *Statist*, and adviser to the U.K. Treasury, wrote on August 1, 1914: "From the standpoint of the immediate future, a great war in Europe probably would bring economic advantage to the people of the United States. It would enable them to sell their great crops at prices which would make them a much greater profit than they would have realized had there been no war."[408]

But before food could work its magic on the dollar, America had to make good on maturing debts in Europe. No one would want to hold dollars if the United States failed to meet its obligations. Paish had calculated that British investors held more than $3.3 billion in American corporate and municipal securities.[409] At the outbreak of the war, no one knew how many of these securities matured in coming months. Corporate America—and their bankers—would have to pay their debts either in gold or British pounds. And not everyone wanted to. In August 1914 the dollar price of sterling served as a barometer of American credibility.

THE BANKERS' WAR

McAdoo's decision to remain tied to gold complicated life for the bankers. Nationally chartered institutions like Vanderlip's National City Bank and Hepburn's Chase National promised to redeem their checking accounts on demand in lawful money—specie, greenbacks, or silver certificates. Banks had to hold reserves in lawful money—equal to 25 percent of their checking deposits for the big New York banks—to guarantee the convertibility. Depositors knew, therefore, that under the gold standard they could always turn their checking accounts into gold, either directly at the bank or by exchanging greenbacks or silver certificates for gold at the subtreasury.

Gold exports at the outbreak of the war removed $50 million of the precious metal from New York bank vaults, leaving them more than 2 percent short of their legal reserve.[410] The bankers needed to prevent further outflows to recover.* The lack of wartime insurance to protect an Atlantic crossing served as an unanticipated ally, shutting down gold exports like a blockade by enemy submarines. But even that did not eliminate the drain. Canadian bankers could get their gold overland, by truck or train. On August 3 they drew $3,025,000 in gold.[411] According to the *Washington Post*, "The attitude of the Canadian bankers during the recent crisis has been regarded as extremely unfriendly and out of harmony with the protective measures adopted by New York bankers."[412]

What protective measures did the New York bankers use to husband their gold? According to Chase's Hepburn, "As soon as clearing-house certificates were resorted to it was easy to prevent gold shipments. A bank receiving large deposits from a depositor could well say, 'we receive for these checks only clearing-house funds, not gold, therefore, we can only pay your checks through the clearing house and not in gold.' "[413] Hepburn's boast overstates his power to shut down gold withdrawals. Chase depositors could always cash their own check drawn against funds already in their Chase accounts and Hepburn would have no choice but to pay legal tender. Nevertheless, the *New York Times* stated, "A practical embargo on gold shipments has been in force ever since the bankers met Secretary of the Treasury McAdoo . . . in this city on August 2."[414]

Some bankers invoked the suspension of the gold standard in most European countries to legitimize their refusal to ship gold. On August 2 an official was quoted: "We do not propose to let Europe give us paper for gold. If they refuse to pay American bills in specie there will be nothing left for us to do but pay European bills the same way."[415]

The *Commercial and Financial Chronicle* editorialized in favor of such measures: "The long and short of the matter, however, is that Europe has actually suspended gold payments. So long as this state of things continues, it is imperative that we shall not sacrifice our own stock and throw it into the sink-holes of Europe."[416] The *Chronicle* then opined: "Contrary to the opinion so generally expressed we have no further gold to spare. The truth is that we dealt far too liberally with Europe in parting with nearly $100,000,000 of our stock during June and July. To go a step further now and let Europe have $50,000,000 to $150,000,000 additional would mean a serious menace to us and threaten the maintenance of gold payments."[417]

---

* According to the National Bank Act (June 3, 1864, section 31), banks with a reserve deficiency could not make new loans or pay dividends. If they failed to meet their required reserves within thirty days the comptroller of the currency had the right to appoint a receiver for the bank.

Not all bankers tried to escape their obligations abroad. Britain had not abandoned the gold standard, thanks to Keynes. According to the *New York Times*,[418] "A minority of bankers have all through the period since the outbreak of the war adhered to the view that so long as we had gold with which to make payment we could not afford to do anything else but send it abroad in any amount in which it might be needed to meet our obligations so far as these are unaffected by the moratoria which have been declared in France and England."*

Private banks, like Kuhn, Loeb and J. P. Morgan, focused on America's promises to pay. They had placed corporate and municipal debt with European institutions. Some of those debts were payable in foreign currency, mostly British pounds and French francs. Kuhn, Loeb sold Pennsylvania Railroad and Southern Pacific bonds in Paris and participated in the sale of New York City obligations in London.[419] J. P. Morgan distributed just about every blue-chip American security through its London affiliate, Morgan Grenfell, and its Paris branch, Morgan Harjes. Failure to pay what was owed would destroy the dollar's credibility.

Honor left America with little room to maneuver, according to Jacob Schiff, head of Kuhn, Loeb. In a speech before the Chamber of Commerce, he said: "Very considerable amounts of corporate indebtedness, of municipal indebtedness, will gradually have to be paid, indebtedness which is payable to some extent in sterling, to some extent in francs and to some extent in marks. The question is should we permit that indebtedness to remain unpaid? The moratoria that have been established in England and France do not cover coupons, corporate or municipal obligations and similar debts payable on stipulated dates. Now, if those debts are not paid the debtor is in default and no sophistry can change this. What does an honest man do if he cannot pay his debts? He tries to borrow it, he makes a note for it. Well that is just what he should do. . . . We must borrow it from our own people who are willing to loan it to us by means of emergency currency, the redemption of which the law protects; and we must pay our debts if we can do it this way."[420]

Schiff complicated his appeal to America's integrity with the then radical proposal to count national bank notes, including emergency currency, as bank reserves.† He garnered no support even among those concerned

---

* The British moratorium read as follows: "The presentation for payment of a bill of exchange, other than a check or bill on demand, which has been accepted before the beginning of the fourth day of August, 1914 . . . shall for all purposes . . . be deemed to be due and be payable on a date one calendar month after the date of its original maturity" (*Economist*, August 8, 1914, 271).

† Only legal tender—gold certificates, silver certificates, and greenbacks—served as reserves for national banks. Not even Federal Reserve notes under the "new currency law" were counted as legal reserves.

with America's obligations abroad. J. P. Morgan partner, Henry Davison, said: "I have seen no disposition on the part of anybody to take advantage of this situation. Every true American will pay his debts when and where due but this [Schiff's] plan would do more to make payment difficult than it would to facilitate discharge of obligations."[421]

The dispute among the bankers remained a classroom exercise as long as the absence of ships and insurance locked the precious metal in New York bank vaults. Then the British found the key. It was called Ottawa. And the bankers' academic debate turned into a street brawl.

THE OTTAWA DEPOSITORY

On Wednesday, August 12, a *Wall Street Journal* headline proclaimed: "Bank of England in Canada."[422] To dispel the initial confusion over whether Parliament had authorized the bank to create a branch on North American soil, the *Journal* explained: "All that's been done . . . is the establishment of a port of receipt for gold, taking away the war risk on gold exports. We may now ship gold [to Ottawa] to the credit of the Bank of England without paying exorbitant rates of insurance or running the risk of confiscation of the gold as contraband."[423]

Max May could not have been happier. The Bank of England had just revived his foreign exchange business. Since August 1 Max had almost no pounds to sell because farmers had no bills of exchange and because he could not create pounds by shipping gold across the Atlantic. He had watched his customers disappear with the jump in the price of sterling. Now Max could please everyone, including himself. He could ship gold to Ottawa and create pounds at a cost of $4.90—the new gold export point.[424] His customers would be more than happy to pay $4.905 or maybe even $4.91 per pound, rather than the $5.00, or more, that had prevailed since the crisis struck. Max could sell more pounds in a day than he had done over the previous two weeks. All he had to do was cash a check at his local bank, take the legal tender to the subtreasury, and exchange it for gold. He could then charter an express company to ship the precious cargo to Ottawa. Max knew that the national banks would not be pleased to give up gold or greenbacks so that he could engage in arbitrage—but they had no choice. He had the legal right.

Max had the law on his side but the banks had the money. They knew that England wanted American gold and had just opened a walk-in safe-deposit box in Ottawa. The combination of Max May and Ottawa made them worry more than ever about their reserves. On August 12 the *New York Times* reported: "The bankers held no conference on the problem [of Ottawa] as far as could be learned but it was decided by a majority to refuse to pay out large sums where it was known that the money was intended for export."[425] No one said how they would do it, but everyone knew they would try.

Chase and National City would redouble their efforts to meet depositor withdrawals with national bank notes rather than lawful money. Their tellers would make it easy for someone wanting to cash a check for $100,000, offering a neat stack, less than an inch high, of 100 national bank notes, each engraved with the imprint of $1,000. Ottawa would not accept national bank notes. Only sterling commanded the same respect as gold in August 1914. A company needing gold to meet obligations abroad could, of course, turn national bank notes into lawful money—and specie—through the Redemption Agency for bank notes in Washington, D.C.* However, Chase and National City could delay gold exports by failing to replenish their Redemption Fund in a timely fashion.† The delay interfered with Max May's arbitrage.

• • •

Confusion between protecting our gold and maintaining our virtue struck like a bout of schizophrenia. The *Wall Street Journal* quoted an anonymous banker confirming the mixed emotions: "It is a problem whether or not we should take advantage of it. . . . Assume that we send gold to Ottawa . . . we will have depleted already inadequate reserves. . . . We must, of course, pay what we owe. We always have. But since England has declared a moratorium, we can certainly take a little time now . . . time enough to perfect a plan whereby our obligations may be met in products we have for sale."[426]

Was the ambivalent banker right? Was time on America's side? McAdoo's conference, to provide "sufficient ships to move our grain and

---

* The redemption process for national bank notes is described in the *Report of the Monetary Commission* (1900, 334ff.). Bank notes may be forwarded to the Redemption Agency in Washington, D.C., either by individuals or banks. Payments are made in lawful money out of the 5 percent redemption fund that each bank is obliged to maintain with the Redemption Agency. The lawful money will be made available at the nearest subtreasury office to the person or bank requesting redemption. A bank would have to replenish its reserve with lawful money if the 5 percent fund were exhausted.

† According to the *Report of the Monetary Commission* (1900, 336), "No notes of any bank will be forwarded to it in excess of the amount credited to it upon account of the 5 per cent redemption fund. In case it appears upon counting the notes that the Treasurer has redeemed notes in excess of the amount on deposit in the 5 per cent fund . . . the excess amount is retained by the Treasurer, and only so many are forwarded as are sufficient to exhaust the bank's credit on the 5 per cent account. The bank is at the same time notified of the shipment and is informed that the amount necessary to restore the fund to 5 per cent of the outstanding circulation must at once be deposited with the Treasurer."

cotton crops to European markets; and [to restore] through the bankers the market for foreign bills of exchange," was scheduled for Friday, August 14, two days after the British bombshell. Europe would have to buy American products to feed itself, as in the past. But agricultural goods remained under the cloud of contraband, susceptible to capture on the high seas if destined to feed an army at war.* And Jacob Schiff had been right about the moratoria in Britain and France. They did not cover interest and dividends on corporate and municipal securities.[427] America's obligations to pay meant that Ottawa came into play immediately. The foreign exchange market shows whether or not virtue triumphed.

VERDICT IN THE COURT OF FOREIGN EXCHANGE

Foreign exchange quotations reappeared on August 8 after a week of behind-the-scenes negotiations. The pound sterling commanded a price of $5.00 on Saturday, August 8, on Monday, August 10, and again on Tuesday, August 11. Rumors about Ottawa circulated in the financial district on Tuesday and appeared in the press the next day. The *New York Times* said, "There were numerous consultations between bankers over the telephone and inquiries were cabled to London as to the truth of the story."[428] The price of sterling on Wednesday, August 12, would indicate whether the announcement of the Ottawa depository had a significant impact on the value of the dollar.

Should the dollar have increased or decreased in response to the British initiative? Companies or municipalities that could exchange their checking accounts for gold would never pay Max May more than $4.90 per pound for a sterling bill of exchange. They could ship the gold themselves if they had to. Thus the reduced demand for a sterling bill would push down the price toward $4.90. On the other hand, the prospect of renewed gold outflows would further threaten America's commitment to the gold standard. The U.S. Treasury might have to suspend convertibility of its paper currency into gold or the banks might fail to honor their pledge to redeem deposits in lawful money. Either outcome would make the dollar less attractive compared with pounds, forcing up the price of sterling in terms of dollars.

Figure 5.2 shows the dollar price of sterling for the month of August 1914. The 1 percent decline in sterling on August 12 to $4.95—from

* The *Wall Street Journal* (August 6, 1914, 1), wrote: "Provisions are conditional contraband. If a cargo of wheat were destined for Portsmouth, obviously it would be for military use, and therefore contraband. But if it were destined for Liverpool it might be contraband, but the presumption would be that it was a commercial transaction."

$5.00 on August 11—represents a significant drop in price.* The foreign exchange market confirmed that Americans could—and would—ship gold to Ottawa. The market also expected the reduced demand for sterling bills of exchange to outweigh any potential damage to American credibility. Ottawa should have made Americans proud—but not too proud.

The *Wall Street Journal* quoted "one of the most important dealers in foreign exchange in New York" as follows: "It [Ottawa] is the single most important announcement since the closing of the stock exchange on July 30. It means that no gold will have to be shipped abroad, but will be deposited to the credit of the Bank of England at Ottawa, and will at once clear our short foreign exchange situation."[429] The expert at the *Journal* was right about Ottawa's importance but was wrong about how completely Ottawa would resolve the problem of America's "short foreign exchange situation." On August 12 sterling remained above the $4.90 gold export point. Ottawa did not eliminate the premium on the British pound compared with the cost of shipping gold. Evidently Max May could not execute his arbitrage as often as he would have liked.† The premium on sterling, and the corresponding discount on the dollar, persisted during the entire month of August—and grew larger.

The absence of ocean transport and insurance cannot explain the high price of sterling. Ottawa removed those excuses. Rather, the premium demonstrated a preference for gold compared with dollars. New York banks preferred gold to paper. The British preferred gold to paper. And American companies and municipalities were prepared to part with extra paper dollars to purchase sterling bills of exchange rather than to pressure their bankers for the gold they were entitled to by law. The entire world preferred gold to American paper currency in August 1914. And sterling shared the exalted status of the precious metal.

Figure 5.2 shows the price of sterling failing to move significantly between August 13 and August 18.‡ The dollar ignored the outcome of

---

* The price movement on August 12 is statistically significant at a confidence level of more than 1 percent. The standard deviation of returns on the dollar price of sterling equals .23 percent per day between August 8, 1914, and December 31, 1914.

† The delay in redeeming national bank notes at the Redemption Fund in Washington (see the preceding notes) explains why Max May could not do the arbitrage in unlimited amounts.

‡ The exchange rate ignored the announcement on August 13 by the British government (see Withers 1915, 64) that it would begin to "discount all approved bills [of exchange] accepted before August 4, without recourse against the holders." The *Wall Street Journal* (August 14, 1914, 8) quoted a "prominent international banker" as saying: "The willingness of the Bank of England to discount approved bills of exchange . . . will go far to reduce the congestion in the London money market but will not materially improve the local situation in exchange."

McAdoo's conference on August 14 "to provide sufficient ships to move our grain and cotton crops to European markets." His press release on August 15 said that "the conference . . . resulted in the appointment of a committee to confer with Congress to . . . insure war risks on ships and cargoes engaged in ocean trade between the United States and Europe."[430] The absence of a favorable reaction reflected a number of uncertainties, including how quickly Congress would act and whether government insurance could overcome the problem of the seizure of contraband by combatants. Despite the tepid response to the initial announcement, McAdoo's Bureau of War Risk Insurance, established in September 1914 as a direct result of the August 14 conference, would trigger the turning point in the crisis.

McAdoo had planted a seed for the dollar's ultimate redemption.

The dollar's progress on August 12 disappeared completely a week later. On August 19 the price of sterling rose to $5.00, a significant jump from $4.96 on August 18.* What caused the reversal of fortune? Did a banker blockade suddenly halt the gold rush to Ottawa or did American credibility suffer a more fundamental blow?

August 19 brought bad news: the first specific report of America's short-term obligations in London. Until then the public did not know how much gold or sterling would be needed to pay foreign indebtedness, nor did it know precisely when those debts matured. On August 19 a *New York Times* headline announced: "New York City Owes $82,000,000 Abroad: All of It in Notes Falling Due in Europe before the End of January 1 Next."[431] The *Times* then quoted City Comptroller Prendergast saying that he had met the day before with leading bankers but "had not yet made arrangements for paying the City's obligations maturing in Europe." A payment of $12,150,000, almost all in pounds, was due in September.

Jacob Schiff unwittingly contributed to the market's negative reaction on August 19 by offering the *Times* background commentary: "He [Schiff] advocated that such of our debts in Europe as are not covered by the moratorium, and in particular the maturing obligations of municipalities like the City of New York or of railroad and other corporations held by the public in Europe, should be paid unquestionably and unhesitatingly when due and that, to the extent that the means for making payment abroad cannot be obtained, . . . they must be provided through the export of gold, even if it involves some strain upon ourselves."[432]

The significant jump in the price of sterling on August 19 left little doubt that the market expected New York City debts to strain America's

---

* The .81 percent price change on August 19 is statistically significant. The daily standard deviation of returns is .23 percent.

gold resources. An editorial in the *New York Times* described the ripple effect: "[The] payment of gold could be enforced by legal procedure of the most embarrassing sort. The largest debtor of gold to be paid abroad and the biggest 'short' of exchange is the City of New York. It is not to be imagined that it will not redeem its bond. Default could be followed not only by a legal proceeding against the city but also by embarrassing demands upon both the banks and the Treasury. If the city were to demand its $30,000,000 bank balances in gold it would embarrass the banks. If the banks were to pay in obligations of the Treasury to deliver gold it would embarrass the Treasury."[433]

Relief from prospective embarrassment remained far off. The potential gold drain that assaulted American credibility on August 19 was about to intensify. The ban on stock trading had suddenly sprung a leak. McAdoo needed help to preserve American honor.

CHAPTER SIX

New Street Defies McAdoo

HENRY NOBLE spent a lifetime at the New York Stock Exchange but never expected to preside over the longest trading suspension in exchange history. He began as a clerk on the exchange in 1880 and two years later purchased a seat from his grandfather, Henry Stebbins, who had been president of the New York Stock Exchange in the 1850s.[434] He became a member of the exchange's governing board in 1898 and served on almost all exchange committees before being elected to the post of president on May 11, 1914. Less than three months later, Henry Noble needed all of his experience to manage an unprecedented problem.

Foreigners owned more than $4 billion railroad stocks and bonds at the outbreak of the Great War, with $3 billion of that in British hands.[435] New York Stock Exchange securities attracted investors from across the Atlantic, in part, because they carried the exchange's seal of approval. The securities could also be sold quickly to raise cash—they were liquid assets. The ready marketability allowed British and French investors to turn their stocks and bonds into dollars on short notice and then demand gold at an American bank. The magnitude of the threat caught Treasury Secretary McAdoo's attention. At the outbreak of the war, gold reserves at New York banks would have been cut in half if the British sold only 5 percent of their holdings.*

McAdoo urged the New York Stock Exchange to close on July 31, 1914, to impede European access to American gold. He had rejected the direct approach, suspending the gold standard, as too costly to American credibility. Instead he froze British and French investments. Europeans could own a piece of America but could not sell it.

McAdoo brandished the New York Stock Exchange like a sledgehammer against the gold drain. He denied everyone a liquid market— Americans as well as Europeans. Not everyone took it lying down. Americans wanted to trade stocks they did not like for those they found attractive. McAdoo did not have the staff or the expertise to suppress

---

* Noyes (1916, 94) put gold reserves in New York banks at $308 million in August 1914. Five percent of $3 billion is $150 million. The burden of gold outflows would fall primarily on New York banks according to the memo by Benjamin Strong, Albert Wiggin, and James Brown (November 2, 1914, Board of Governors, Central Subject File, 1913–1954, box 1470, National Archives II, College Park, Maryland).

them. He left that task to Henry Noble and the New York Stock Exchange. That was like putting Willie Sutton in charge of security at Fort Knox. No wonder the trading ban buckled under pressure, endangering McAdoo's defenses.

MONITORING THE STREET

Henry Noble led the meeting of the New York Stock Exchange Governing Board on the morning of July 31. Fifteen minutes before the ten o'clock opening bell, Noble received a call from J. P. Morgan relaying Treasury Secretary McAdoo's message to close the exchange.[436] A motion to "shut the Exchange until further notice" passed by a large majority.[437]

Immediately after the meeting, Henry Noble established the Committee of Five to oversee exchange business during the suspension of trading.[438] He appointed exchange members Ernest Groesbeck, Donald G. Geddes, H. K. Pomroy, and Samuel F. Streit to join him on the committee. Formal approval of the Committee of Five came in a vote by the governing board on August 3. The committee started work immediately. It met with bank representatives regarding certifying checks drawn on exchange members, it dealt with the issue of clearing transactions completed before the suspension of trading, and it confronted the problem of trading exchange-listed securities outside of the New York Stock Exchange.

Plans to circumvent the suspension of trading began the very first weekend of August. The *New York Times* carried an advertisement on Monday, August 3, announcing: "Emergency Stock Market: Pending the resumption of trading on the New York Stock Exchange and other markets, we are prepared to buy and sell all classes of securities on the following terms and conditions: Bids must be accompanied by cash to cover; offers to sell must be accompanied by the securities properly endorsed."[439] It was signed: "New York Curb."

The New York Curb Market, located outdoors on Broad Street near the New York Stock Exchange, normally traded "unseasoned" securities that were not listed on the New York Stock Exchange. The daily newspapers published transactions from the Curb in stocks like United Cigar Stores, Otis Elevator, and the various Standard Oil Companies, under the heading "Outside Securities." In 1921 the Curb Market moved indoors and became the American Stock Exchange. [440]

An uneasy truce had reigned between the New York Stock Exchange and the New York Curb, as though they were neighboring feudal estates. The less powerful Curb showed its respect by not trading a security after it joined the Big Board, as the New York Stock Exchange was called. But when the New York Stock Exchange closed for business on July 31, at least some Curb members felt that it was permissible to poach. Trading profits and commissions on exchange-listed securities, forbidden by informal treaty under normal conditions, posed a tempting target for Curb traders on the prowl.

The Curb members responsible for the encroachment must have been quickly disciplined because the confrontation dissipated on August 4. A notice in the *Wall Street Journal* carried the following retraction: "No Dealings on the Curb: Advertisements which appeared in papers which may mislead the public regarding the attitude of the New York Curb market association in regard to dealings in securities are herewith absolutely repudiated."[441] It was signed: E. R. McCormick, Chairman, New York Curb Market Association.

The *Wall Street Journal* weighed in with a front-page headline: "An Appeal to Wall Street's Patriotism."[442] The *Journal* urged: "Every banking and brokerage house in Wall Street . . . should cooperate with the Stock Exchange in a real suspension of the market for stocks. . . . Any banking house with a membership on the regular board [NYSE] or on the Consolidated board, attempting to make a market where the wisdom of the best financial intelligence has suspended such a market . . . should be summarily and disgracefully expelled."[443]

Wall Street's appeal to patriotic discipline extended beyond the narrow streets of lower Manhattan. Back then nearly every major city had a stock exchange of its own, trading securities of local companies as well as stocks listed on the New York Stock Exchange. The *New York Times* reported on August 1 that all regional exchanges voted to close along with the New York Stock Exchange, including Boston, Philadelphia, Pittsburgh, Baltimore, Detroit, Indianapolis, St. Louis, Chicago, Cincinnati, Columbus, Washington, and San Francisco.

According to Henry Noble, a flood of communications inundated the Committee of Five urging it to modify the suspension.[444] On August 5 the Baltimore Stock Exchange reported to the committee that a member of the New York Stock Exchange had "been guilty of going directly to the trust companies and making offerings of bonds." The committee responded that it would like the name of the member so that it could take appropriate action. Instead, on August 7 the Baltimore Stock Exchange forwarded an urgent request to reopen the exchange.

By August 11 Noble cites a nagging distraction near the New York Stock Exchange: "The growth of an unregulated outside market began to force itself upon the attention of the Committee . . . an occasional group of mysterious individuals were seen loitering in New Street behind the Exchange. A member of the Committee of Five . . . remarked as he observed them late one afternoon, 'the outside market seems to consist of four boys and a dog.' "[445]

Noble makes New Street sound like a dusty alley in the Casbah, where hashish-laden smoke blankets questionable transactions. In fact, New Street is the very first intersection on Wall Street, less than a flurry of ticker tape off Broadway. The stone siding of the New York Stock Exchange served as a convenient facade for New Street traders.

The press reported that New Street challenged local traffic regulations: "Two big policemen [were] stationed during trading hours in the very heart of the market, which is on the asphalt pavement at the end of the stock exchange building, in order that no groups may obstruct traffic. This was the result of a raid made by the Central Office detectives designed to break up the cash trading in stocks that has gone on in the rear of the stock exchange building since the official market was closed."[446]

Despite the harassment from local police, Noble confirms that "this furtive little group developed into a good sized crowd of men who assembled at ten o'clock in the morning and continued in session until three o'clock in the afternoon."[447] In fact, Noble was somewhat schizophrenic toward New Street. He recognized that "irregular dealing, as long as it remained within narrow limits and was not advertised in the press, furnished a safety valve"; but he then concludes, "the Stock Exchange authorities must do all in their power to hold the development of this market in check."

Who was this "furtive little group of mysterious individuals" that challenged the authority of the New York Stock Exchange and sparred with the local police? No one knows for sure because Noble withheld their names as though they were confidential trade secrets. Stockbrokers on all exchanges had the motive to sneak outside for a quick trade because without trading they had no income. But members of the New York Stock Exchange had the most to lose. George W. Ely, secretary of the exchange, admonished member firms with a public proclamation: "Attention of members is called to section 4, article XX, of the Constitution, which reads: 'Dealings upon any other exchange either directly or indirectly in securities listed on the [New York Stock] Exchange is forbidden. Any violation of this rule shall be deemed an act detrimental to the interest or welfare of the Exchange.' "[448]

Members of the Curb had the least to lose and the most to gain from working the crowd on New Street. And they did. When the *New York Times* published its annual review of financial developments of 1914, it included a table of "High and Low Prices" on New Street compiled with the help of "quotations supplied directly to the *Times* by George S. Crap, a dealer in outside securities who participated in New Street trading."[449] Members of the Curb traded "outside securities."

The Committee of Five took a number of steps to restrain New Street.[450] It silenced the New York Stock Exchange ticker that normally disseminates prices to investors throughout the country. To isolate further the upstart market from the public's view, the committee convinced the press to ignore New Street transactions. The *Wall Street Journal* quoted Henry Noble's plea: "I must ask the newspapers of New York to cooperate with the officials of the Exchange in preventing these [unauthorized trading] practices."[451]

The leading newspapers, including the *New York Times*, the *Wall Street Journal* and the *Commercial and Financial Chronicle*, embargoed New Street quotations as though they were privileged military communiqués. A report from Boston confirms the widespread success of the boycott: "Outside brokers are getting out circulars offering to deal in stocks on a cash basis, as one would deal in real estate; and quoting prices. They complain that the newspapers refuse their advertisements and are cooperating with the stock exchanges and that the financial news agencies are cooperating with the [New York] Stock Exchange in suppression of prices."[452]

The *New York Times* justified its prior restraint: "Despite the wider publicity given quotations on transactions alleged to have been made in the street market, dealings in listed securities have not yet reached a scale that justifies the acceptance of prices made outside the Stock Exchange as a basis for buying and selling."[453] This self-serving description shortchanges New Street and fails to explain why the upstart market would soon provoke the New York Stock Exchange itself into modifying the trading ban.*

Henry Noble recognized New Street's threat to the New York Stock Exchange: "On all previous occasions when the facilities of the Exchange had been inadequate, or had been shut off, an unregulated market had established itself in public places and proceeded uncontrolled. During the Civil War . . . a continuous market developed, partly in the street and partly in a basement called the 'coal hole' and flourished during the day, while in the evening it was continued in the lobby of the Fifth Avenue Hotel. This market did more business than was done upon the Exchange itself, and a few years after the war, many of its members were admitted to the Stock Exchange."[454]

THE NEW YORK STOCK EXCHANGE DEFENDS ITS TURF

The Committee of Five launched a frontal attack to deflect New Street's challenge. On August 12, 1914, it authorized trading through the New

---

* New Street, in fact, provided economically meaningful liquidity services to investors (see Silber 2005).

York Stock Exchange's Clearing House at prices "no less than the closing prices of Thursday, July 30, 1914." The committee released the following guidelines: "Members of the Exchange desiring to buy securities for cash may send a list of same to the Committee on Clearing House giving amounts of securities wanted and the prices they are willing to pay. Members of the Exchange desiring to sell securities, but only in order to relieve the necessities of themselves or their customers may send a list of same giving the amounts of securities for sale. No prices less than closing prices of July 30, 1914, will be considered."[455] The committee left unspecified exactly what qualified as "only in order to relieve the necessities."

The New York Stock Exchange Clearing House normally settled trades completed on the exchange's trading floor. It employed hundreds of clerks to process the paper fluttering behind every transaction. As Wall Street's back office, the Clearing House would receive the stock certificates from those who have sold on the exchange floor and then transfer those certificates to the buyers after accepting their payments. The trading suspension on July 31, 1914, left the Clearing House without any new business.

According to Noble, the trading system inaugurated at the Clearing House on August 12 required "a large clerical force [to] tabulate the orders received and bring purchasers and sellers together who were willing to trade in similar amounts and at similar prices. . . . To consummate a trade the Clearing House would notify both parties, leaving it to them to carry out the delivery and payment, and requiring them to inform the Clearing House when the transaction had been completed." Somewhat ironically, the address given for communicating with the Clearing House was 55 New Street.

From the outset, the Clearing House trading facility maintained a low profile. The August 13 *Wall Street Journal* reports: "The Stock Exchange authorities refuse to divulge the amount of bids and offers for stocks in accordance with the rule adopted yesterday. Nor will they give out the stocks for which offers or bids were made, nor the prices. It is only known that advantage of the rule has been taken by a number of [brokerage] houses."[456]

Did behind-the-scenes trading at the Clearing House smother New Street?

Noble conceded a seesaw battle between the trading forums: "A very considerable amount of business [at the Clearing house] began at once. Many people with ready money   appeared as purchasers and relieved the necessities of those who had been embarrassed by the war. A little later, when progress on the war took on a more discouraging aspect, this 'Clearing House Market' fell to the arbitrary minimum of the [July 30] closing prices, with a large excess of selling compared to buying orders, and the New Street market grew in proportion. During the darkest days of depression in prices . . . business in the Clearing House almost ceased. [When] New Street prices rose again to the Clearing House level a relatively small business on the 'outlaw' market was transformed into a relatively large business conducted under the supervision of the Exchange."[457]

According to Henry Noble, the Clearing House generated significant trading activity. He also notes that nearly all of the business shifted to New Street when stock prices in the street fell significantly below the July 30 quotes permitted in the Clearing House. All black markets behave this way—activity jumps with the difference between free market prices versus "officially sanctioned" prices. And New Street was, in fact, a black market. But how did Noble know the details without observing New Street transactions? Was he simply speculating based on "first principles" or did he follow New Street quotations more closely than he cared to admit?

Stock prices were unavailable to the general public because Noble himself convinced the major newspapers of their patriotic duty to suppress New Street quotes. But people really needing the information, including those charged with administering the trading suspension, could find it. The Records of the Committee of Five contain news clippings giving price quotations from the New Street market.[458] Those clippings came from the *Morning Telegraph*, normally a "theater and turf paper."[459] Evidently, the New York Stock Exchange could not muscle the *Morning Telegraph*, which did not depend on Wall Street for regular news.

The *Telegraph* usually published New Street quotations on between 60 and 110 securities, compared with 100 to 150 securities quoted regularly in the *New York Times* before trading was suspended.[460] The number of quotations on New Street depended primarily on the source. More than 100 stocks were usually listed when the table cited "Quotes by Beekman Underhill, 16 Beaver Street." About 60 stocks appeared when Edward F. Breen (44 Broad Street) was the source.*

STOCK PRICES MOLLIFY McADOO

Treasury Secretary McAdoo closed the New York Stock Exchange on July 31, 1914, to hamper Europe's access to American gold. He did not expect to transform New Street from an asphalt roadway into an open-air

---

* Neither Edward F. Breen nor Beekman Underhill belonged to the New York Stock Exchange. Breen applied for membership at the exchange in 1922 but his meeting before the Committee on Admissions was canceled on June 8, 1922. No explanation given for the cancellation, but given the "clubby" nature of the exchange, it would not be surprising if Breen's price quotations for New Street worked against his admission prospects.

stock market. McAdoo relied on the expertise of New York Stock Exchange president Henry Noble to administer the trading ban. He did not expect Noble to launch trading-by-appointment at the New York Stock Exchange Clearing House to protect the exchange's franchise. New Street and the Clearing House provided American and overseas investors with an all-weather trading complex, undermining McAdoo's objective. Why didn't McAdoo put some teeth into his trading ban?

McAdoo pursued a policy of benign neglect toward the trading violations because the makeshift markets deflected the pressure to reopen the exchange. Henry Noble had observed that New Street "furnished a safety valve." New Street and the Clearing House kept investors from open rebellion. In addition, prices on New Street confounded predictions of a stock market crash, a fact that McAdoo did not want to hide. Governments often tolerate black markets that serve their purpose. In the 1950s Britain permitted a parallel black market in the Hong Kong dollar to modify the fixed exchange rate policy of its colony. Some claim that this parallel market "contributed to stability in Hong Kong and resistance to communist forces."[461]

Stock prices dropped by an average of 6 percent on Thursday, July 30, 1914.[462] Fear that the collapse in prices would continue the following day contributed to the decision to close the Exchange. The evidence suggests, however, that buyers outnumbered sellers on the morning of July 31, as reported in the *Wall Street Journal*: "Most of the brokers in the Street had large volumes of buy orders and much disappointment was expressed by bargain hunters that the Exchange failed to open."[463] Were the sellers simply waiting for a more opportune moment to pounce?

Stock prices could not respond to the actual declarations of war. Every major stock market in the world had closed by July 31.[464] Diplomats held out prospects for peace among the Great Powers until Saturday, August 1, when Germany declared war on Russia.[465] France entered the conflict on August 3 and Britain joined on August 5. New Street prices did not appear in the *Morning Telegraph* until three weeks later, on August 25. By that date America had undertaken measures to defend itself from financial panic. How did the New Street market weigh this combination of events?

Figure 6.1 shows the behavior on New Street of the index of twenty railroad stocks and twelve industrials from August 25, 1914 through the end of October, when price quotations ceased.* Stock prices were

---

* Price movements in the indexes are all relative to the July 30 close. The indexes were constructed from an equally weighted average of the returns on stocks that were traded on New Street. Prices on New Street came from the New York Stock Exchange Archives and the *Morning Telegraph*. Nine of the twelve industrial stocks and nineteen of the twenty railroad stocks were quoted on New Street.

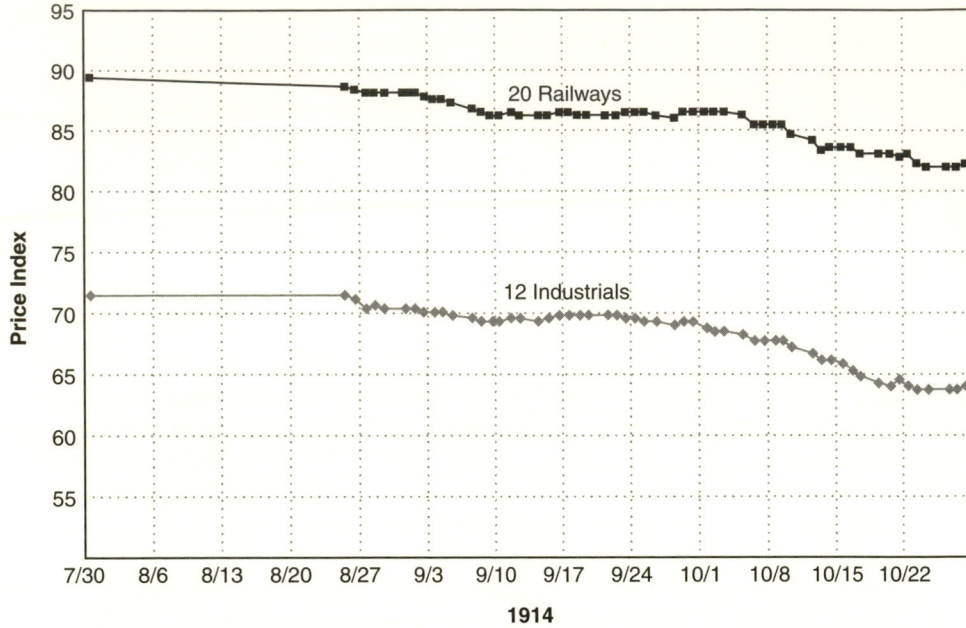

Figure 6.1. Stock Prices on New Street versus July 30, 1914, on the New York Stock Exchange.

Data Source: New York Stock Exchange Archives and the *Morning Telegraph*.

unchanged when quotations began on August 25 compared with prices on July 30. American neutrality combined with McAdoo's successful launch of emergency measures offset the initial apprehension concerning world conflict. Recall the favorable greeting the stock market had given to the mere prospect of an Aldrich-Vreeland rescue in June 1913.

The stock market does not react predictably to war. Prices usually decline when the market is caught by surprise. Stocks on the New York Stock Exchange fell 3.5 percent on Monday, December 8, 1941, the day after Pearl Harbor, and prices dropped 4.65 percent on June 25, 1950, when North Korea invaded its southern neighbor.[466] On the other hand, the Tokyo Stock Exchange rallied when Britain declared war on Germany on September 3, 1939, presumably in anticipation of additional military spending.[467]

New Street did not completely ignore wartime news. By the end of October prices were more than 9 percent below their July 30 close. In its retrospective on 1914, the *New York Times* cited the fall of Antwerp as responsible for the October drop in prices on New Street.[468] The German capture of Antwerp, rumored in the press on October 10, was confirmed on October 11 with the following headline: "Sees England Invaded: That Will Follow the Fall of Antwerp."[469] Both the railroads and the industrials dropped significantly between Friday, October 9, and Monday, October 12.*

Perhaps it is no coincidence that the *Morning Telegraph* succumbed to renewed pressure to stop reporting New Street prices at the end of October. The bearish turn in prices wore out New Street's welcome mat.

DID THE TRADING SUSPENSION WORK?

New Street flattered McAdoo in August 1914 by advertising the absence of a stock market crash. McAdoo allowed New Street to flourish and permitted the New York Stock Exchange to defend itself through the Clearing House. Did New Street and the Clearing House open the alley door for European access to American gold?

European investors would have preferred to sell their securities at the Clearing House, under the imprimatur of the New York Stock Exchange, but they could not ignore New Street. Potential buyers of stock migrated to New Street when prices in the street fell below the July 30 minimum permitted at the Clearing House. The well-known contemporary Yale economist, Irving Fisher, commented on the mounting pressure from both markets: "The closure of the stock exchange . . . cannot completely or permanently prevent the transactions which so many people on both sides are anxious to consummate. Curb markets and limited cash sales on the exchanges themselves are doing some of this business, and sooner or later, much more will be done whether the exchanges are open or not."[470]

A comparison of the combined trading volume on New Street and the Clearing House with trading on the New York Stock Exchange prior to July 30 provides a rough estimate of the effectiveness of McAdoo's trading ban. The *New York Times* Financial Review of 1914 estimated that New Street traded a maximum of 40,000 shares during the busiest days in October.[471] The *Times* also reported that "as many as 30,000 shares were handled on the busiest days" in the Clearing House.[472] We know from Henry Noble's description of the competition between the two trading venues that New Street's business shriveled when the Clearing

---

* The two day return on the railroad index is minus 1.52 percent. The daily standard deviation of returns on New Street between August 25 and October 28 equals .355 percent, implying a two-day standard deviation of returns equal to .502 percent. The t-statistic of the two-day return equals 3.03. The two-day return on the industrials is minus 1.33 percent. The daily standard deviation is .402 percent and the two-day standard deviation is .5685 percent. The t-statistic of the two-day return is 2.34.

House flourished and vice versa. Thus total trading volume even on the busiest days never exceeded 40,000 shares.

During the entire month of July 1914 the New York Stock Exchange traded an average of 250,000 shares per day.[473] Daily volume soared to 894,000 shares during the last week of the month, when war fever agitated investors. How many shares would have traded per day had the New York Stock Exchange conducted business as usual after July 31? Pent-up trading interest from every stock exchange in the world would have swelled New York Stock Exchange volume. The July average of 250,000 shares per day is a minimum estimate of the trading that would have taken place on the New York Stock Exchange. Thus McAdoo's closure of the New York Stock Exchange cut trading from a minimum of 250,000 shares to a maximum of 40,000 shares. Trading after July 31 fell to less than one-sixth of what it would have been.

How much gold could have gone abroad if the New York Stock Exchange had remained open? No formal estimates connect stock trading directly with gold outflows, but a suggestive calculation provides an idea of the magnitudes involved. Approximately 20 percent of American railroad securities, the largest category of publicly traded securities, were held by foreign investors in 1914.[474] Applying that fraction to the minimum estimate of 250,000 shares of daily trading on the New York Stock Exchange means that at least 50,000 shares would have been traded by foreign investors each day. If all of those foreign transactions after July 31 represented Europeans liquidating their American securities, the sales would have generated dollar proceeds of approximately $3,100,000 per day and $74,400,000 per month.* These dollars could have all been presented at local New York banks with a polite but firm demand for specie.

How much gold did New Street and the Clearing House actually provide to Europeans? Trading in these makeshift markets was at most one-sixth the NYSE figures. If foreign investors sold the same 20 percent of the total volume, the actual proceeds to overseas investors on New Street and the Clearing House amounted to $516,666 per day and $12,400,000 per month. Thus McAdoo's policy of shutting the New York Stock Exchange avoided a potential gold outflow of $62 million per month ($74.4 million minus $12.4 million). Between August and October the outflow would have totaled $186 million. New York City banks held $308 million in gold in August 1914.[475]

Avoiding $62 million in gold outflows per month justifies McAdoo's decision to close the exchange, but the total could have been even larger.

---

* Shares are translated into dollars using the $62 average price of the seventy securities quoted on New Street. Daily numbers are translated into monthly figures assuming 24 trading days per month (the New York Stock Exchange closed only on Sunday).

Sales by foreign investors could have easily surpassed $74 million per month had the exchange remained open and Europeans probably sold fewer than $12 million on New Street and the Clearing House. Foreign selling would have exceeded $74 million because it would have totaled more than 20 percent of trading volume. The *New York Times* reported on August 2: "It was estimated by foreign stock exchange houses that from $100 million to $150 million worth of American stocks and bonds were thrown on the market [last week] for whatever they would bring by European investors."[476] The $100 million estimate of stock sales by Europeans translates into 45 percent of total shares traded during the last week of July.[477] Actual sales by Europeans on New Street were probably less than $12 million because foreigners accounted for less than 20 percent of the volume. New York Stock Exchange members that normally handled foreign business were precluded from trading on New Street.

Gold exports did not disappear after the war began. The outflows of $15 million in August and $19 million in September were large by historical standards.[478] The $44.4 million drain in October was the largest monthly drain since 1900. McAdoo knew those outflows would have been much greater had he not padlocked the New York Stock Exchange on July 31, 1914. But closing the exchange did not solve the problem of how American debtors would pay the gold that was coming to British and French investors.

CHAPTER SEVEN

Rescue

J. P. Morgan Jr. labored in the shadow of a giant. The Panic of 1907 had transformed his father, J. P. Morgan Sr., from controversial financier to public hero. Morgan Sr.'s obituary on April 1, 1913, read: "The pinnacle of his power was reached in the Panic of 1907 when he was more than 70 years old, and to some extent withdrawn from participation in active affairs. By general consent he was put at the head of the forces that were gathered together to save the country from disaster, and men like John D. Rockefeller and E. H. Harriman, to say nothing of Presidents of banks and trust companies, put themselves and their resources at his disposal."[479] Morgan Sr.'s legend grew despite his failure to prevent the panic in October 1907 from tumbling into an economic horror.

Morgan Jr. followed the accepted practice of dropping Jr. from his name after his father's death. He also succeeded "the Senior," along with the title, at the head of the partner's table in America's most prestigious banking firm. And he inherited his father's bulky frame. The similarities in their lives help to explain the public's propensity to merge the two men into a financial Methuselah, as though a single J. P. Morgan reigned as king of American finance from the 1860s to the 1940s.

The confusion fails to give Morgan Jr. the credit he deserves for helping to tame the crisis at the outbreak of the Great War. Perhaps Morgan Jr.'s less overbearing personality explains the dominance of his father's reputation. When asked to give his recipe for success, he said: "Do your work; be honest; keep your word; help when you can; be fair."[480] In August 1914, less than eighteen months into his tenure as head of J. P. Morgan & Company, Morgan Jr. found his country on the verge of its second panic in seven years. Unlike his father, he succeeded in helping America avoid financial collapse.

A VULNERABLE NEW YORK CITY

New York City led a parade of worried debtors at the outbreak of the war. According to the *Wall Street Journal*, "the running expenses of the city amount to approximately $190,000,000 [per year], or more than the gross earnings of the Pennsylvania Railroad."[481] Financing those expenses placed a considerable burden on city residents. The *New York Times* estimated that "a family of five can live comfortably in the Borough of Manhattan" on an annual income "between $1,050 and $1,150."[482] The city collected an average of $129 in taxes a year per household—more than 10 percent of the average family's income.[483] The federal government took only 3 percent in taxes and the state demanded even less than that.[484]

Taxes were insufficient to run the largest city in America. New York had incurred more than $1.1 billion of indebtedness, with maturities ranging from one month to more than fifty years.[485] The city had followed the practice of selling short-term notes to finance day-to-day expenditures, expecting to repay the obligations with tax receipts coming due. New York had reduced its reliance on such "tax anticipation notes" a few years before 1914 by collecting taxes twice a year, in May and November, rather than annually. The shift to semiannual tax collections saved the citizens of New York City more than $3 million a year in interest.[486]

Borrowing in anticipation of future revenues is not inherently evil. Creditworthy municipalities currently rely on TANs, the same type of tax anticipation notes issued by New York City in 1914. Had the city sold its short-term notes during the first half of 1914 on Wall Street, rather than in London and Paris, it would not have needed gold when the war broke out. American investors would have accepted national bank notes if they wanted to cash in their bonds. In the spring of 1914, New York comptroller William A. Prendergast shipped the city's debts across the Atlantic. Were there no buyers in New York?

A worldwide search for the lowest possible interest rate motivated New York to sell its debts abroad. According to J. P. Morgan partner Thomas Lamont, "It has long been the custom of the City of New York to issue short-time notes in anticipation of taxes. . . . Usually these short-time notes would be sold in the New York money market. . . . However, because of the more advantageous rates of interest prevailing abroad, the City had issued its notes, in 1914, in pounds and francs and had discounted them in London and Paris. It was consequently under obligation to pay off these notes in pounds sterling and in francs."[487] Reducing interest expense had always been a high priority with the city.*

New York advertised its creditworthiness in Europe as though it were selling Coca-Cola. On May 1, 1914, the city entered an exhibit at the International Urban Exposition in Lyon, France. According to the city's Finance Department, "the plan has been developed to emphasize the credit

* The source of the reduced expense associated with borrowing in Europe came from the city's foreign exchange transactions. According to the *Wall Street Journal* (August 24, 1914, 5), "By careful buying and selling exchange to cover the foreign transactions the city officials have been credited with making a substantial saving on the interest they have to pay."

of the City, correlating the various items exhibited with the financial fabric which they support."[488] Some of the city's most important initiatives decorated the pavilion at the exposition, including, "pictures of the Catskill Aqueduct and watershed, the new subways . . . views at Coney Island, the Metropolitan Museum of Art. . . . [And] not to overlook the main point, photographic reproductions of the City's revenue bonds."[489]

Under normal circumstances these marketing efforts might have helped New York to rollover its maturing debt at favorable interest rates. But August 1914 intruded. British and French investors liked the pictures but wanted gold. And no amount of advertising could convince them otherwise.

Treasury Secretary McAdoo had watched the dollar take a beating on August 19, the day Comptroller Prendergast announced that the city owed $82 million in short-term debt, denominated in pounds and francs, to British and French investors. No one knew how many other municipalities and corporations had tapped European markets for the same reason as New York—to lower borrowing costs. McAdoo needed numbers. He also wanted a detailed plan and decided to put the Federal Reserve Board to work on the problem.

McADOO ENLISTS THE FEDERAL RESERVE BOARD

Members of the Federal Reserve Board had been sworn into office on August 10, 1914. Since then they resembled newly minted generals waiting for armies to command. The board's power stemmed from its role in monitoring the activities of the Federal Reserve Banks. The regional banks, not the board, could issue Federal Reserve notes, discount commercial paper, and clear checks. Considerable disagreement among strong-minded personalities within the system would delay the opening of the individual banks until November 1914. Meanwhile, board members bickered with Treasury Secretary McAdoo over housekeeping matters.

The Federal Reserve Act had, by law, installed the treasury secretary as chairman of the Federal Reserve Board and the comptroller of the currency as a member of the board. The act also authorized the treasury secretary to arrange for the board's offices.[490] McAdoo cleared space in the Treasury to house the five other members of the board. The new offices were located on the second floor of the Treasury building, flanked on one side by McAdoo and on the other by Comptroller John Skelton Williams.

Charles Hamlin had been appointed governor of the Federal Reserve Board by President Wilson. In those days the governor of the board served as the chief operating officer and chaired meetings of the board in

McAdoo's absence. Hamlin felt right at home in the Treasury building, having served as an assistant secretary under McAdoo. But the other board members—Paul Warburg, Adolph Miller, Fredrick Delano, and W.P.G. Harding—resented their status as tenants. They worried that McAdoo wanted to make the Federal Reserve Board nothing more than an appendage of the Treasury Department, like the Bureau of Engraving and Printing.[491]

Members of the board fretted over their office space, in part, because it reflected their Washington status. According to W.P.G. Harding, who succeeded Hamlin as governor in 1916, "There had been a good deal of discussion, before the appointments [to the board] were made of the importance and dignity of the Board, and it was often alluded to as the Supreme Court of Finance. This was obviously a misnomer . . . [but] it was thought by some that the Board would rank in importance and dignity next to the Supreme Court and the Cabinet."[492] Without a building of their own, however, members of the Federal Reserve Board would have difficulty advancing in diplomatic receiving lines.

Twenty years would elapse before the Federal Reserve Board broke free from the U.S. Treasury. In the Banking Act of 1935, Congress removed the secretary of the Treasury and the comptroller of the currency from the board.[493] After 1935 the president designated a chairman from among his seven appointees. Going forward, the title of governor applied to each member of the board of governors of the Federal Reserve System. While the reorganization was underway, the board of governors conducted a competition to design a building of its own. It is no accident that the marble edifice on Constitution Avenue, completed in 1937, competes in grandeur with the Supreme Court building.

In August 1914 McAdoo harnessed the board's expertise in money and finance. Paul Warburg had been a partner at the Kuhn, Loeb banking firm; Adolph Miller had been an economics professor at the University of California; and W.P.G. Harding had been a commercial banker in Birmingham, Alabama. McAdoo asked the board to invite the leading bankers in the country to the Treasury for a meeting on Friday, September 4, 1914, to discuss American obligations abroad.[494]

THE GOLD POOL

McAdoo and the Federal Reserve Board worried that New York City's $82 million of indebtedness led a parade of claims that were due in Europe before the end of the year. To determine the magnitude of the problem, the board sent invitations to representatives of bank clearing houses throughout the country. Clearing houses in cities with substantial potential for foreign exposure—New York, Chicago, Boston, Philadelphia, St. Louis, and San Francisco—received invitations to send two representatives. Other bank clearing houses, including those from Cincinnati, Denver, Omaha, Pittsburgh, and Portland, received invitations to send one representative.

The Federal Reserve Board hoped to determine how much gold was needed and then to mobilize the precious metal locked away in the American heartland. Paul Warburg had written a memo to McAdoo at the end of August on the importance of consolidating gold holdings in the Federal Reserve and the Treasury and "to get it away from the cash vaults of the National banks, the state banks and the trust companies."[495] The regional disparity in representation at the September 4 conference undermined Warburg's goal. It stoked the resentment of banks in the interior of the country toward their Big City counterparts.*

Albert Wiggin, chairman of the New York City Clearing House Committee and president of Chase National Bank, and Benjamin Strong Jr., at the time president of the Bankers Trust Company, were appointed representatives of the New York Clearing House. On September 2 they sent a letter to financial institutions in New York requesting details from each bank on: "Credit balances due to Canada, Great Britain, Germany, France, and other countries; Amount of commercial credits still unused and likely to be availed of; Amount loaned here for account of European clients; Amount of exchange you are obligated to deliver."[496] Wiggin and Strong also said, "Banking houses that have placed corporate obligations abroad are requested to state whether obligations are securities, dividends or coupons and whether demand is due in September, October, November, or later."[497]

The information sought by Wiggin and Strong invaded a bank's privacy. The press reported the discontent: "There is some well defined opposition to supplying the information regarding the exchange position of the banking institutions. . . . At the bottom of this opposition is the feeling that some might place themselves at a disadvantage in supplying this information. It would, for one thing, disclose the hands of those who may have supplies of exchange against which they can draw and this might lead to pressure upon them to surrender these funds to those who may need them to cover obligations incurred before the outbreak of the war."[498]

Bankers guard the details of their investments with well-deserved paranoia. Most financiers expect competitors to exploit every scrap of

---

* The *New York Times* (September 2, 1914, 10), reported that the Federal Reserve Board was expected to counter the resentment: "It has been suggested that the Federal Reserve Board could help materially in recommending to the banks of the interior that they share in the task of supplying the gold for the settlement of these claims to Europe."

information, as though they were planning a military assault. Did the bankers suppress their fears in early September for the common good? According to the *New York Times*, some did and some did not: "Messrs Wiggin and Strong carried with them to Washington data supplied by *most* [emphasis added] of the international banking houses showing the amount of money owed Europe and the amounts of credit available for settling it."[499]

Wiggin and Strong may have arrived in Washington with incomplete data, but there was enough to confirm everyone's fears. The Federal Reserve Board compiled the reports of all Clearing House representatives and determined that America owed Europe $500 million coming due before the end of the year.[500] That obligation would deplete all of the gold reserves of New York banks and leave an unpaid bill of $200 million.

America needed a plan and Wiggin and Strong had brought one with them. A *New York Times* headline on September 4 announced: "Gold Pool Proposed for Foreign Debts: Clearing House Committee Will Suggest It to the Federal Reserve Board Today."[501] The *Times* explained: "It was understood in the financial district that A. H. Wiggin and Benjamin Strong Jr. will propose the formation of a gold pool to provide at least $200 million in gold for shipment abroad."[502] The president of a large downtown bank said: "It would seem practical in liquidating this country's indebtedness to form . . . an underwriting to a gold pool with the various financial centers of the United States and the Treasury Department [contributing]. . . . This would give a stability to our securities and our credit. . . . Spread out over the country the amount of gold that would have to be supplied by each bank would not be so large as to embarrass it."[503]

The meeting on September 4 established a committee, chaired by James B. Forgan, president of the First National Bank of Chicago, to implement the Gold Pool. Four bankers, in addition to Forgan, served on committee: Benjamin Strong Jr. of New York, L. L. Rue of Philadelphia, Sol Wexler of New Orleans, and Thomas P. Beal of Boston. They planned to raise $150 million in gold, rather than the $200 million reported in the press, and recommended that "The Federal Reserve Board take the steps to ascertain the amount of gold that will be contributed by the banks in the respective cities and that it use its influence to have said banks contribute their proper pro-rata [share]."[504]

The foreign exchange market registered its immediate approval. Figure 7.1 shows the dollar price of the British pound for September 1914. Sterling started out the month at a lofty $5.065, having risen steadily in value since New York City announced the scope of its debt on August 19. The figure shows a dramatic turnaround since September 1, when the Federal Reserve Board's initiative began. On September 4, the

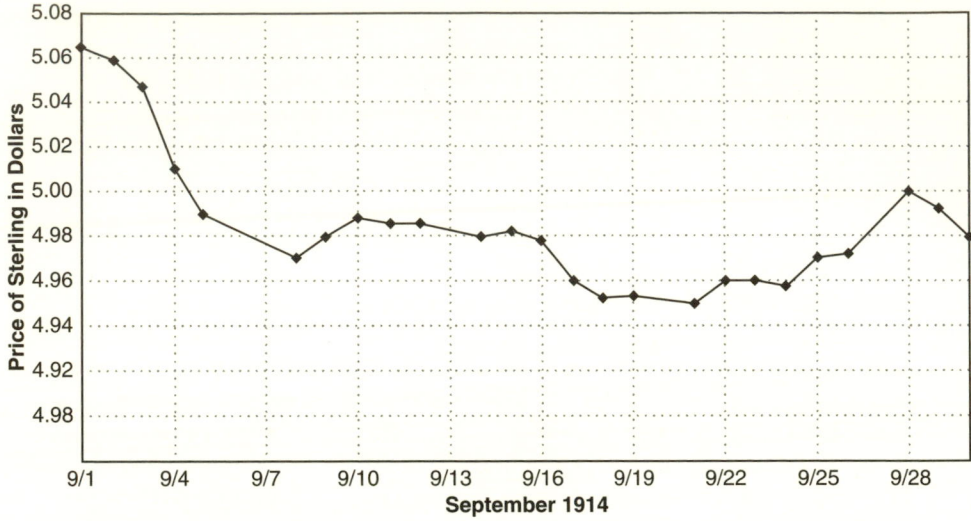

Figure 7.1. Sterling Exchange Rate, September 1914.

Data Source: *Wall Street Journal*.

day of the meeting at the Treasury Department in Washington, sterling fell to $5.01, a significant decline of about three-quarters of 1 percent from $5.0475 the previous day.* As the *Wall Street Journal* reported, "There is a good deal easier tone to the foreign exchange market. This is attributed in large measure to the meeting now taking place at Washington between New York bankers and the Federal Reserve Board over the exchange situation."[505]

It is somewhat surprising that the Federal Reserve's initiative bore fruit even before a definitive plan had been approved. How could the foreign exchange market expect the Federal Reserve Board to insure participation in the Gold Pool by banks throughout the country when New York suffered from an undercurrent of resentment? Without the help of their country cousins, the banks of New York did not have the necessary gold reserves to establish a fund.

The *Wall Street Journal* may have been too quick to credit the Gold Pool with the dollar's revival on September 4. Something else that had been percolating in the background spilled into public view. And the prestigious investment house of J. P. Morgan & Company stood behind it.

---

* The return of minus .743 percent on September 4 has a t-statistic of 3.23, which is statistically significant at conventional levels of confidence. The standard deviation of returns on the dollar price of sterling equals .23 percent per day between August 8, 1914, and December 31, 1914.

NEW YORK CITY BAILOUT

J. P. Morgan had asked Treasury Secretary McAdoo to arrange a private meeting with the Federal Reserve Board on August 20, the day after New York City publicly confessed its foreign debts. Morgan needed Washington's cooperation in a rescue he had discussed with New York City comptroller William A. Prendergast. Morgan told McAdoo that the banks in New York could form a syndicate to issue short-term dollar denominated notes for the city and manage the proceeds to pay the city's European obligations in gold and sterling, but they "could not do anything on such a scale without the knowledge of the Secretary of the Treasury and the Comptroller of the Currency."[506] In particular, Morgan said the Treasury had to agree that "the banks might be obliged to further reduce their cash reserves in order to protect the city's credit. . . . [In addition] it would be necessary for the Treasury Department to permit New York City obligations to be used as security for emergency currency to a somewhat larger extent than might have been expected."

Morgan also saw an opportunity to promote fiscal responsibility in New York. He said that the rescue should be undertaken only if "the finances of the City are to be conducted upon a policy different from that followed during many years . . . and should lead to the stopping of debt increase and gradually, by additional taxation, to a reduction of the debt."[507] Some sixty years later, in 1975, with New York City once again on the verge of bankruptcy, the Municipal Assistance Corporation was established to monitor the city's compliance with federal and state budgetary restrictions.* Morgan's suggested fiscal reforms in 1914, unlike the modern bailout of New York, resembled boilerplate in a prospectus. Morgan knew that the country had to ignore New York's fiscal laxity. He said: "The failure of the greatest city in America to meet its obligations punctually would . . . have dealt an almost irreparable blow to the credit of New York City, as well as cast discredit on the United States."[508]

Treasury Secretary McAdoo had no difficulty accommodating Morgan's request to expand the collateral value of New York City securities for emergency currency. He had already extended a similar privilege to southern states by approving cotton warehouse receipts as acceptable collateral.[509] But Morgan's request to allow New York City banks "to further reduce their cash reserves" would set a dangerous precedent.

New York City banks had not met their legal reserve requirements since August 1, 1914.[510] According to the *Commercial and Financial Chronicle,*

---

* The Municipal Assistance Corporation (MAC) came into existence on June 10, 1975, to supervise New York City's finances. MAC issued bonds backed by a dedicated portion of the city's sales tax. The proceeds from these bonds were used by the city. MAC, together with federal loan guarantees, helped the city avert bankruptcy.

"It is one of the remarkable features of the present situation that absolutely no attention is being given to the necessity of removing this deficiency in reserves. At all previous periods of financial disturbance where a serious deficiency in reserve developed [1893 and 1907], it was at once recognized that the dislocation must be corrected before tangible improvement in affairs could be counted on."[511] Could McAdoo promote the New York City bailout by allowing New York banks to violate further the regulatory safeguards?

McAdoo knew he would come under fire by approving this implicit subsidy to New York City. Treasury Secretary Leslie M. Shaw had been attacked nearly a decade earlier for relieving banks of the necessity to hold reserves against government deposits.[512] McAdoo made no formal declaration in response to J. P. Morgan's request. He and Comptroller of the Currency John Skelton Williams simply ignored bank violations of legal reserve requirements. However, the *Commercial and Financial Chronicle* noticed: "Such a situation must inevitably tend to create additional distrust."[513] McAdoo did not care. The stakes were simply too great.

McAdoo's assistance to New York City in 1914 marks the birth of the "Too Big to Fail" doctrine in American finance. The federal loan guarantees during the 1970s to the Lockheed Corporation, a giant defense contractor, and to the Chrysler Corporation, at the time an *American* car manufacturer, and the bailout of Continental Illinois bank, the seventh largest bank in the United States in 1984, continued a tradition that began with McAdoo's decision to rescue New York City in 1914.

William G. McAdoo followed his entrepreneurial instincts by taking a calculated risk. His actions encouraged Morgan to form a syndicate with Jacob Schiff's Kuhn, Loeb & Company to redeem New York's credit. For two weeks after the meeting at the Federal Reserve Board on August 20, 1914, Morgan, together with his partner Henry Davison, hammered out an acceptable agreement.[514] On September 4, the same day that Wiggin and Strong proposed the Gold Pool, syndicate managers J. P. Morgan & Company and Kuhn, Loeb delivered a letter to Comptroller Prendergast outlining the terms and conditions of the bailout.[515]

The syndicate agreed to place, at par, city notes maturing over the next three years and to use the proceeds to repay the city's obligations in Europe. To counter the city's complaint that a 6 percent interest rate on the dollar-denominated notes was too high, the syndicate capped New York's foreign exchange exposure at a rate of $5.035 per pound sterling.[516] The syndicate would absorb any costs above that figure, and the city would receive a rebate if the obligation could be repaid at a lower foreign exchange rate.

On September 5 the *New York Times* hailed the syndicate's proposed transaction as "one of the most important financial operations ever undertaken, and it is expected to exert a most beneficial influence."[517] The *Times* went on to say: "The information which the banking community has received regarding the city plan has resulted in a sharp drop in exchange. Three days ago demand sterling was above $5.05. Yesterday it sold as low as $5.00."[518] The favorable reaction reflected the market's belief that the two leading investment banks, Kuhn, Loeb and J. P. Morgan, would get the funds needed to repay New York City's obligations without driving up the price of sterling. They had an economic incentive to acquire gold to make the payments, having protected the city against price increases in sterling above $5.035.

The *New York Times* credited the New York City bailout with precipitating the significant drop in sterling—and the increased value of the dollar—on September 4. The *Wall Street Journal* attributed the currency movement on September 4 to the Gold Pool proposal by Wiggins and Strong. The price movement on September 4, 1914, cannot disentangle the relative contribution of the two financial packages.* But within a week another announcement would resolve the dispute over the source of America's improved credibility.

MOBILIZING THE PRECIOUS METAL

The foreign exchange market approved of the Gold Pool and the New York City bailout, but the bankers had to make them work. Both plans relied on gathering the yellow metal from bank coffers to ransom America from the Europeans. No one really wanted to ship gold abroad. According to the *New York Times*, the bankers hoped that "the mere fact that this market stands ready to make these payments is expected to . . . make it possible to cover nearly all the amount in bills of exchange instead of in gold."[519] The bankers wanted to assemble a gold hoard and display it like a stack of chips at a high-stakes poker game.

The overlap between the two plans raised sufficient concern to force Benjamin Strong, representing the Gold Pool, and Morgan and Schiff, representing the New York syndicate, to meet with the secretary of the Treasury and the Federal Reserve Board on Thursday morning, September 10, to coordinate the defense of America's virtue. Strong sent McAdoo a telegram two days before, suggesting that Strong arrive early

---

* A third announcement was released on September 4 by the Bank of England (*New York Times*, September 5, 1914, 3), saying that it will "Provide acceptors [of bills of exchange] with the funds necessary to pay at maturity all bills contracted for before the moratorium was declared." None of the commentary related the movement in the price of sterling on September 4 to this announcement.

to brief him.[520] McAdoo invited Strong to his home the day before Morgan and Schiff were scheduled to arrive.

The meeting that took place between McAdoo and Strong on Wednesday evening, September 9, was the first of their many conversations about gold. McAdoo urged the banks to pay it out freely, while Strong emphasized the difficulty of doing so.[521] Their debates would continue after Strong became governor of the Federal Reserve Bank of New York. He would lock horns with McAdoo to foster a delay in opening the Federal Reserve Banks until they could accumulate sufficient gold. For now they both wanted to use the precious metal to guarantee America's credibility.

At the September 4 conference, Wiggin and Strong had suggested, as part of their Gold Pool plan, that the Federal Reserve Board use its influence to mobilize gold reserves throughout the country. Reality set in after the September 10 meeting among Morgan, Schiff, Strong, and the board. J. P. Morgan and Jacob Schiff described the negotiations they conducted to form the syndicate to meet New York City's obligations. Members of the Federal Reserve Board wanted to do the same for the Gold Pool, but they had no troops to command. The board also knew that resentment toward New York would hamper any effort at moral suasion. The Federal Reserve Board approved of the Gold Pool in principle but admitted that it "found it difficult to arrange the details for carrying it out."[522]

The Federal Reserve Board stumbled publicly on September 11 by issuing the following statement: "In view of the announcement that New York City has completed arrangements for paying of her maturing obligations . . . the Board felt that it may not be necessary to create the proposed fund of $150,000,000 in gold and decided to await further developments before giving the matter further consideration."[523] Three days later, a *Wall Street Journal* article placed the Gold Pool on the inactive list: "The Federal Reserve Board has for the time being abandoned the consideration of the bankers plan to form a Gold Pool. . . . This action is taken in view of the fact that the situation has been so materially relieved by the arrangements in New York City to meet its $82,000,000 foreign indebtedness."[524]

The foreign exchange market dispelled any doubt about the relative importance of the New York City bailout versus the Gold Pool. Figure 7.1 shows that the dollar price of the pound remained virtually unchanged between September 10 and September 15. The market greeted the cancellation of the Gold Pool with a giant yawn.

What accounts for the success of the New York City rescue? J. P. Morgan & Company and Kuhn, Loeb knew how to raise money for corporations and municipalities. Morgan's list of satisfied companies included

U.S. Steel, and Kuhn, Loeb's began with the Pennsylvania Railroad. Before bringing a new bond issue to market, the two investment banks usually consulted with their customers—wealthy individuals, insurance companies, and trusts—to set the interest rate that would attract investors. They then organized a group of selling banks, the syndicate, to distribute the public offering throughout the country. Members of the syndicate earned a commission—sometimes called an underwriter's fee—for participating in a public offering of newly issued securities.

Henry Davison, the J. P. Morgan partner in charge of organizing the syndicate, employed charm, personality, and the prospect of participating in future public offerings, to convince a total of 124 banks in New York to subscribe to the city's bonds.[525] The banks agreed to pay their obligation in gold or sterling on a schedule determined by syndicate managers, J. P. Morgan & Company and Kuhn, Loeb. Davison allocated the bonds within the syndicate in proportion to each bank's deposits. The largest institution, National City Bank, subscribed to $7,800,280 of the city's bonds and the smallest, the Tottenville National Bank in Staten Island, committed to $3,005.[526] J. P. Morgan and Kuhn, Loeb each took $694,155 bonds. The syndicate raised a total of $100 million—a sum that would repay all of the city's obligations maturing before the end of the year, including $82 million held in Britain and France.

Success in redeeming the city's credit depended not only on raising the money but in delivering gold or sterling to British investors. The first test came on September 15, 1914, when the syndicate managers demanded a total of $8,257,400 for obligations coming due through the end of the month. J. P. Morgan & Company called for the gold to be delivered to 23 Wall Street before the end of the day. Bank messengers arrived at the House of Morgan starting at ten o'clock in the morning, usually with a police escort, carrying satchels and handbags that looked as though they had seen years of commuter service on the city's subways.[527] The bags contained packets of gold certificates, along with a few gold coins, that summed to each bank's required contribution. Tellers at the Morgan bank combined the gold certificates from several messengers and then delivered them across the street to the subtreasury office, where they were redeemed for gold bars. The bars returned to the bank under guard and were sealed in kegs. Within an hour of closing on September 15, an express company loaded the cargo onto trucks and delivered it to the railway station for shipment to Ottawa. The Bank of England depository took possession of the precious metal twelve hours later.

The syndicate's efficiency in raising and transferring the gold generated an optimism usually reserved for opening day of a new baseball season. A prominent banker sounded the appropriate note: "There is now a big rift in the clouds and I would not be surprised if conditions improved rapidly from this time. . . . The big demand for the New York City notes was one of the most pleasant surprises which we have had recently."[528] J. P. Morgan wrote a note to McAdoo confirming the success of the city's financing: "The entire issue is oversubscribed. The net result is that the banks will be relieved of a very considerable amount of the loan which they are carrying and will only be left with that which they wish to hold."[529] Nothing pleases syndicate members more than buying securities from the issuer and reselling them to ultimate investors before the ink is dry on the prospectus. All that's left in banker pockets are the profits.

The spillover from New York City's success created a financial frenzy. The *Wall Street Journal* reported on September 15: "Consummation of the plans to meet the $100 million of New York City's maturing securities, $80 million of which are held in England and France, was the most constructive development that has taken place since the war started. . . . There has been evidence that England, the largest foreign holder of our securities, is not as anxious to liquidate as might be supposed. About 75% of the holders of the £420,000 Lake Shore one-year notes elected to take new notes . . . in exchange for maturing securities. One of the bankers in charge of that financing said: 'When they know they can get their money, they are not so eager to have it.' "[530]

The Lake Shore one-year notes were obligations of the Lake Shore & Michigan Southern Railway. The refinancing of these securities attracted British investors for two reasons: America showed a willingness to pay its debts in gold and the interest rate jumped to attractive levels. The new Lake Shore notes carried an interest rate of 6.75 percent. They replaced maturing securities that had been issued at an interest rate of 4.5 percent in March 1913.[531] The more than 2 percent jump in rates reflected the precautionary demand for cash since the war began.[532] All borrowers felt the pinch. New York City had to pay an interest rate of 6 percent to its new investors, compared with 4 percent in the last city borrowing.[533] The city comptroller—and the mayor—had complained about the cost of the financing to McAdoo. They should not have taken it personally.

A PREMATURE CELEBRATION

The triumph of the New York rescue meant that America had defended its credit reputation. Predictions of a quick return to normalcy followed. A member of the New York Stock Exchange said on September 19: "I am told that . . . in the past few days such progress has been made that we can expect something tangible in the near future. Those who attempt a forecast regarding a resumption of business on our Stock Exchange . . . think there will be a reopening . . . by October 15."[534]

McAdoo confounded predictions of a speedy reopening of the exchange. The New York Stock Exchange remained padlocked until December 12. McAdoo also surprised the handicappers of finance by announcing a revival of the Gold Pool a week after its reported demise. On September 21 the *Wall Street Journal* reported: "Secretary McAdoo late Friday gave out the following statement: 'J. B. Forgan of Chicago, A. H. Wiggin and Benjamin Strong Jr. of New York, and L. L. Rue of Philadelphia, representing the committee appointed by the conference of bankers . . . today conferred with the [Federal Reserve] Board in further consideration of their proposed plan to create a gold fund. . . . The act of New York City in completing its arrangements . . . relieved one phase of the situation and made it desirable to further consider the subject. . . . The Bankers' Committee has considered the developments and is of the opinion that it may be desirable to create such a fund of $100,000,000 to meet the situation at the present time.' "[535]

What cloud in the New York City rescue forced the "Bankers Committee" to resurrect a slimmed-down version of the Gold Pool? They had abandoned the Gold Pool on September 14 because the "situation has been so materially relieved." Was the situation less "materially relieved" than appeared to the naked eye?

Benjamin Strong, a member of the Bankers' Committee, had the vision of an eagle when it came to gold. He had watched members of the New York City syndicate delivering what they owed to the House of Morgan at 23 Wall Street on September 15. He did not like what he saw.[536]

The city's obligations to British investors were denominated in sterling. The syndicate organized by J. P. Morgan and Kuhn, Loeb needed £2,150,000 to cover obligations coming due in the month of September.[537] Banks could pay their quota to the syndicate either in gold or foreign exchange. Gold could be shipped to Ottawa and turned into sterling at a cost of $4.90 per pound. On September 15, the day banks had to deliver their first installment to 23 Wall Street, a sterling bill of exchange cost $4.985 per pound. Every bank should have delivered gold rather than a bill of exchange. Sterling bills of exchange cost an extra 8.5¢ per pound sterling. Nevertheless, 20 percent of the total payments on September 15 arrived at the House of Morgan in the form of sterling bills of exchange.[538] Bankers wanted their gold and were prepared to pay a penalty of nearly 1.75 percent to keep the precious metal.*

---

* The additional 8.5¢ per pound sterling (.085) divided by 4.90 = .0173, which is 1.73 percent.

Benjamin Strong knew that the banker preference for gold would keep the price of the British pound above the $4.90 gold export point. He promoted the Gold Pool as a second line of defense—to show the British that America had additional reserves to commit, beyond the New York City syndicate, in the battle for credibility. But he worried that the pressure to export gold would continue as long as sterling remained above $4.90. Gold exports posed a very special danger in the life of Benjamin Strong.

CHAPTER EIGHT

End Game

TREASURY SECRETARY McAdoo's finger-in-the-dike policies had plugged the holes threatening American finance. He aimed the Aldrich-Vreeland Act at the banking system's currency drain. He shored up gold supplies at subtreasury offices around the country to defend the government's promise to redeem paper currency. He shuttered the New York Stock Exchange to halt the hemorrhage of the precious metal to Europe. And he called in J. P. Morgan to protect America's credit from foreign attack. But the danger had not passed. Six weeks after the crisis began the dollar price of sterling remained above $4.90, provoking gold exports.

McAdoo needed a fundamental adjustment in the American economy to restore normalcy. He had sought to establish the Federal Reserve Board to accomplish the task. During the first week of August, McAdoo had put the finishing touches on the Federal Reserve Board by lobbying Wilson's final nominees—Paul Warburg and Fredrick Delano—through the Senate Banking Committee. On August 10, McAdoo had announced: "We are going to be able to make this System a bulwark against financial disaster. . . . These banks could have been organized by the 1st of August, but due to causes over which we had no control the organization was not perfected by that date. The fact that the Board itself has been organized means that the Banks can certainly be organized by the 1st of October, or sooner."[539]

McAdoo committed publicly to establishing the regional Reserve Banks by October 1 because the banks, not the board, were authorized to issue Federal Reserve notes and to establish the discount rate that could attract deposits from abroad. Two powerful Federal Reserve officials, Paul Warburg and Benjamin Strong, prevented McAdoo from launching the system in time to tame the crisis. They worried that rushing the banks into operation would endanger the new currency system.

McAdoo had to defeat the crisis on his own. He would triumph with an exit plan he had set in motion during the first week of August.

DISSENSION FROM WITHIN

On September 1, 1914, the *New York Times* summarized the case for caution: "There have come to Secretary McAdoo and the members of the Reserve Board many letters from bankers of prominence urging that the Board proceed very slowly with the organization of the new system. These bankers argue that now is a very inauspicious time to set up the new system because of the chaotic conditions due to the war. . . . Mr. Warburg is credited with fully sharing this view of the situation. Being a banker of international reputation and having a scientific grasp on the whole subject, he is said to have made his position very strong with Secretary McAdoo and other members of the Federal Reserve Board."[540]

The press drew the battle lines: "Paul Warburg and Comptroller [of the Currency] Williams have locked horns over the big question of whether the Reserve Banks shall be organized at all at this time."[541] The newspaper account indicated that the comptroller had powerful support from the "Treasury-alliance" within the board: "It is understood that Secretary McAdoo, Comptroller Williams and [Governor] Hamlin have taken the position that there should be no delay in organizing the new reserve system."[542]

Warburg's "scientific grasp" of the principles of central banking had encouraged Wilson to nominate the Wall Street banker to the board. The president liked Warburg's preference for an independent central bank and hoped it would offset McAdoo's efforts to dominate the board. McAdoo had lobbied for a board that "would work in harmony with the Treasury Secretary."

The day after the dispute spilled into public view, the New York Times reported that "McAdoo denied that there were any differences among the members of the Federal Reserve Board."[543] McAdoo also announced that October 1 remained his target date for opening the banks.[544] Warburg supported the chairman of the board by issuing the following statement: "I have noticed with extreme regret a statement by the Washington correspondent of the New York Times concerning differences of opinion reported to exist between the Comptroller of the Currency and myself. These statements are absolutely unwarranted. The Federal Reserve Board has acted with complete unanimity on all questions which have so far come up for action and discussion and it is a great satisfaction to state that that the Board finds itself in complete harmony as to the questions now pending."[545]

Warburg's public truce fooled no one, least of all McAdoo. He recalled Warburg's criticism of the Federal Reserve Act during the congressional debate, arguing that the proposed legislation would bring about "direct government management."[546] After reading a 5,000 word memorandum from Warburg in opposition to many features of the pending legislation,[547] McAdoo had said: "Mr. Warburg's argument was so remote from actuality, and rested on ideas so foreign to anything in my own mind that I could only stare at it in astonishment."[548] Nevertheless,

McAdoo helped circumvent the Senate Banking Committee's blockade of the Warburg nomination:[549] "Personally, I favored his appointment. It seemed just and right that a member with the Wall Street point of view should be on the Board, if it was to be well rounded and representative of all classes of American finance."[550] McAdoo could be generous as long as he expected to control the board.

After his appointment, Warburg did not hide his reservations from his colleagues about rushing the banks into existence. On August 27 he wrote a memo to McAdoo outlining his arguments. No one knows whether the *New York Times* received a purloined copy, using it as a basis for its September 1 report on dissension within the board, but the memorandum contained clear evidence of Warburg's opposition to opening the regional banks.

Warburg's seven-page memo reads as though he were paid by the word. The following excerpt summarizes his position: "The main problem to be considered by the Federal Reserve Board is the question whether the Federal Reserve Banks should be opened in the near future or whether the opening of these Federal Reserve Banks should be indefinitely postponed. I say indefinitely because I believe that if these Federal Reserve Banks are not opened now it may be impossible to open them for a year, or possibly even longer. . . . But we could not think of opening now unless the law [is] radically amended in some respects. If the bank opened under the present law it would have capital of about $19,000,000 and deposits [in gold] of about $250,000,000. . . . Past and present experience shows conclusively that a gold reserve of $250,000,000 is not sufficient to safeguard the immense financial structure of currency and bank credits of the United States."[551]

Warburg did not reject opening the banks immediately but said the law had to be amended or the system would fail to safeguard American finance. Warburg devoted five pages to explain the amendments needed to rectify his perception of a key shortcoming in the Federal Reserve Act: "The entire gold holdings of the United States, taking the holdings of all the banks, the free Treasury balance, and gold in circulation, is estimated to amount to upwards of $1,500,000,000. It is apparent how insufficient is a system which assembles only $250,000,000 of this gold and leaves about $1,250,000,000 free as an absolutely useless and wasted asset of the nation."[552]

McAdoo had no patience with Warburg's grand design for accumulating as much gold as possible within the Federal Reserve System. And neither would Congress. America's central bank, voted into existence on December 23, 1913, germinated for years before becoming the law of the land. The Aldrich-Vreeland Act of 1908 had established the "National Monetary Commission . . . to inquire into and report to Congress at the earliest date practicable, what changes are necessary or desirable in the monetary system of the United States."* Republican Senator Nelson Aldrich, joint sponsor of the 1908 legislation and chairman of the National Monetary Commission, introduced a bill to create an American central bank on January 9, 1912. The "Aldrich Plan" had been designed in a meeting on Jekyll Island off the Georgia coast among the senator and a few bankers, including Henry Davison, who had just become a partner at J. P. Morgan, and Paul Warburg, then a partner at Kuhn, Loeb.[553] According to Warburg, "A plan had been outlined which provided for a 'National Reserve Association,' meaning a central reserve organization with an elastic note issue based on gold and commercial paper."[554] Carter Glass called the plan "a central bank of banks, for banks and by banks."[555]

Aldrich's bill disappeared, along with the Republican senator, when the Democrats captured the White House and the Congress in November 1912. A month after the election, President-elect Wilson met with Carter Glass, soon to become chairman of the House Banking and Currency Committee, to make certain that America's central bank would be responsible to the people and not just the financiers. Wilson's input resulted in the inclusion, as part of the December 1913 legislation, of a board in Washington to monitor the regional Reserve Banks.[556]

Both McAdoo and Warburg knew that Congress would not amend the Federal Reserve Act to accommodate Warburg's obsession with gold. Warburg's support for opening the banks immediately, but only with appropriate congressional amendment, meant exactly what the September 1, 1914, *New York Times* headline said: "Warburg Favors Delay."[557]

The Federal Reserve Act conferred on McAdoo the right to choose the date to open the Federal Reserve Banks. McAdoo agreed with Warburg's concern that the "immediate drain on our gold supply might prove very embarrassing." He knew that when commercial banks became members of the system they would need gold to meet their required reserves and capital contributions with the regional Federal Reserve Banks. The Reserve Banks needed gold to back the new Federal Reserve notes that would circulate as currency. McAdoo had padlocked the New York Stock Exchange to protect the gold in bankers' vaults, in part, to pave the way for the birth of the Federal Reserve System.[558]

McAdoo also shared Warburg's concern for the danger from America's indebtedness to Europe. He orchestrated the New York City syndicate to demonstrate America's willingness to pay, expecting that to

---

* Warburg (1930, 23) considered this the most important paragraph in the Aldrich-Vreeland Act.

dampen European demands for the precious metal. The foreign exchange market's blessing for the New York City rescue should have advanced McAdoo's timetable for opening the regional Reserve Banks. Instead, it brought Benjamin Strong into the fray as a powerful ally to Paul Warburg.

BENJAMIN STRONG, CENTRAL BANKER

Before becoming the first governor of the Federal Reserve Bank of New York, Benjamin Strong spent a decade at Bankers Trust Company. He joined Bankers Trust as secretary in April 1904 and became president in January 1914.[559] In October 1914, after nine months as president of Bankers Trust, Strong became governor of the Federal Reserve Bank of New York. He served as chief executive officer of the New York Reserve Bank until his death in October 1928. Chase National Bank's Albert Wiggin said after Strong died: "His administration of the Federal Reserve Bank during the critical period of the Great War and the following period of adjustment demonstrated his ability and fine force of character. His death is a great loss to the banking world."[560] Paul Warburg added: "The New York Reserve Bank will stand as a monument to his genius."[561]

At Bankers Trust Company, Benjamin Strong learned to be a banker's banker even before he arrived at the Federal Reserve. Bankers Trust occupied a unique position in New York's financial community. It was incorporated as a trust company, just like the Knickerbocker Trust Company that closed its doors during the Panic of 1907, but was owned by a consortium of banks, hence the name Bankers Trust Company. Henry Davison, vice-president at First National Bank of New York in 1903, conceived of Bankers Trust as a vehicle for banks to participate in the trust activities that were forbidden to them by law. Davison installed his Englewood, New Jersey, neighbor, Benjamin Strong, as secretary of his brainchild.[562]

During the Panic of 1907, J. P. Morgan Sr., a stockholder in Bankers Trust, drafted Henry Davison to help orchestrate a rescue of the failing trust companies. Davison tapped Strong to examine the books of the Knickerbocker Trust Company, but the company suspended operations before Strong could decipher its balance sheet. Strong watched the doors close on the line of depositors and recalled: "The consternation on the faces of the people on that line, many of them men that I knew, I shall never forget. I know that Harry [Henry Davison] left the building with a sense of dejection and defeat which it is quite impossible for me to describe."[563]

The Panic of 1907 turned Strong and Davison into supporters of a central bank.[564] Davison, after becoming a partner at J. P. Morgan & Company in 1909, participated in what he called the "duck shooting trip" to Jekyll Island with Aldrich and Warburg.[565] Strong spoke in favor of the "Aldrich Plan" at the American Bankers Association convention in 1911.[566]

After the Democrats replaced the Aldrich bill with Carter Glass's Federal Reserve Act in mid-1913, Strong worked to alter the legislation before it took final form. He feared that twelve regional banks "would prevent the effective pooling of reserves."[567] He worried that the bill "placed too much power in the hands of political appointees and denied to bankers the representation to which they were entitled."[568] And he complained "that Federal Reserve notes were to be obligations of the United States government."[569] On November 1, 1913, Strong wrote to his fellow New York banker, Paul Warburg: "In my opinion, if the United States government embarks once more upon the expedient or experiment of issuing fiat paper, although in this case supported by bank assets and a percentage in gold reserve, the day will come when we will deeply regret it."[570]

Neither Strong nor Warburg liked the Federal Reserve Act, but both men were drawn to public service. Days before the final vote on December 23, 1913, Strong said: "We are all citizens of the United States, and must put our citizenship above our convictions in matters of this kind. If this bill is enacted, as I presume it will be, we must all bend our energies in making the best of it."[571]

Warburg accepted Wilson's nomination to the Federal Reserve Board on July 31, 1914, in part, because "of the seriousness of the present emergency."[572] Warburg then tried to convince Strong to accept the offer of governor of the Federal Reserve Bank of New York. On August 27 Strong wrote to Warburg explaining his reasons for declining: "Our talks have been quite personal and unofficial so I feel at liberty to write you personally and confidentially. . . . Let me assure you that no selfish consideration has led me to come to this decision. . . . I would vastly prefer undertaking this important constructive work in the public interest to making money for myself. . . . [But] we are facing problems here in New York not only in regard to our own business, which I am glad to say gives me no concern, but in regard to the affairs of clients, of friends and of this city and country which lead them and me to believe that it would be unfair for me to give up my present work [as president of Bankers Trust] just now."[573]

Strong's letter of August 27 disappointed Warburg, but gave him a glimmer of hope. Benjamin Strong would have to accept the position as governor of the Federal Reserve Bank of New York if Warburg could convince him that it was in the country's best interest. While Warburg fought to delay the timetable for opening the Reserve Banks, he gathered ammunition to bludgeon his friend into joining forces with him in the new Federal Reserve System. It did not take long.

On October 5, 1914, Benjamin Strong became governor of the Federal Reserve Bank of New York. How did Warburg change Strong's mind?

THE THREAT

Benjamin Strong shared Paul Warburg's obsession with gold. As a central banker, he believed that the Federal Reserve Banks should hold far more gold than required by law. He said: "We need an immense safety factor beyond the legal minimum and it is for this reason that I have been so urgent about accumulating gold."[574] Strong also wanted to make the dollar "an international currency by [creating] confidence in the redeemability of dollars in gold at all times."[575] August 1914 threatened to derail those goals.

The Federal Reserve Act provided for the accumulation of gold in the central bank by requiring commercial banks to contribute capital and reserves to their regional Federal Reserve Banks. Chase National Bank and National City Bank would pay the Federal Reserve Bank of New York, the Continental and Commercial National Bank would settle with the Federal Reserve Bank of Chicago, and the Girard National Bank would contribute to the Federal Reserve Bank of Philadelphia. Warburg had estimated in his August 27 memo to McAdoo that the regional Reserve Banks would accumulate "capital of about $19,000,000 and deposits of about $250,000,000." He suspected the Reserve Banks would accumulate only a fraction of that total in gold.

According to the Federal Reserve Act, commercial banks had to pay only half their reserves in gold or lawful money.[576] The other half could be satisfied with discounted commercial paper. The Reserve Banks agreed to pay the express charges for shipments of gold to induce commercial banks to tender the precious metal rather than commercial paper.[577] Under normal circumstances even that minor incentive would be more than enough to bring in gold. But with sterling above $4.90 in the foreign exchange market, gold was too valuable; banks would ship the commercial paper to the Federal Reserve Banks and keep the gold. Warburg's memo to McAdoo had said as much: "Under present circumstances a very large portion of these [$250,000,000] deposits would be paid in the form of rediscounts, so that one might expect that the actual gold held in the aggregate by the new Banks would amount to about $150,000,000."[578] Warburg had warned earlier that "a gold reserve of $250,000,000 is not sufficient to safeguard the immense financial structure of currency and bank credits of the United States." A gold reserve of only $150 million would leave the Federal Reserve System with the power of a welterweight.*

Paul Warburg surely shared his concerns with Benjamin Strong at the September 4 meeting in Washington among bankers and the Federal Reserve Board. They had exchanged confidences before. Treasury Secretary McAdoo had announced his intention, two days earlier, to open the Reserve Banks on October 1. Strong recognized that Warburg's calculations could turn McAdoo's schedule into a time bomb. Sterling above $4.90 would nullify Strong's objective of accumulating enough gold to serve as "an immense safety factor beyond the legal minimum."

Benjamin Strong wanted the Federal Reserve System to succeed, despite his reservations about the original legislation. He knew the United States needed a central bank and that Warburg's analysis meant it would start on a starvation diet. Warburg's warnings gained urgency when Strong saw how the commercial banks responded to J. P. Morgan's call for gold contributions in connection with the New York City rescue.

Recall that on September 15, 1914, the day banks had to deliver their first installment of sterling or gold to J. P. Morgan & Company, a sterling bill of exchange cost $4.985 per pound, 8.5¢ per pound above the gold export point. Every bank should have delivered gold rather than a bill of exchange. Nevertheless, 20 percent of the total payments on September 15 arrived at the House of Morgan in the form of sterling bills of exchange. Bankers wanted their gold and were prepared to pay a penalty of almost 1.75 percent to keep the precious metal.[579] Banks would surely keep their gold and deliver commercial paper to the Reserve Banks when there was no penalty for doing so.

On September 22, 1914, shortly after Paul Warburg and Henry Davison kidnapped Strong for a weekend of friendly persuasion, a delegation from the board of directors of the Federal Reserve Bank of New York met with Benjamin Strong.[580] He agreed to accept the position of governor "if the directors were unanimous."[581] Apparently they were. Strong presided over his first board meeting at the Federal Reserve Bank of New York on October 5, 1914, the same day he became governor of the bank.[582]

---

* Warburg's concerns with the gold provisions of the Federal Reserve Act had been reinforced by Sir George Paish, editor of the *Statist* and adviser to the U.K. Treasury. Warburg had sent Paish a copy of the Federal Reserve Act during December 1913. He had received a note from Paish, dated January 8, 1914 (Papers of Paul Warburg, box 1, Yale University), saying: "The provision I am still most dubious about is the gold reserve against the note circulation. . . . The discovery that only a small part of the notes were covered by gold might cause great uneasiness and lead to withdrawal of all gold held against the notes."

THE CONFLICT

William Gibbs McAdoo could not ignore both Benjamin Strong and Paul Warburg. The unlikely duo—Warburg, a German-Jewish immigrant with a central banking mission, and Strong, of Puritan stock with a patrician's sense of obligation—formed a powerful counterweight to McAdoo. Warburg knew more about central banking than anyone in the system but operated within McAdoo's sphere of influence. Strong's position as governor of the New York Reserve Bank gave him a measure of independence, like the viceroy of some distant province. McAdoo had the authority to choose opening day for the banks, but Strong, the chief executive officer of the most important Reserve Bank, could drag his heels.

Benjamin Strong pushed Warburg's argument for delay beyond the initial doubts about gold contributions. He argued that the premium on sterling in the foreign exchange market would damage the ongoing viability of the system: "If the Federal Reserve Banks refuse to pay gold they will be discredited at the outset, and gold will certainly be demanded of them if they expand their note issues when gold will be at a premium . . . the premium as reflected in the price of sterling."[583] Strong worried that, even if the Federal Reserve System started with sufficient gold reserves, the precious metal would leech away as the banks issued paper currency convertible into gold. Failure to keep its currency in circulation would defeat the new currency system.

Warburg and Strong's misgivings restrained McAdoo. Figure 8.1 shows the British pound above the $4.90 gold export during the entire month of September. McAdoo's October 1 target date for opening the banks slipped away under the weight of the sterling premium. Strong and Warburg would have liked McAdoo to delay plans to open the banks until the premium disappeared completely. McAdoo did not want to wait that long. He had the legislative authority to open the banks, and public pressure to fulfill his obligation mounted. McAdoo remembered his slogan as president of the Hudson & Manhattan Railroad Company, "Let the Public Be Pleased."

Unlike central bankers Warburg and Strong, many commercial bankers, especially in the West and South, wanted the Federal Reserve Banks to open quickly to expand credit and to facilitate crop movements. Twenty bankers in the State of Virginia addressed a letter to the chairman of the Federal Reserve Board: "The annual convention of the American Bankers Association will be held in Richmond on October 12. The member banks of Richmond believe that it will exercise a most helpful and beneficial influence upon the business sentiment of the entire country if prior to or during that convention the organization of the Federal

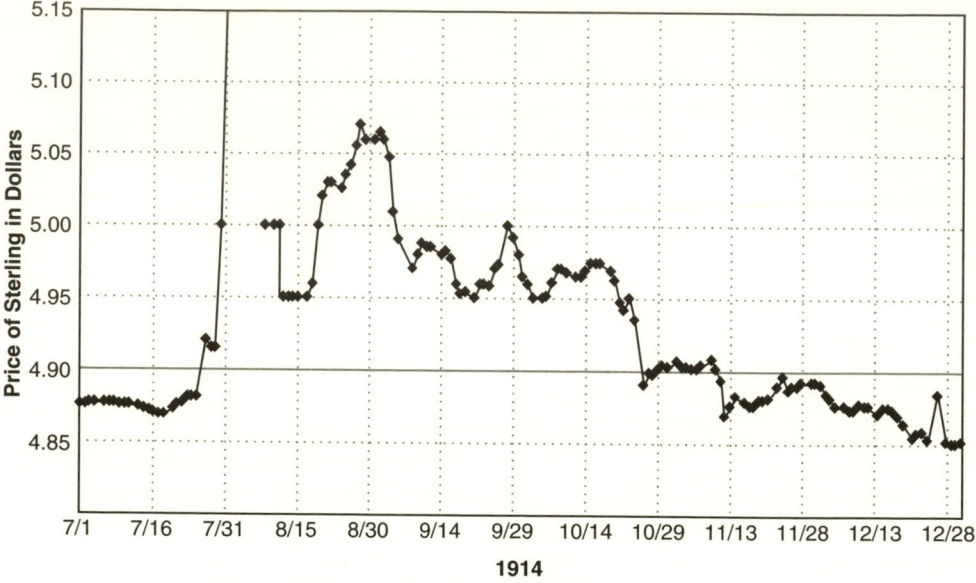

Figure 8.1. Sterling Exchange Rate, Second Half of 1914.

Data Source: *Wall Street Journal.*

Reserve Bank of Richmond can be effected. . . . We have the profoundest conviction that the operation of [the Federal Reserve Act] . . . will bring more widespread relief to the situation than all the expedients hitherto tried or suggested."[584] The governor of Florida sent a telegram to Washington saying: "On behalf of the people of Florida, I urge the Federal Reserve Banks be put in operation immediately and the Reserve board act immediately to protect the cotton crop."[585]

A resolution, passed by the Texas legislature and delivered to the Federal Reserve Board, summarized the argument for opening the banks without delay: "Whereas . . . Texas will produce four million bales of cotton . . . Whereas approximately 95 percent of the Texas crop is annually shipped and used beyond the limits of the state, and there is now no appreciable export demand . . . Whereas the effect of these conditions is to seriously threaten the cotton growers . . . Resolved . . . the Legislature of the State of Texas . . . urge[s] you to expedite as much as may be possible the establishment of the Regional Reserve Banks to be organized under the provisions of the Federal Reserve Act."[586]

Cotton touched McAdoo's southern core. He recognized that "a world at war needs more cotton than a world at peace,"[587] He also knew that

American exports would create a demand for dollars and a supply of British pounds in the foreign exchange market, driving down the premium on sterling. McAdoo had targeted the cotton crop for aid at a conference in Washington on August 24.[588] He had also authorized emergency currency based on cotton warehouse receipts.[589] The key to overcoming the sterling premium that threatened the birth of the Federal Reserve extended to all agricultural exports. McAdoo pushed ahead with plans to open the Federal Reserve Banks because he had already launched a program to stimulate shipments of American goods to Europe.

THE RESOLUTION

During the first week of August 1914 McAdoo had recognized the need for an exit plan, rooted in economic fundamentals, to resolve the threat to America. He knew that the emergency measures he had already instituted—closing the New York Stock Exchange and pumping Aldrich-Vreeland currency into the banking system—would damage the American economy if they remained in place. On August 8 McAdoo had scheduled a foreign exchange conference for August 14 to provide "sufficient ships to move our grain and cotton crops to European markets."

The August 14 conference proposed that Congress establish a Bureau of War Risk Insurance, housed in the Treasury Department, to protect American shippers and to encourage exports. Congress passed the legislation on August 29 and the bureau was organized on September 3.[590] On September 12 the New York Times reported: "No branch of the Government service is busier these days than the newly established Bureau of War Risk Insurance. The transfer of vessels to American registry has suddenly brought a large volume of underwriting business to the government's insurance office. . . . applications had been received for policies on hulls alone amounting to more than $5,000,000."[591]

McAdoo announced on September 28, 1914, that insurance policies would become effective the following day.[592] Vessels incorporated under the American flag were eligible for coverage. However, the rules of U.S. neutrality imposed severe limitations on what could be covered. Contraband, such as armaments, gun powder, and military clothing, obviously could not qualify. But many seemingly innocuous items, including, clothing, telephones, horseshoes, food, grain, and, unfortunately, cotton, were designated conditional contraband if destined for the armed forces of a belligerent.[593] Combatants could exercise considerable discretion in confirming the status of a particular consignment of grain or cotton. The limitations imposed by conditional contraband slowed the healing power of the Bureau of War Risk Insurance. Sterling stood at $4.98 on September 30, 1914.

• • •

Progress in opening the Reserve Banks remained under a cloud. On October 3 the *New York Times* reported: "There was no prospect that the new Federal Reserve System would be put into operation by December 1."[594] The very next day the *Times* reversed itself: "Members of the Federal Reserve Board insisted today that there would be no serious delay in putting the new Reserve Banks in operation. The purpose was, it was explained, to have the banks in New York, Chicago, and St. Louis begin business as soon as possible, and it was expected that they would be started by October 15."[595] The confusion at the *Times* reflected the smoldering debate within the Federal Reserve System about when to open the Regional Banks. The disagreement exploded like a time bomb at a meeting of the board on October 10, 1914.

Governor Hamlin presided at the meeting of the Federal Reserve Board on Saturday, October 10.[596] McAdoo made a brief appearance, recommending some changes in the draft of a memorandum, penned by Warburg, on a plan to raise $150 million to aid cotton exports. Hamlin agreed to redraft the memorandum in light of McAdoo's suggestions. As McAdoo left the meeting, he said he hoped the board "would use every endeavor to open the Banks as soon as possible." Hamlin replied: "This would be done."

Hamlin described Warburg's reaction after McAdoo left the room: "Warburg paced up and down violently angry, attacking me, for my conduct as Governor in bull-dozing the Board; he said it was absurd to open before a conference with the Governor of New York and other banks; [he said] that I often forced the Board to change its views to please the Secretary [of the Treasury] . . . and that he did not intend to stand it any longer."[597]

Hamlin answered Warburg: "I had never and would never influence the Board to vote against its conviction. . . . [Comptroller] Williams and I, who had fought and bled with the Secretary, had great affection for, and respect for, his opinion."[598] Warburg then implied that Hamlin and Williams deferred to McAdoo out of affection. Hamlin responded: "The most significant deference to any others opinion was our deference to [yours] in the appointment of Strong as Governor after we had reason to fear that choice might be attacked on the ground that Strong would not have the courage to withstand New York capitalistic influence."[599]

Hamlin's disclosure "staggered Warburg." Warburg thought he had performed a public service by convincing Strong to accept the job as governor of the Federal Reserve Bank of New York. His colleagues on the board, according to Hamlin, acquiesced to Warburg's wishes, despite their concern over Strong's independence. Strong's tenure at Bankers Trust, courtesy of J. P. Morgan partner Henry Davison, gave the board reason to worry. The revelation may have disappointed Warburg, but it failed to deter him from pursuing his objective of delaying the birth of the Reserve Banks.

McAdoo arrived at the board meeting on October 15 armed like a gladiator. He read a letter from the president addressed to him as chairman of the Federal Reserve Board: "Many complaints had been made . . . by Senators . . . that the Board was deliberately holding back in organization of the reserve banks . . . that in order to show it to be untrue . . . the Board should use every effort to expedite the opening."* McAdoo then distributed a two-page letter of his own to the board: "At our last meeting I suggested to you the importance of opening at the earliest possible date. . . . So impressed am I with the supreme importance of doing this that I want to urge immediate action. . . . As Chairman of the Organizing Committee, I have deferred calling a final meeting of that Committee for the purpose of winding up its affairs, but the time has now arrived when I feel that this should be done. As you are aware, the duty devolves upon the Secretary of the Treasury, under the Act, of announcing 'in such manner as he may elect the establishment of the Federal Reserve Bank in any district.' I am now prepared to make this announcement."[601]

McAdoo sprinted toward the finish line like a champion and then tripped, as though he had been felled by bullet. He completed his announcement as follows: "I would suggest that Monday, November 2, be fixed as the date when the Federal Reserve Banks shall be declared established for business . . . but I think that it should take the form at the moment of being . . . preliminary."

Why did McAdoo pull up short? He had been decisive since the crisis began. He had the right to establish November 2 as opening day. He also had Wilson's support. But McAdoo could not ignore Warburg's warning, especially with sterling selling at $4.975, well above the gold export point. On October 13, two days before the board meeting, Warburg sent McAdoo a fourteen-page memorandum, prepared jointly with board member W.P.G. Harding.[602] The memo listed sixteen steps needed before the Reserve Banks could open, ranging from the receipt of "about $200,000,000 to $300,000,000 million in lawful money" to the

---

* Hamlin described this incident in his Diary (vol. 2, October 10, 1914, p. 172, Library of Congress). There is no record in McAdoo's files or in the Papers of Woodrow Wilson of the president's letter that McAdoo read to the board. McAdoo addressed the board, but exactly what he read from is unclear.

requirement of "a double set of vaults" at each bank. The memo offered ways to accommodate each of the sixteen points but ended with a query that only McAdoo could answer: "It would be very helpful to know on how much gold from the Treasury the Federal Reserve Banks could count when opening."[603]

McAdoo had no authority to offer the Treasury's gold to the Federal Reserve Banks. His response to Warburg's October 13 memo consisted of waffling on the November 2 date. McAdoo also heard Benjamin Strong add a practical dimension to the problem. Strong told the board on October 15 that "it would be an error to attempt to begin without having in readiness the machinery for doing the work. To open the banks within two to four weeks would be impossible."[604] McAdoo had heard enough but decided to wait until after the meeting of representatives of all the Reserve Banks, scheduled for October 20, before making his final decision.

McAdoo found allies at the October 20 conclave when he proposed November 16, 1914, as the date to open. The Federal Reserve Banks of Dallas, Richmond, Atlanta, and Kansas City stood solidly with the treasury secretary, making the farmers in their districts proud. New York, Minneapolis, and San Francisco all preferred January 1, 1915, or later.[605] A compromise—November 30—received approval by a narrow margin, seven districts in favor and five against.[606]

McAdoo had compromised enough. On Sunday, October 25, 1914, he ignored the vote and announced that all Reserve Banks would open on November 16. McAdoo quoted President Wilson as giving the best reason for avoiding further delay: "An effort to protect the System against the strains of the emergency which it is designed to relieve is to cast doubt on the System itself."[607]

The November 16 date set by McAdoo held firm despite delaying tactics within the system. McAdoo singled out "the representative of the Federal Reserve Bank of New York (FRBNY)," in an almost comical interchange, as trying to overturn the decision:[608]

FRBNY: The bank has no vault or safe place for keeping . . . gold.
McAdoo: There is a sub-Treasury in New York . . . [use] its vault.
FRBNY: Our bookkeeping system is not . . . ready for the printing of forms.
McAdoo: Surely you can have enough printing done by November 16 . . .
FRBNY: We can't get our office furniture by that time.
McAdoo: Buy a few chairs and pine-top tables.

Benjamin Strong did not want to derail the Federal Reserve System. He, like other bankers, sought the delay because "the whole future of the System might be jeopardized if the Reserve Banks were subjected to heavy demands when they were . . . weak in resources and prestige."[609] McAdoo recognized that the New York bank faced legitimate resource shortages. It needed vault space. McAdoo arranged vault space at the New York subtreasury.[610] It needed gold. McAdoo kept the New York Stock Exchange under lock and key to curtail the gold outflow while sterling remained above $4.90. He decided to open the Reserve Banks because that was his job. He thought they would serve as the future "bulwark against financial disaster." And he expected growth in U.S. agricultural exports to turn the tide in America's favor, sooner rather than later. McAdoo did not have to wait long for events to confirm his judgment.

THE PAYOFF

On October 26, 1914, the foreign exchange market gave McAdoo good reason to celebrate. The dollar price of sterling declined significantly, by nearly 1 percent, on this memorable Monday, the day after McAdoo's announcement that the Reserve Banks would open on November 16.* Moreover, as shown in figure 8.1, sterling's closing price of $4.89 on October 26 represents the first dip below the gold export point since the crisis struck. According to the Wall Street Journal: "There is now a greater approach to normal market conditions in exchange than any time since the outbreak of the war. . . . Another important result from the decline in exchange below $4.90 is that it automatically shuts off gold exports."[611]

McAdoo had the right to celebrate on October 26, but contemporary news stories do not credit the spectacular move in foreign exchange to his revelation, the evening before, that the Reserve Banks would open on November 16. Instead, another announcement released on October 26 received all of the accolades.

The New York Times front page carried the headline, "England Opens Seas to Cotton: Exchange Rate Drops on Heavy Discounting of Bills."[612] The article explains that the British ambassador to the United States, Sir

---

* Sterling closed at $4.935 on Saturday, October 24 (see Wall Street Journal, October 26, 1914, 8), and closed on Monday, October 26, at $4.89 (see Wall Street Journal, October 27, 1914, 1), a drop of .911 percent. The standard deviation of returns on the dollar price of sterling equals .23 percent per day between August 8, 1914, and December 31, 1914. The return of minus .911 percent has a t-statistic of 3.96, which is statistically significant at conventional levels of confidence. On October 28 the Wall Street Journal (p. 8) refers to a "three cent decline on Monday." A three-cent decline would have a t-statistic of 2.64, also statistically significant.

Cecil Spring-Rice, delivered a note to Acting Secretary of State Lansing, dated October 26, 1914, saying: "Dear Mr. Counselor: In compliance with your request, I telegraphed on the 23rd to my government to inquire . . . whether or not they considered [cotton] to be contraband. Last night I received a reply from Sir Edward Grey, in which he authorizes me to give the assurance that cotton will not be seized."[613] The *Times* then adds: "Bills drawn against exports of cotton appeared in the foreign exchange market yesterday [October 26] and were of first importance, according to exchange brokers in bringing about another abrupt fall of rates."[614] No mention of McAdoo's announcement opening the Reserve Banks appeared in the *New York Times* or the *Wall Street Journal* in connection with foreign exchange.

McAdoo's Bureau of War Risk Insurance supported the dollar's redemption on October 26. The bureau, which had opened for business on September 28, began a new trajectory after the removal of cotton from the contraband list. The *New York Times* reported that McAdoo gave "widest publicity" to the development: "Definite assurance has been received by the British Government that cotton will not be treated by Great Britain as contraband. . . . The Bureau of War Risk Insurance of the Treasury Department is writing insurance freely on cotton when carried by American vessels."[615]

The British proclamation freed cotton from confiscation but did not eliminate the risks of war. Only the Bureau of War Risk Insurance could do that. Increased underwriting by the bureau would expand cotton exports.[616] According to McAdoo, "Marine insurance companies were willing to insure ships and their cargoes against ordinary hazards of the sea, such as shipwreck collision and foundering; but they declined to undertake insurance against floating mines, or capture or torpedoes, or any other perils of war."[617]*

Benefits to cotton farmers from the British announcement arose in surprising quarters. According to the *New York Times*, "Buying for cash at the direction of the German Government was reported as the day's feature of operations in the 'spot' cotton market. German buyers have been placing contracts on a moderate scale for several weeks, but the decision of the British authorities not to interfere with shipments of cotton to any of the European countries evidently lent a spur to purchases yesterday [October 26]. It was said in shipping circles that several cargoes of the staple would leave southern ports this week for Italy and Denmark . . . although the cotton was intended for trans-shipment to German mills."[618]

---

* According to Wilkins (2004, 15), the Bureau of War Risk Insurance had to compensate for "the absence of adequate facilities for insurance of American vessels and their cargoes against the risk of war."

McAdoo had suspected all along that the solution to the financial crisis lay in agricultural exports in general, and cotton in particular. He had launched the initiative with his August 14 conference, designed to provide "sufficient ships to move our grain and cotton crops to European markets." According to McAdoo, "The work of the bureau, with its insurance against every imaginable war disaster, sent timid ships to sea. . . . [I]t was a financial success from beginning to end."[619] The Treasury reported that more than twelve hundred ships secured insurance from the bureau between September 1914 and the end of 1915.[620]

Figure 8.1 puts the sterling price movement on October 26 into context. The dollar price of sterling stood at $4.97 on Monday, October 19, the day before representatives of the Federal Reserve Banks gathered in Washington for their meeting. The price of sterling closed at $4.935 on Saturday, October 24, a drop of 3.5¢ over the five days prior to the British contraband announcement. No significant daily price changes occurred during this period, but the *New York Times* gave special attention to Saturday's decline of 1.5¢. On Sunday the *Times* said: "Reports of the conference on Friday [October 23] between Treasury officials, Sir George Paish [representing the U.K. Treasury], and New York bankers had a favorable bearing on the foreign exchange market [on Saturday]. News from Washington made it appear that financiers felt that the arrangements made to send out of the country $80,000,000 to meet maturing obligations of the City . . . together with the $100,000,000 raised in the country wide [Gold] pool, had gone far to square up the pressing indebtedness of the United States abroad."[621]

The Friday conference among British and American officials did not produce a significant price decline on Saturday, October 24—0.3 percent is small by historical standards—but it seems to have shifted market sentiment. The favorable report by the *Times* on October 25 set the stage for the powerful response to the contraband announcement the following day. The decline in sterling below the gold export point on October 26, 1914, marked a turning point in the battle for financial credibility. McAdoo could have declared victory.

Instead, he waited—and worried.

RETURN TO NORMALCY

A victory celebration would have required McAdoo to relax his grip on the New York Stock Exchange, or to establish a timetable for doing so. The onset of the crisis had been defined by the closure of the exchange. On August 1, the *Wall Street Journal* had said that President Wilson "directed Secretary of the Treasury McAdoo to take all possible steps to insure the financial stability of the nation and he approved the closing of the New York Stock Exchange."[622]

Why didn't McAdoo set a date for opening the New York Stock Exchange on October 25, just as he had done for the Reserve Banks? A month earlier the *Washington Post* carried a headline connecting the two events: "Stock Exchange May be Ready to Resume November 1: Awaits Reserve Bank Board."[623] The *Post* quoted an unnamed governor of the exchange saying: "If the Federal Reserve Board gets in full operation by that time, it would not be at all unlikely."[624]

The simplest answer is that McAdoo had stuck his neck out on August 10, 1914, by promising to open the Federal Reserve Banks on or before October 1.[625] He had never said anything publicly about the exchange, except to approve its closure on August 1. Contrary to the Federal Reserve Banks, he did not have the legislative responsibility to open the stock exchange. But McAdoo could have used the same influence to open the exchange as he had used to keep it shut. On August 27 the *Wall Street Journal* had observed: "Intimations have been received from Washington to the effect that the opening of the Exchange would be considered undesirable by the Government officials who realize that . . . every effort should be made to relieve the strain on the country's monetary system."[626]

McAdoo kept silent about the exchange on October 25 because the strain had not yet disappeared. Sterling had closed above the gold export point the day before. Even after sterling dipped below the magic number on October 26, McAdoo worried that it might not stay there. It did not. Two days later the British pound poked its head above $4.90 and did not drop back. Sterling above the gold export point rekindled the risks that haunted Paul Warburg and Benjamin Strong. The governor of the Federal Reserve Bank of New York shared his concerns with the chairman of the Federal Reserve Board.

At a meeting of the Federal Reserve Board on October 31, Strong reiterated his suspicion that the banks could not maintain the convertibility of the new currency into gold: "The reserve banks could not safely guaranty to deliver gold in the future. If the system were successfully established they could do it but would not agree to do it."[627] Strong doubted that the November 16 timetable that McAdoo had just released would produce favorable results. In a memorandum dated November 2, he wrote: "It must be born in mind that there is no certainty as to the amount of gold which will be paid into the Federal Reserve Bank [of New York] at the commencement of its operation."[628] Strong demanded the stock exchange remain shut as a safety net. In the same November 2 memo, he said: "Until . . . the commercial situation has been adjusted, and the exchanges [sterling] have turned in our favor, any discussion bearing on the opening of the New York Stock Exchange to a free and unrestricted market of American securities . . . would be premature."[629]

McAdoo had already risked his reputation by overriding the consensus about when to open the banks. He could not ignore Strong's warnings. Nor did he want to. Gold exports during October totaled $44.4 million, the largest monthly outflow since 1900.[630] McAdoo understood the fundamental risks of shifting to a new monetary regime: "The entire scheme was novel and untried. We were dealing with experimental formulas, with principles that had existed only in theory and which were to be put to the most practical of tests."[631] McAdoo kept the New York Stock Exchange closed as his insurance policy. On November 7 the *Wall Street Journal* quoted McAdoo as saying: "The chief thing that is needed [to reopen the exchange] is a restoration of international confidence. This is, in my opinion, almost an accomplished fact." "Almost" was not quite there yet.

Less than a week later, the foreign exchange market signaled the end of the crisis. On November 11 sterling again dipped below the gold export point, closing at $4.8938. On the following day the pound dropped another 2.5¢ to $4.86875, encouraging the belief that the rate would remain below the gold export point. The *Wall Street Journal* reported: "The foreign exchange market broke sensationally . . . to well within the present gold export basis, which is usually considered to be $4.90. The present level of exchange is the lowest point the market has touched since before the declaration of war, and marks the restoration of normal conditions."[632] No specific news announcement accompanied the significant drop in sterling on November 12, but the *Journal* noted that "the large supply of credits on the other side, created in the exports for account of belligerent nations, has been the chief factor in the amelioration of the situation."[633] Figure 8.1 shows that sterling remained below the gold export point through the end of the year.

On November 16, 1914, opening day for the Federal Reserve Banks, sterling stood at $4.87875. It had been below the gold export point for nearly a week. Commercial banks tendered more than 80 percent of the $245 million of paid-in-capital and required reserves in gold and gold certificates.[634] The Federal Reserve's incentive plan—paying the express charges for shipping gold—worked to perfection. The foreign exchange market no longer discouraged commercial bankers from accommodating the central bank's plea for gold. Were Warburg and Strong wrong to worry as much as they did? If the banks had opened earlier, when sterling was at a premium, the outcome could easily have been very different.

Was the delay in opening the Reserve Banks really necessary to protect the system? O.M.W. Sprague, the contemporary crisis expert from Harvard, concluded: "It is probably fortunate, however, that the new banks did not begin business as originally expected, in June or July. While they might have been helpful, it is unlikely they would have been able to maintain the normal course of banking operations. Partial failure might have lessened the confidence in the new system, and such confidence, it hardly need be said, is absolutely indispensable if it is to perform the functions for which it has been designed."[635]

The New York Stock Exchange took advantage of the favorable turn of events. Bond trading resumed on the exchange floor on November 28.[636] Stocks that were "not international in character" started on December 12.[637] All stocks were admitted for trading on December 15.[638]

November 11, 1914, the day the discount on the dollar disappeared for good, marks the turning point in U.S. financial credibility. Within a few months, America would challenge Britain as the world's financial superpower.

CHAPTER NINE

Birth of a Financial Superpower

ACCORDING to John Maynard Keynes, Britain ruled world finance with the pound sterling. At the outbreak of the Great War, he said: "Foreign countries have been keeping a substantial part of their ultimate monetary reserves in London. . . . This is profitable and enormously enhances London's position as a monetary center. . . . Its existence depends very directly on complete confidence in London's unwavering readiness to meet the demands upon her. . . . The existence of this confidence in the past has been one of the most important differentiations between London and Paris or Berlin. . . . It ought not to be endangered except for the very gravest cause. . . . The evils of the suspension of cash payment are very great."[639]

The British pound was more than a reserve currency in 1914. Sterling also served as a vehicle for international exchange, as a means of finalizing payments among businesses.* A Philadelphia grocery chain, The Acme Coffee and Tea Company, would pay for tea from China by instructing its London bankers to transfer pounds to the account of the Chinese exporters.

Keynes's reverence for the role of the British pound as international money led to his recommendation to preserve the convertibility of the pound into gold. He worried that countries would not use sterling to settle trading balances with each other if sterling were not viewed as a reliable store of value. The "future position of the City of London," according to Keynes, depended on the pound sterling continuing to serve the business world as the equivalent of gold.[640]

London provided more than just a first-class currency in its role as the world's financial superpower. The British had excess capital to invest and the banking expertise to price and distribute newly issued securities. Sir George Paish, an adviser, along with Keynes, to the U.K Treasury in 1914, reported that between 1908 and 1910 issuers from fifty different

---

* An international medium of exchange is sometimes called a vehicle currency (see Chrystal 1977). Kindleberger (1967, 4) attributes the term "vehicle currency" to Robert Roosa, under secretary of the Treasury in the Kennedy administration. Roosa (1966, 5) says: "My own feeling is that the reserve currency role . . . has been an integral part of the trading [vehicle] currency role." I will refer to sterling as international money as a shorthand.

countries marketed securities in the City of London, raising a total of £288 million.[641] The United States led the list with issues totaling more than £73 million. The British colonies raised an additional £228 million in London, led by Canada with £101 million.[642] Paish summarized the impact of British finance: "The large amounts of capital that Great Britain has supplied to individual colonial and foreign countries . . . [shows] the powerful influence which Great Britain has exerted in developing the world's natural resources by supplying other countries freely with the funds for railway construction, mining, and for production of every kind of natural wealth."[643]

Two characteristics—sterling as international money and London as global money lender—qualified Britain for the world financial crown in 1914. The pound sterling served as the currency of choice for international transactions, just like the dollar does today, and borrowers throughout the world visited the City of London, rather than Wall Street, to raise capital. Sterling's role as an international medium of exchange set it apart. The reduced cost of repetitive transactions allows a single currency to dominate world commerce.[644] Entrenched payment habits make it difficult to dethrone the king of international exchange.[645]

Paris and Berlin might have contested the view that the City of London reigned supreme in world finance, but no one proposed New York as a serious competitor.[646] Wall Street does not even make Keynes's list of alternatives. Before the war, New York and the dollar represented no threat to British monetary power.[647]

McAdoo changed everything. At the outbreak of the Great War he honored America's commitment to gold, just like Britain, and turned the United States into a contender for the international financial crown.

EARLY HOPES DASHED

During the first few years of the twentieth century, Americans viewed world finance through the narrow streets of lower Manhattan. A flurry of foreign government bonds sold in New York during August and September 1900, by Germany, Sweden, and Britain, prompted the *Wall Street Journal* to report on September 15, 1900: "The announcement that Kuhn, Loeb & Company and others had taken $20,000,000 of the German loan [denominated in marks] was additional evidence of the new position taken by the United States among the great powers. . . . Probably the factor of principal importance in connection with these foreign loans is the outlet which seems to be opening for the surplus wealth of the United States."[648]

Repeated financings by the British in connection with the Boer War suggested that America had entered the major leagues of finance. Between August 1900 and April 1902 the exchequer raised approximately $150 million in sterling-denominated bonds on Wall Street.[649] J. P. Morgan & Company's role as underwriter, alongside the Rothschilds and Baring Brothers, led Carl Hovey, the contemporary biographer of J. P. Morgan Sr., to say: "This underwriting was very successful. . . . The transaction ranked this country for the first time among the money powers of the world."[650]

Two years after the British loan of April 1902, America helped the imperial Japanese government fight its war with Russia. Jacob Schiff's Kuhn, Loeb & Company led the underwriting along with the Hong Kong and Shanghai Banking Corporation, now known as HSBC, and Parr's Bank of London.[651] Kuhn, Loeb marketed half of the total £10 million issue to American investors.

Raising funds for European and Asian governments brought increased respect to American capital markets.[652] Secretary of State John Hay qualified as head cheerleader when he said: "The 'debtor nation' has become the chief creditor nation. The financial center of the world, which required thousands of years to journey from the Euphrates to the Thames and the Seine, seems to be passing to the Hudson between daybreak and dark."[653] Hay made his poetic—but premature—proclamation on February 27, 1902, in an address before Congress commemorating the death of President William McKinley. Had he known at the time about the future loan to Japan he might have referred to New York as the "financial center of the universe."

What happened between 1904 and 1914 that allowed Keynes to ignore the American threat? The short answer is 1907. American capital attracted foreign governments to Wall Street but the U.S. banking system repelled them. Europeans might want to borrow money in New York, but they certainly would not want the dollar as an international medium of exchange. Americans could hide behind the claim that banking panics were a nineteenth-century phenomenon—until October 1907. O. M. W. Sprague, in his classic 1910 study of crises, explained the consequences of the panic for America's influence in world finance: "London holds its commanding position because it is known that money lent there can be instantly recalled. Similarly, New York is not meeting the obligations as our domestic money center, to say nothing of living up to future international possibilities, so long as it is unable to respond to any demand, however unreasonable, that can lawfully be made upon it for cash."[654]

The weak foundation of America's early claim to financial maturity should have been obvious. The governments of Sweden, Germany, and Britain tapped U.S. capital but did not have to cater to the American public by issuing dollar-denominated bonds.* The British bonds were denominated in sterling and the German bonds in marks.[655] The Swedish bonds were issued in Swedish kroner and in all the major currencies—pounds, marks, and French francs—but not in dollars.[656] Japan's 1904 issue was denominated in sterling, with payments in dollars tethered to the exchange rate of $4.87 per pound.[657]

The dollar did not serve the world as an international currency before the Great War. Keynes had good reason to ignore American claims to world financial leadership.

THE TRANSFORMATION

The outbreak of war in August 1914 highlighted U.S. monetary vulnerability. The combination of gold outflows and maturing obligations in Europe taxed America's ability to pay. The discount on the dollar in the foreign exchange market measured the loss in credibility.† A suspension of payments in 1914, coming seven years after the embarrassment of 1907, could have delivered a knockout punch to America's international financial dreams.

Some financiers recognized that America could register a monetary coup by conquering the threat posed by the Great War. Every country of the world except for Britain had suspended gold payments. America would take a giant leap forward if it could remain true to gold, just like a financial superpower—just like Britain.

On August 20, 1914, while chaos reigned in foreign exchange, Henry Lee Higginson, an investment banker from Boston, had written to President Wilson: "We can take [England's] place if we choose; but courage, willingness to part with what we don't need at once, real character, and the living up to all our debts promptly will give us this power."[658] Higginson suggested that "the government should offer American bankers the gold necessary to pay American debts maturing in Europe" and "should keep the stock exchange closed."[659] Wilson forwarded the letter to McAdoo on August 22.[660]

---

* The articles in Eichengreen and Hausmann (2005) discuss the denomination of debt issued across national borders. See especially Eichengreen, Hausmann, and Panizza, "The Pain of Original Sin"; Bordo, Meissner and Redish, "How Original Sin Was Overcome: The Evolution of External Debt Denominated in Domestic Currencies in the United States and British Dominions"; and Flandreau and Sussman, "Old Sins: Exchange Clauses and European Foreign Lending in the Nineteenth Century."

† The discount on the dollar reflected a preference for gold, or sterling, compared with dollars. The *persistence* of the discount reflected the difficulty of foreign exchange dealers, like Max May, in executing the gold arbitrage as often as they wished (see chapter 5).

Figure 9.1. Sterling Exchange Rate, September 1, 1914, through August 31, 1915.

Data Source: *Wall Street Journal.*

McAdoo had already decided to padlock the exchange for as long as necessary before he had received Higginson's note, but he saw no need to follow the suggestion that the government lend gold to the bankers. McAdoo had discussed the New York City problem with J. P. Morgan and had received a letter outlining the rescue from Morgan on August 21, the day before Higginson's note arrived on his desk.[661] The city bailout would nullify the most prominent financial threat and serve as a model of American financial propriety. But if Higginson were right about the potential benefits from "living up to all our debts promptly," McAdoo had the opportunity to turn potential monetary disaster into a financial triumph. Higginson's letter may have pushed McAdoo, a week later, to call the meeting for September 4, 1914, that led to the Gold Pool proposal by Strong and Wiggin.

The foreign exchange market served as the barometer of American financial credibility. Figure 9.1 shows the behavior of sterling exchange between September 1, 1914, and August 31, 1915. The horizontal line at

$4.90 represents America's gold export point and the horizontal line at $4.833 represents the gold import point.* On September 1 the pound's 3.4 percent premium above $4.90 darkened the dollar's reputation like a storm cloud. By the end of October, however, the sky had cleared and all but a fraction of the premium disappeared.[662] Market participants felt the shift in the center of financial gravity. On October 27, 1914, Max May, the treasury secretary's favorite foreign exchange expert at the Guaranty Trust Company, said: "The situation is encouraging. One of the most encouraging signs of the times is that South America, China, and Japan are increasingly drawing their bills on this market directly instead of on London."[663]

Sterling's role as an international currency meant that countries settled their trading obligations with each other in British pounds. A Japanese importer of U. S. cars would pay the Ford Motor Company with a sterling bill of exchange drawn on N. M. Rothschild. An American importer of Japanese toys would pay the same way. Max May observed that London bills of exchange no longer sat at the center of every transaction. Japan had begun to draw bills directly on New York.

Britain recognized the sea change as well. The *New York Times* reported on November 1 that "there will *not* be an immediate demand by Great Britain for payment of current and accruing obligations of American business firms . . . [because] the balance of trade may turn in favor of the United States, and . . . it will only be a matter of a few weeks until the pressing necessity to consider the export of gold is removed."[664] A week later, the *Washington Post* quoted a U.K. Treasury official on America's potential as a source of world capital: "Sir George Paish, in his conferences in Washington . . . has spoken cautiously and yet optimistically of this opportunity which is now open to the United States. . . . He is reported to have intimated to some of those with whom he had been in conference that we have it within our power to amass such supplies of fresh capital as will enable us to serve for some years as the chief financial money lender."[665]

The syndicate of banks paying New York City's debts in London shipped its last consignment of gold on November 9, 1914.[666] Sterling dipped below the gold export point on November 11, and a day later, plunged a significant one-half of 1 percent.[667] The *Wall Street Journal* noted the transformation: "It is the consensus of opinion that the backbone of the extraordinary demand for exchange . . . has been broken."[668]

The disappearance of the discount on the dollar on November 11,

---

* I set the gold import point, the lower bound of the exchange rate band, at $4.833, or .68 percent below the $4.8665 mint parity. This is the same percentage deviation as the $4.90 upper bound. The *Economist* (August 1, 1914, 253) set the lower bound at $4.827.

1914, four years to the day before the Armistice that ended the Great War, marks the beginning of America's ascent to international financial leadership. The United States weathered an attack on the dollar's credibility by meeting its obligations under the gold standard. William G. McAdoo avoided a replay of 1907 that could have shattered American aspirations. And the world had begun to notice. According to Max May, the dollar had gained a toehold as an international medium of exchange.

February 1915 confirmed the dollar's metamorphosis. Figure 9.1 shows sterling falling through the lower bound of the exchange rate bands in the middle of the month. The pound dropped below the "gold import point" because Britain refused to permit unlimited gold exports, despite remaining legally tethered to gold.* The *Wall Street Journal* described the role reversal between the two currencies: "Within six months foreign exchange has swung around from the highest to the lowest level ever recorded [until this point]. That is to say, demand sterling has declined from about $6.50 to $4.79."[669] The *Journal* offered an explanation: "Some international banking authorities were quite outspoken in expressing the opinion that the break in exchange was due, in part, to withdrawals of balances from the other side by people who think it a part of wisdom to take their capital out of Europe and transfer it to a place of greater safety in the United States."[670]

The dollar had replaced sterling as a safe-haven currency.

THE CONFIRMATION

Countries of the world quickly verified Sir George Paish's prediction of America's role as "chief money lender." The United States had excess capital and did not have a war to fight. It could lend its funds rather than spend it on munitions. On January 5, 1915, the press reported: "Canada on the north of the United States and Chile, far to the south of us, are now facing emergencies created by the European war, which relatively speaking are quite as great as those which the United States faced and overcame in the first two months of the war. . . . The chief emergency which Canada now faces has been occasioned by the difficulty of approaching the London money market. . . . Recently there has been marketed in the United States . . . nearly $7,000,000 of notes representing

---

* A British Importer of American goods should never accept less than $4.833 per pound. Instead, the importer should take a pound sterling to the Bank of England, exchange it for an ounce of gold, ship the gold to the United States (hence the gold import point), and exchange the gold for $4.8665 at the U.S. Treasury. After deducting .68 percent for shipping costs the pound produces $4.833. Britain short-circuited the arbitrage by refusing unlimited exchanges of pounds for gold.

Canadian indebtedness. . . . The ease with which this transaction was completed is of itself an indication that . . . we can hereafter do a great deal in the way of taking the place of London in supplying financial assistance to Canada. . . . When Chile has exhausted her London credit . . . she must turn elsewhere for assistance. Presumably she will turn to the United States."[671]

Canada and South America were natural outlets for U.S. capital. Argentina borrowed $15 million from a Wall Street syndicate three days after the Canadian loan. The press noted that "For many years Argentina was accustomed to look to London for capital."[672] America turned into a true global financier two months later, when Switzerland visited New York in March and issued dollar-denominated bonds with a face value of $15 million.[673] By way of contrast, when Sweden and Germany issued bonds in New York in 1900, they sold mark- and kroner-denominated bonds. The Swiss financing in March 1915 elicited the following commentary: "This transaction [is] . . . without precedent. Before the European war, Switzerland, if in need of funds, would have applied to Great Britain or to France."[674]

The transaction that dwarfed all others, both in size and importance, occurred in October 1915. J. P. Morgan & Company managed a $500 million bond issue for Britain and France.[675] The joint Anglo-French loan was tailor-made for the American public. Most importantly, the securities were issued in units of $100, $500, and $1,000 (fig. 9.2).[676] Unlike the bonds issued by Britain to finance the Boer War at the turn of the century, these securities were denominated in dollars rather than sterling. The U.S. dollar no longer took a back seat to the British pound.*

America's new role as an international money lender compared favorably with British experience. Between January 1, 1915, and April 5, 1917, when the United States declared war on Germany, foreign entities—mostly governments—issued $2.6 billion dollar-denominated securities in New York.[677] Recall that foreign issuers, including the British colonies, sold a total of £516 million (approximately equal to $2.5 billion) securities in London between 1908 and 1910.[678]

But the United States could not lay claim to the world financial crown unless the dollar emerged as a full-fledged international medium of exchange. Britain reigned as the king of international finance for two reasons: because it acted as moneylender to the world and because its currency served as a vehicle currency. The dollar's progress would encounter resistance from deeply entrenched payment habits.

---

* For a discussion of the importance of debt denomination, see the articles cited earlier by Eichengreen, Hausmann, and Panizza; Bordo, Meissner, and Redish; and Flandreau and Sussman in Eichengreen and Hausmann (2005).

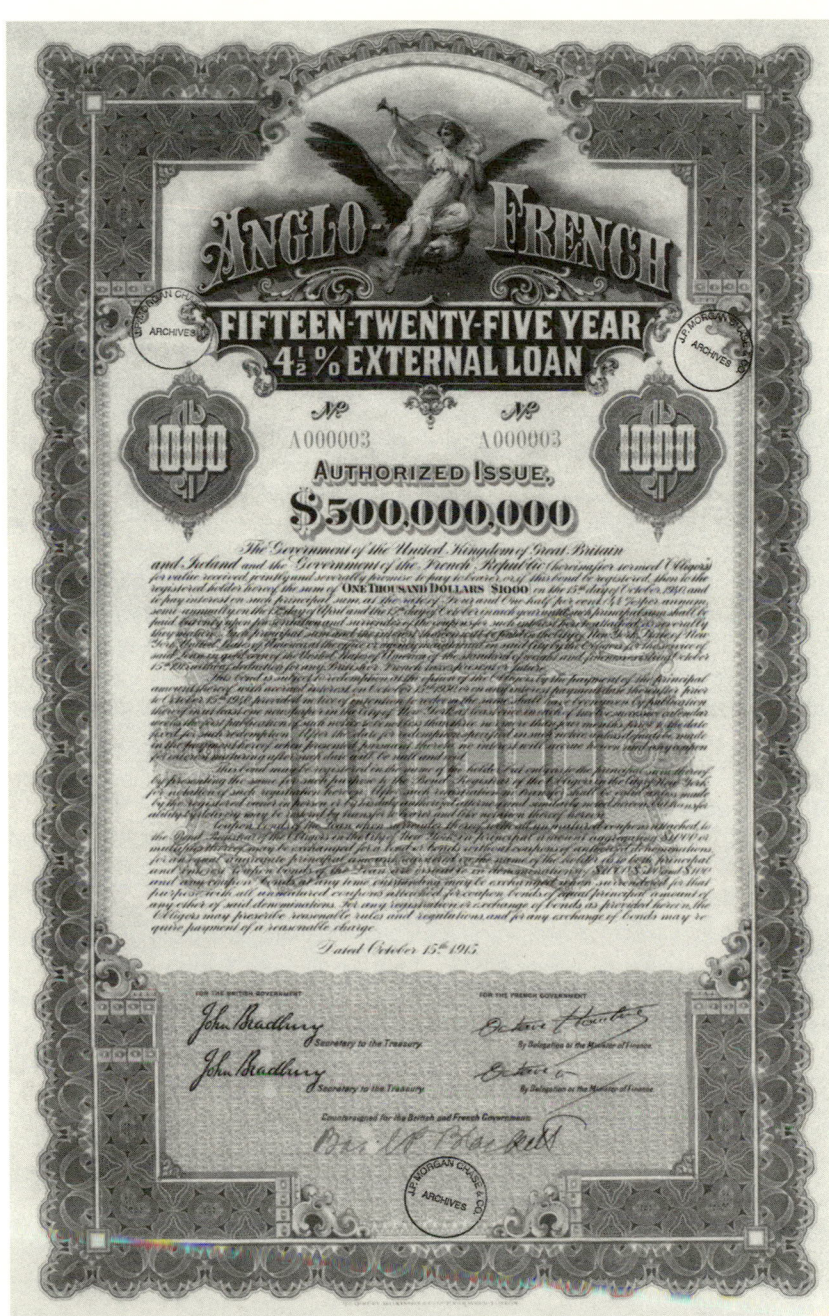

Figure 9.2. Anglo-French Loan $1,000 Certificate, October 15, 1915.

Source: JP Morgan Chase Archives, JP Morgan Chase, New York.

Dollar balances held abroad to facilitate international transactions would confer potential benefits on American consumers. When Brazilians ship coffee to the United States and receive payment from Americans, they would normally want to use the cash for American products, like cars or cotton. But if Brazilians held dollars as cash balances, like checking accounts, America gets to keep the coffee, the cars, and the cotton for itself. A financial superpower can live off its currency, at least for a while. America did precisely that during the last half of the twentieth century, sending dollars into permanent residence in foreign countries to pay for the excess of imports over exports.

When the Great War erupted, Keynes rightfully dismissed New York as a money center because no one held the dollar as international money. In January 1915 Elisha Jay Edwards, a financial columnist widely known under the pen name "Holland," marked the birth of the dollar as an international medium of exchange.*

On January 18, 1915, a *Washington Post* headline announced: " 'Holland' Writes of China's Change from the London to United States Markets: The Action Means the Eventual Shift of the World's Financial Center from the English Capital to New York."[679] The article elaborated: "The mere fact that China has sent and is about to send gold to the United States aggregating $3,000,000 would itself be of no special importance. In normal times that might represent a special transaction. But there seems to be related to this movement . . . the first on record . . . various features which are regarded in the financial district . . . as of the highest importance. . . . China has sent gold in [such] large amounts to the United States for the purpose of facilitating transactions between her merchants and those of other parts."[680]

"Holland" explained the importance of this development by contrasting it with China's practices before the war began: "China and the merchants of that country have long been accustomed to establish or buy credit in London. . . . Against these credits the merchants were able to draw bills of exchange with which they could pay their obligations in London or elsewhere."[681]

"Holland" concluded with the following observation: "The exchange drawn against this gold will be what is called dollar exchange, that is to say, represented in terms of dollars. When the time comes that the majority of exchange of the world is represented by dollars rather than

---

* "Holland" served as a financial columnist from 1909 until his death in 1924 (see *New York Times*, April 27, 1924). Except for a brief interlude between August 1914 and March 1915, when his column appeared in the *Washington Post*, he wrote three or four articles per week for the *Wall Street Journal*. A search of the *Wall Street Journal* turned up 74 articles written by "Holland" during 1909, 301 articles in 1912, 201 in 1916, 156 in 1920, and 39 in 1924, the year he died.

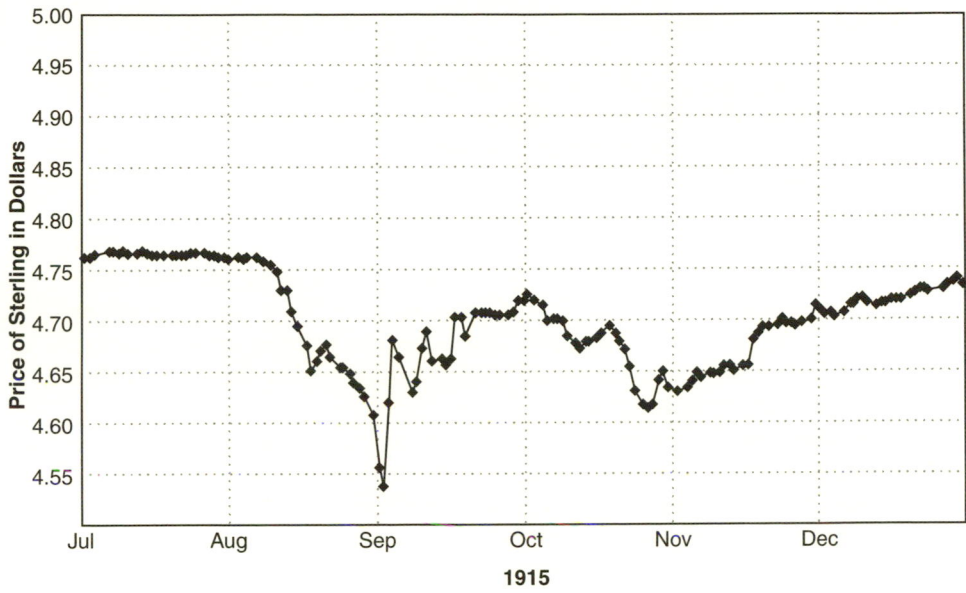

Figure 9.3. Sterling Exchange Rate, July 1, 1915, through December 31, 1915.

Data Source: *Wall Street Journal.*

pounds sterling the money center of the world will be regarded as having shifted from London to New York."[682]

New Zealand and Chile followed China's lead and established dollar-exchange facilities during the second half of 1915. As one banker noted,[683] "Already the dollar is recognized as the medium of exchange between ourselves and our South American customers who have been forced to use dollar acceptances owing to chaotic conditions in the sterling market. . . . There is, of course, prejudice against the idea in London, but I hardly think the opposition can hold out in face of what is obviously an inevitable solution of the present situation."[684]

Figure 9.3 confirms the "chaotic conditions in the sterling market" during the last half of 1915. The dollar price of sterling fell from $4.76 on August 1, 1915, to $4.54 on September 1, 1915—nightmare price levels that had not been witnessed in nearly a century.[685] Prospects for the Anglo-French loan rescued sterling from the free fall in September. The $500 million loan, consummated on October 15, 1915, helped the British pound recover to $4.73 by December 31.

Sterling's vulnerability should have completed the transfer of power to the American dollar. It did not. The United States had to share financial superpower status for a decade. How did sterling manage to stay alive?

THE LAST BATTLE

Money is a social contrivance. A car dealer in Chicago accepts dollars for the latest model in the showroom because the dealer can pass those dollars on to the local department store to pay for a brand new suit. Paper dollars have no value by themselves but serve Americans as the medium of exchange because dollars are generally accepted in payment.[686] How does something become the medium of exchange? Gold and silver coins gained acceptance as media of exchange because they had intrinsic value—they could be worn as jewelry if necessary.* Cigarettes served as a medium of exchange in prisoner of war camps because they served up nicotine if needed. Dollar bills gained credibility because they were convertible into gold.

Once established as legal tender in payment of all obligations, a domestic medium of exchange tends to remain in place. It has the law on its side, like the incumbent sheriff in a small-town election. In addition, entrenched payment habits make it difficult to replace whatever is accepted as money.† Fluctuations in the value of money usually fail to dislodge it from general use. The Federal Reserve note has served as America's currency for nearly one hundred years despite losing more than 95 percent of its purchasing power since its introduction in 1914, despite the suspension of its convertibility into gold in 1933, and despite two years of double-digit inflation (1947 and 1980) in which it lost more than 12 percent of its value. Only hyperinflation poses a threat to an established currency system.

The persistence of payment habits among countries promotes a similar durability to the established international medium of exchange, despite the absence of the legal tender feature. As Paul Krugman, the Princeton University economist, said, "it seems clear that history will matter; once an exchange structure is established, it will persist unless the structure of payments shifts enough to make it untenable."[687] The International Monetary Fund created special drawing rights (SDRs) in 1969 to serve

---

* Karl Menger, the founder of the Austrian school of economics, observed (1892, 252): "The reason why the precious metals have become the generally current medium of exchange . . . is because their saleableness [sic] is far and away superior to that of all commodities. . . . There is no center of population which has not . . . come keenly to desire and eagerly covet the precious metals . . . for their utility and peculiar beauty."

† Menger (1892, 249) says: "In this way practice and habit have certainly contributed not a little to cause goods, which were most saleable at any time, to be accepted . . . in exchange for less saleable goods; and . . . to be accepted from the very first with the intention of exchanging them away again." Modern treatments emphasize low transactions costs and economies of scale; see Swoboda 1968, Brunner and Meltzer 1971, Chrystal 1977, and Krugman 1980.

as a reserve currency alongside gold and the dollar. The SDR never succeeded despite its impressive lineage.*

Not surprisingly, America emerged from the Great War as money-lender to the world, but it needed more time to dislodge the British pound as the international currency of choice. The enhanced credibility of the dollar could not destroy the pound's advantage from an entrenched century of tradition. In addition, sterling's role in financing trade between the United Kingdom and the British colonies conferred a special franchise on the pound among the Commonwealth countries.† The United States had no empire to bolster the dollar's role.

On November 30, 1918, three weeks after the armistice, Leopold Fredrick, a director of the American Smelting & Refining Company, and promoter of dollar exchange in Chile in 1915,[688] confessed to sterling's dominance. He said: "The popular belief is that New York today is the center of world finance and that we have succeeded in wresting from London that position. I have made a careful investigation and ascertained . . . [that] only so far as loans made by the United States to the Allies are concerned, has the financial center been shifted to New York; however, so far as the financing of exports and imports of the world are concerned, London is still supreme."[689] Frederick canvassed London dealers and found that they had approximately $500 million in sterling-denominated foreign trade acceptances outstanding at that time compared with $210 million in dollar-denominated foreign trade acceptances for New York dealers.[690]

London's perseverance had been anticipated by some. J. P. Morgan observed during the 1915 negotiations over the Anglo-French loan: "When the war is over you will find the United States settling down again into using the European money markets as a clearing house, very much as before."[691] At the beginning of 1916, Clarence W. Barron, proprietor of the Boston News Bureau and future founder of *Barron's*, the well-known

---

* The SDR was created by the International Monetary Fund in 1969 to support the Bretton Woods fixed exchange rate system. The value of the SDR was initially defined as equivalent to 0.888671 grams of fine gold—which, at the time, was also equivalent to one U.S. dollar. After the collapse of the Bretton Woods system in 1973, the SDR was redefined as a basket of currencies, today consisting of the euro, Japanese yen, pound sterling, and U.S. dollar. According to H. Robert Heller (in Mussa, Boughton, and Isard 1996, 329), "the SDR has been less than a resounding success . . . [because of] the absence of a true payments function for the SDR."

† Chinn and Frankel (2005), list four factors that promote a country's currency as international money: (1) patterns of output and trade—a country with a large share in international trade has an advantage; (2) the country's financial markets—a large and liquid financial market is a plus; (3) confidence in the value of the currency—the currency should not fluctuate erratically; and (4) network externalities—a currency that has been in use will continue (i.e., inertia helps).

financial weekly, said: "Whether or not the future of United States banking 'lies on the seas' remains to be seen. There is no denying the fact that after the war we must be prepared to face very lively competition on the part of Europe in this regard, and especially England, who should be jealous of her prestige as world banker. The sterling bill has heretofore ruled supreme but our bankers are sure to find a place for dollar exchange in foreign commerce. We have already made a good beginning in South America but the real competition will come after the war."[692]

Barron's prediction that Britain would try to jealousy guard its financial supremacy proved accurate. As part of postwar planning, the U.K. government appointed the Committee on Currency and Foreign Exchanges after the War, under the chairmanship of Lord Cunliffe, the governor of the Bank of England. The Cunliffe Committee's First Interim Report in August 1918 left no doubt about the importance of the gold standard in postwar Britain: "In our opinion it is imperative that after the war the conditions necessary to the maintenance of an effective gold standard should be restored without delay. Unless [this] machinery . . . is once more brought into play, there will be grave danger of a progressive credit expansion which will result in a foreign drain of gold menacing the convertibility of our note issue and so jeopardizing the international trade position of the country."[693]

Less than six months after the war ended, the United Kingdom took a giant step backward before going forward. The British government suspended its ceremonial adherence to the gold standard on April 1, 1919.[694] The dollar price of sterling, which had been pegged during most of the war by the U.K Treasury at $4.76, fell to $3.30 in February 1920.[695] Holders of sterling balances suffered a loss of 30 percent in less than a year. The *Wall Street Journal* confirmed the damage, as well as the persistence of sterling as an international medium of exchange: "Many cotton merchants suffered loss when sterling dropped from around $4.60 to its recent low level because contracts covering the consignments were drawn in terms of sterling."[696]

Currency instability should, at some point, overwhelm entrenched payment habits. Why did sterling refuse to die?

New York failed to deliver the coup de grace because the Cunliffe committee had assured the world of Britain's commitment to gold. The suspension on April 1, 1919, was viewed as a tactical withdrawal. It would pave the way, after wringing the wartime inflation out of the economy, for Britain's return to the former $4.8665 parity with the American dollar. Britain had a tradition to uphold. Montagu Norman, governor of the Bank of England from 1920 to 1944, said that failure to restore convertibility meant "the world-centre would shift permanently from London to New York."[697]

Six years later, on April 28, 1925, Britain confirmed its monetary credibility and returned to the gold standard. But the pound had already suffered irreparable damage.

THE WINNER IS

Preparations for England's return to gold began a year before the final decision was made. In the spring of 1924, a committee was appointed to chart Britain's monetary course, chaired by Sir Austen Chamberlain, former chancellor of the exchequer, and then by Sir John Bradbury, former permanent secretary to the Treasury during the war.[698] On June 27, 1924, the first witness before the Chamberlain-Bradbury committee, Bank of England Governor Montagu Norman, left little doubt about the declining status of sterling. Norman said that "the shrinking from sterling of which I have experienced from many parts of the world" is an important reason for returning to the gold standard.[699] Sir Charles Addis, a director of the Bank of England, testified after Norman. He said that the return to gold would help "the recovery by the City of London of its *former* [emphasis added] position as the world's financial centre."[700]

Britain's return to gold failed to achieve its objective. The *Wall Street Journal* reported on March 26, 1925, a month before Britain restored the $4.8665 parity: "An outstanding feature of the Wall Street money market is the large volume of world commerce which is being financed through the American acceptance market. Dollar credits have become firmly established in all commercial centers of the world. . . . The principal reason for the growing use of American bills is the stability of the dollar and its absolute gold redemption if so demanded. . . . The return of sterling to par, and the complete restoration of a free gold market in London, will not in the least militate against the steady development of the American acceptance market."[701] Three years later the *Journal* evaluated the progress: "Although accurate figures are not available showing the volume of bills in the London market, it is reliably estimated that the present total dollar volume of acceptances is very close to, if not actually more than, the volume of sterling bills in the British market."[702]

The dollar's enhanced credibility finally dethroned sterling as the dominant international medium of exchange. America's commitment to gold had paid a major dividend.

The second half of the 1920s witnessed America's push to power. New York dominated London as moneylender to the world. The three-year period after Britain returned to gold provides a basis for comparison. Between 1926 and 1928, foreign issuers sold a total of $4 billion securities in the United States, about double the sum raised in the United Kingdom.[703]

Government borrowings in America included the Kingdom of Belgium ($50 million), the Dominion of Canada ($40 million), the Republic of Chile ($36 million), the State of Bavaria, Germany ($20 million), the Commonwealth of Australia ($40 million), and the City of Tokyo ($20 million).[704] New York had become the premier global money lender, sprinkling capital in British fashion around the world to promote economic development. By the end of 1928 the dollar had also surpassed sterling as the international money of choice.[705]

Britain and America remained locked in financial combat until World War II destroyed the illusions of British power. During the last half of the twentieth century, the dollar steamrollered sterling to the sidelines. How important was the summer of 1914 to the dollar's destiny? The financial burden of the Second World War and the erosion of the British Empire probably doomed sterling, but the 1920s—and even the 1930s—might have evolved quite differently had William G. McAdoo not preserved American financial credibility at the outbreak of the Great War.

WHAT MIGHT HAVE BEEN

London's reign as king of world finance began on August 12, 1870, during the Franco-Prussian War.[706] According to Walter Bagehot, author of *Lombard Street*, the central banking manual written in 1873, the suspension of specie payments by the Bank of France marked the turning point: "All great communities have at times to pay large sums in cash, and of that cash a great store must be kept somewhere. Formerly there were two such stores in Europe, one was the Bank of France and the other the Bank of England. But since the suspension of specie payments by the Bank of France, its use as a reservoir of specie is at an end. . . . London has become the sole great settling house of exchange transactions in Europe, instead of being formerly one of two. And this preeminence London will probably maintain."[707]

Bagehot correctly predicted London's victory, but the Bank of France did not seem to deserve its fate. Capital markets forgive a country that suspends specie payments during wartime as long as it resumes its obligation after the emergency has passed.[708] What provoked Bagehot's conclusion? He felt that a financial superpower must meet a higher standard. He said that "the note of the Bank of France has not . . . been depreciated enough to disorder ordinary transactions. But any depreciation, however small . . . is enough to disorder [foreign] exchange transactions."[709] A country that wants its currency as an international medium of exchange cannot behave like everyone else. It must foster super-credibility.*

Keynes invoked the same wisdom when recommending that Britain stay true to gold at the outbreak of the Great War: "London's position as a monetary center . . . depends very directly on complete confidence in London's unwavering readiness to meet the demands upon her."[710] He reiterated that position in 1917 in his "Memorandum on the Probable Consequences of Abandoning the Gold Standard." Keynes said: "No one will send balances here unless they are free to take them away again, should they desire to do so. That is the essence of banking. A bank which has suspended payment does not receive fresh deposits. Not only would a blow have been struck at the post-bellum position of the City of London. We should also have thrown away a great financial asset for immediate purpose."[711]

The consequences of the Great War and the tactical withdrawal from the gold standard in April 1919 altered Keynes's thinking. He argued against the return of sterling to parity in 1925 because, among other things, it would overvalue sterling in the foreign exchange market.[712] At the prewar exchange rate of $4.8665 per pound, British goods were too expensive because prices in the United Kingdom rose faster than in America during the war. Reestablishing the old parity would lead to a chronic excess of imports over exports in Britain. Keynes also sensed danger in the plan to embrace the gold standard straightjacket simply to retake first place in world finance. He wrote to Sir Charles Addis, after Addis testified before the Chamberlain-Bradbury committee supporting the return to gold: "Are you quite sure that the rigid linking up of the London and New York markets is all honey? The magnitude of the New York money market is quite different in relation to ours [compared] to what it was in pre-war days and in pre–Federal Reserve Bank days. . . . Are you sure that you want London to be at any time the dumping ground of unlimited cheap American money liable to be withdrawn at a day's notice?"[713]

The newly established status quo in world finance undermined the benefits of Britain's return to gold. Keynes judged the battle for financial supremacy as too costly in 1925.

America emerged from the Great War prepared to usurp the monetary crown. The war had transformed the United States from a debtor into a creditor nation. But excess capital does not produce a monetary superpower. Saudi Arabia financed American trade deficits during the 1970s

---

* Bagehot's argument ignores the bimetallic standard of the Bank of France before the Franco-Prussian War. It was not clear whether France would abandon bimetallism in favor of gold after the war. See Ferguson (1999, 208–9). Also see Flandreau (2004) for a more complete discussion.

with petrodollars—earnings from the quadrupling of oil prices. No one suggested that Riyadh would replace New York as financial capital of the world. Moreover, Britain did not need an abundance of capital to retake first place as moneylender to the world. Financial institutions, like banks and insurance companies, lend money by mobilizing the savings of others, committing only a few cents of their own in the process. Britain had the financial machinery and expertise to do the same.

American capital, by itself, could not buy the credibility needed to challenge sterling as international money—only the gold standard could. William G. McAdoo paved the way for the dollar to dislodge sterling as the world's currency by remaining true to gold. Alexander Noyes, the contemporary financial editor of the *New York Times*, recognized the power of McAdoo's actions: "The importance of that decision to maintain gold payments, in the face of suspension of such payments and of resort to inevitably depreciated money in practically every other country of the world, it would be difficult to exaggerate. It is not too much to say that as a matter of financial history, the United States stood during those two or three weeks of August at the parting of the ways. The promptness of the decision . . . had as much to do with the subsequent financial strength and prestige of the United States . . . as did the turn in Europe's conduct of the war. . . . Almost immediately, it made New York the banking center of the world."[714]

The Federal Reserve helped advance America's assault on British financial supremacy. The new currency system promised to protect American banks from the crises that plagued the United States since the Civil War. The Reserve Banks also promoted the market in acceptances that spread the use of dollar exchange.[715] Paul Warburg championed the central bank's influence: "The day of the opening of the Federal Reserve Banks will mark the advent of our financial independence."[716] But the Federal Reserve System needed the nurturing of a newborn to stand on its own. McAdoo's initiatives restored the dollar's credibility on November 11, 1914, four days before the banks opened. Without that credibility the new currency system might have taken years before promoting America's cause in international finance.

America gained a semblance of British respectability in August 1914. The embargo on gold exports, imposed when the United States entered the war in 1917, failed to detract from the dollar's progress.* America

---

* The United States did not leave the gold standard in 1917. Gold continued to circulate freely within the country. Under the gold embargo, exports were permitted under license, as indicated in the following quote (*New York Times*, September 16, 1917, E4): "Japan . . . has sold [Russian] rubles in New York for the purpose of getting gold. Ordinarily these transactions are put through London but in view of the British prohibition against gold exports the Japanese have resorted to this market. . . . H. Hikosaka, the New York agent of

had earned a reputation for meeting its obligations under the most trying circumstances. Branding gold as contraband of war, just like Britain did, left no imprint.

Would a rejection of the gold standard at the outbreak of the Great War have changed history? A suspension of convertibility in 1914, the second American panic in seven years, could have been a decisive setback, like the one-two punch that halts a challenger for the heavyweight crown. Britain could have easily remained the undisputed, if somewhat battered, champion of international finance until the Second World War. It almost happened.

At the outbreak of the war, some bankers wanted to suspend the commitment to pay American debts in gold. On August 2 an official was quoted: "We do not propose to let Europe give us paper for gold. If they refuse to pay American bills in specie there will be nothing left for us to do but pay European bills the same way."[717] The *Commercial and Financial Chronicle* editorialized in favor of such measures: "The long and short of the matter, however, is that Europe has actually suspended gold payments. So long as this state of things continues, it is imperative that we shall not sacrifice our own stock and throw it into the sink-holes of Europe."[718]

William Jennings Bryan's position as secretary of state lends credibility to reports that the Wilson cabinet discussed the matter. Bryan had denounced the precious metal in his Cross of Gold speech to the Democratic convention in 1896.[719] Charles Hamlin, governor of the Federal Reserve Board, wrote in his diary on August 28, 1914, that McAdoo had come to the board and said "We ought seriously to consider the propriety of the U.S. suspending gold payments."[720] Hamlin commented that "He [McAdoo] did not say this had been considered by the cabinet but from his manner this seemed clearly to have been the case."[721]

If Wilson had allowed Bryan's view to prevail, the United States would have joined the entire world—save for Britain—in rejecting gold. After the war everyone would have forgiven America, but they might not have trusted the United States—like they trusted Britain—to behave like a monetary superpower. Sterling would have reclaimed almost all of its business after the war, just as J. P. Morgan had suspected. Bank of England Governor Montagu Norman would not have worried that "the world-centre would shift permanently from London to New York." And John Maynard Keynes might have carried the day. Britain would have been under little pressure to return to gold in 1925.

---

the Japanese institution said: 'I do not understand that the President [Wilson] has any intention of interfering with the course of legitimate trade, consequently we have no expectation of trouble.' "

Keynes preferred not to restore sterling to the gold standard in 1925, but most of all he counseled patience. He testified before the Chamberlain-Bradbury committee at the hearings to evaluate plans for Britain's return to gold. During the proceedings on July 11, 1924, Sir Austen Chamberlain asked Keynes: "It is an essential part of your views that we ought not attempt to restore the old parity of the sovereign?" Keynes responded: "No, that is not an essential part of my views. My own belief is that the policy I advocate—price stability—would almost certainly lead to a restoration of the parity of the sovereign, because I find it hard to believe that American prices will not rise in time. . . . I am against hurrying the day, but I regard it as probable that if we concentrate on a price stability policy we shall probably find ourselves at no very distance from par."[722]

Keynes's view gained adherents on the committee. Sir John Bradbury, who succeeded Chamberlain as chairman after Chamberlain became secretary of state for foreign affairs, wrote a few days after Keynes's testimony:[723] "I am so far impressed by the views of McKenna [former chancellor of the exchequer] and Keynes that it may be wise not to pursue a policy of restoring the dollar exchange to parity at the cost of depressing home prices. . . . My present feeling is rather in favor of pursuing a credit policy which will aim at keeping the exchanges in the neighborhood of 4.40 . . . and working back to par."[723]

Had Britain waited, abandoning the plan to force the pound back to $4.8665 in 1925, it might never have returned to the gold standard. The crash of October 1929 came less than five years after the return to parity. More than twenty years had elapsed before Britain returned to gold after suspending in 1797, during the Napoleonic Wars. The speculative excesses that led to the 1929 crash might have unfolded the same way but, without the constraints of gold, the monetary authorities would have had greater freedom to act. And the Great Depression might have been much shorter.*

Britain left the gold standard for good on September 21, 1931.[724] After the British announcement, America faced a foreign demand for gold by countries worried that the United States would also suspend convertibility. At the same time, the American public demanded cash because the people did not trust the banks. Walter Bagehot, the oracle of central banking, had warned about the dangers of an "internal panic and external demand for bullion."[725] He said: "The holders of reserves have to treat two opposite maladies at once—one requiring stringent remedies,

---

* Peter Temin (1989) argues that the Great Depression was a result of the unyielding commitment to the gold standard when it was no longer appropriate.

and the other an alleviative treatment with large and ready loans."[726] Bagehot's now classic prescription reads: "We must first look to the foreign drain and raise the rate of interest as high as may be necessary. . . . And at the rate of interest so raised, the holders . . . of the final bank reserve must lend freely."[727]

The Federal Reserve System followed Bagehot's textbook instructions.[728] The New York Reserve Bank raised the discount rate, the interest rate on its loans of reserves to member banks, from 1.5 percent to 2.5 percent on October 9, 1931, and raised it another full percentage point a week later.[729] The Federal Reserve System's lending of reserves to commercial banks jumped to a monthly average of $694 million during October, November, and December, compared with an average of $223 over the previous three months.[730]

The increased supply of reserves conforms to Bagehot's remedy "to lend freely." But the Federal Reserve did not expand credit fast enough. Despite the increased lending of reserves, the money supply fell by 8.8 percent from the end of September 1931 through December 1931, a 35 percent annual rate of decline that belongs in the record books.[731]

What caused the shortfall? One culprit—along with others—is that lending at 3.5 percent attracts fewer borrowers than lending at 1.5 percent. Bagehot's classic prescription for dealing with an internal and external drain fails to recognize that central bankers can control either credit or interest rates, but not both. Milton Friedman and Anna Schwartz, in their classic, *A Monetary History of the United States*, discuss the increase in U.S. interest rates after Britain left the gold standard. They say that rates rose because "they reflected the liquidity crisis and the unwillingness or inability of banks to borrow even more heavily from the Reserve System."* The "unwillingness of banks to borrow" should have come as no surprise. The jump in the discount rate restrained the demand for credit.

Had Britain not returned to the gold standard in 1925, it would not have been forced off in September 1931. Under those circumstances, America would not have had to defend itself from a rush to gold by countries worried that the United States would also suspend. The Federal Reserve would not have raised the discount rate in October 1931. The Great Depression was more than just a speck on the horizon at the

---

* See Friedman and Schwartz (1963, 319). Meltzer (2003, 342ff.) also discusses the reaction to the British devaluation in great detail. He points out (p. 348) that "federal reserve credit expanded by $1 billion after the crisis." The problem is that the amount of Federal Reserve credit outstanding (bank borrowing plus open market securities held plus float plus other assets) that is consistent with a level of interest rates of 3.5 percent is less than it would have been with rates at 1.5 percent.

time. Bank borrowing from the Federal Reserve would not have been discouraged. No one knows how much shorter the Depression might have been without the distraction of Britain and the gold standard.

In August 1914 William G. McAdoo confronted Bagehot's "internal panic and external demand for bullion." Unlike in 1931, the United States overcame the twin dangers and challenged British monetary supremacy. November 11, 1914, four years to the day before the Armistice, marks the birth of America as a financial superpower.

Blueprint for Crisis Control

AMERICA benefited from decisive financial leadership during the last two decades of the twentieth century. Paul Volcker confronted a runaway inflation when he became chairman of the Federal Reserve Board on August 6, 1979. Two months later, in October 1979, he adopted a controversial plan to curb spiraling prices by controlling the nation's money supply.[732] Volcker stuck to his principles of price stability and established the central bank's credibility as a bulwark against inflation. The victory set the stage for a generation of economic prosperity. Alan Greenspan succeeded Paul Volcker on August 11, 1987. Two months later, on October 19, 1987, the largest one-day decline in stock market history threatened to bring the American financial system to a standstill. Greenspan met the crisis head on by committing to lend freely at the Federal Reserve's discount window to support the integrity of the nation's payments system.[733] Alan Greenspan's success at avoiding a collapse in the economy after the 1987 crash, and his subsequent achievements at crisis management during the 1990s, sustained American economic stability during his tenure in office.

Volcker and Greenspan brought economic sophistication to their jobs. Paul Volcker had completed all but his doctoral dissertation at Harvard and served in senior positions at the Chase Manhattan Bank and the U.S. Treasury. Alan Greenspan ran a successful economic consulting firm for many years and then received his doctorate from New York University's Graduate School of Business Administration.* But the determination and initiative they brought to the central bank mattered as much as their training in economics. The failure of the Federal Reserve to control inflation under the chairmanship of Arthur Burns during the 1970s testifies to the limitations of intellect alone.

Arthur Burns, chairman of the Federal Reserve Board from February 1, 1970, until January 31, 1978, knew far more economics than either Paul Volcker or Alan Greenspan. He was an expert in business cycles

---

* Alan Greenspan was one of fifteen students in my Advanced Theory of Money and Income class in 1966. I had just arrived at NYU as a twenty-three-year-old assistant professor. Greenspan was already a well-known forecaster with his own consulting firm, Townsend-Greenspan & Company. I don't remember much about what I taught, but the future Federal Reserve chairman got an A.

and served as president of the National Bureau of Economic Research, the institution that designates peaks and troughs in the American economy. He failed to translate his expertise into action. According to Milton Friedman, an important theme in Burns's writings before he became Federal Reserve chairman was avoiding inflation.[734] Arthur Burns also knew how to control prices. He said: "It [The Federal Reserve] could have restricted the money supply and created sufficient strains . . . to terminate inflation with little delay."[735] Burns refused to stem the inflationary spiral because of the political costs.* William Poole, president of the Federal Reserve Bank of St. Louis, and a distinguished economist in his own right, said: "The Great Inflation was understandable but was not unavoidable. Stronger leadership . . . could have stopped it."[736] An important distinction between a great thinker and a great leader is that a leader knows when to get the job done—and does it.

William G. McAdoo had no formal economics education. He was a lawyer by training and an entrepreneur by vocation. By virtue of his position as treasury secretary he became the first chairman of the Federal Reserve Board. None of the central bank's crisis management tools were in place when the European conflict threatened American finance in August 1914. McAdoo triumphed, in part, precisely because he did not have an operational central bank. The absence forced McAdoo to improvise, allowing his practical bent to flourish. He also had the confidence to act. Political columnist Walter Lippmann described McAdoo as "A man who makes his way in the world, not by conformity, but by initiative."[737]

McADOO'S ROAD MAP

In August 1914 William G. McAdoo responded immediately to the twin threats, the external gold drain to Europe and the internal drain of currency from banks, triggered by the outbreak of war. The delay in opening the Federal Reserve Banks allowed McAdoo to apply the modern principle of training an independent weapon on each policy target. He closed the New York Stock Exchange to curtail gold exports and in-

---

* Christina Romer (Federal Reserve Bank of St. Louis Review 2005, 177) argues that the root of the 1970s inflation stemmed from a "fundamentally misguided economic framework" employed by policy makers, rather than an absence of political will. However, even she agrees that politics intruded part of the time. She said that during 1976, when "inflation was rising and unemployment was falling . . . Burns may have expanded in an effort to win re-nomination [as chairman] from President Carter. Thus, this appears to be one episode when politics or personal ambition, rather than economic beliefs drove policy." See Romer and Romer (2004, 142).

voked the Aldrich-Vreeland Act to expand domestic currency. These emergency measures controlled potentially fatal hemorrhages in America's financial system. Failure to respond promptly could have spelled disaster. O.M.W. Sprague cited a four-day delay in 1907 as a critical mistake.*

William G. McAdoo never hesitated. Walter Lippmann parodied McAdoo's impetuousness in the press: "It may not be quite true . . . that Secretary McAdoo made eight or nine decisions one day going down in the elevator of a building in Washington, but it is in the general direction of the truth."[738] During the crisis of 1914 McAdoo balanced impulse with reflection.

McAdoo knew that his emergency measures would damage America if they remained in place for an extended period. He responded with an exit plan to rectify the underlying economic imbalance. McAdoo recognized that the gold drain could be reversed by promoting American exports of agricultural commodities to offset European sales of U.S. securities. On August 8, 1914, he called a meeting for the following week at the Treasury to provide "sufficient ships to move our grain and cotton crops to European markets."[739] The Treasury conference created the Bureau of War Risk Insurance. When the British announced on October 26, 1914, that cotton was no longer considered contraband, the availability of insurance supported the dollar's redemption in the foreign exchange market. McAdoo's preparation turned happenstance into good fortune.

The existence of an exit plan permitted a sledgehammer approach to crisis control. Flooding the country with emergency currency threatened, in McAdoo's own words, "to wreck the United States of America."[740] Shutting the stock exchange for four months left the capital markets without a rudder for the longest stretch in history. The exit plan encouraged bold initiatives by promising to limit the collateral damage of potentially lethal medicines.

McAdoo's victory in 1914 serves as a blueprint for crisis management. He would probably insist on including instructions that come with a tourniquet: apply the restraint quickly to stop the hemorrhaging, repair the wound, and then restore normal functions.

Hesitation at any stage can prove fatal.

* Sprague (1910, 257) says: "The failure to issue clearinghouse loan certificates as early as Tuesday was the most serious error made during the crisis." The "Tuesday" in this quote refers to October 22, 1907. According to the *New York Times* (October 27, 1907) the New York Clearing House declared on Saturday, October 26, that banks could use Clearing House loan certificates to dispense their obligations.

Notes

1. Lewis (1938, 533) reports an estimate of $4.1 billion in railroad securities held by foreigners as of June 30, 1914. The U.S. Department of Commerce (1975, 2:735) reports a total value of railroad securities equal to $20.2 billion at the end of 1914. Thus, $4.1 divided by $20.2 equals 20.3 percent.

2. Letter from Higginson to Wilson, August 20, 1914, Papers of William G. McAdoo, Library of Congress.

3. Note from Wilson to McAdoo, August 22, 1914, Papers of William G. McAdoo, Library of Congress.

4. See Conant 1915.

5. See *Wall Street Journal*, January 5, 1915, 5; January 8, 1915, 5; and January 18, 1915, 8.

6. Memorandum, August 3, 1914, in Keynes 1971, 11.

7. See Bordo and Rockoff 1996.

8. See Bagehot (1873, 32) for a similar argument.

9. The details of McAdoo's life are from his autobiography, *Crowded Years* (1931). Specific quotations will be cited explicitly.

10. McAdoo 1931, 25.

11. Ibid., 31.

12. Ibid., 50–53.

13. *New York Times*, August 1, 1914, 3.

14. The announcement of the meeting appeared in the *Wall Street Journal*, August 8, 1914, 4.

15. Noyes 1926, 86–88.

16. See the letter from Keynes to Sir Charles Addis, a director of the Bank of England, dated July 25, 1924, in Keynes (1981, 271).

17. See Eichengreen 1992, 13; Kindleberger 1973, 295; Temin 1989; and chapter 9.

18. See Taylor 2002, 7.

19. Ibid., 8.

20. Noyes 1926, 86–88.

21. Six percent is the average of a 6.9 percent decline in the index of twelve industrial stocks and a 5 percent decline in the index of twenty railroad stocks. The data on stock price averages come from the daily *Wall Street Journal*.

22. Sprague 1910, 255.

23. *New York Times*, July 31, 1914, 1.

24. Noble 1915, 87.

25. *New York Times*, August 1, 1914, 1.

26. Chernow 1990, 125.

27. Sprague 1910, 251.

28. *New York Times*, August 1, 1914, 1.

29. Noble 1915, 9.

30. *New York Times*, June 29, 1914, 1.

31. *New York Times*, June 30, 1914, 1.

32. Lewis (1938, 533) reports an estimate of $4.1 billion in railroad securities held by foreigners as of June 30, 1914. See calculations in note 1.

33. For a similar view, see Ferguson 2006.

34. *New York Times*, July 24, 1914, 1.

35. *Wall Street Journal*, July 24, 1914, 8.

36. *Wall Street Journal*, July 31, 1914, 4.

37. The *New York Times* reported on August 2, 1914, 4: "It was estimated by foreign stock exchange houses that from $100 million to $150 million worth of American stocks and bonds were thrown on the market [last week] for whatever they would bring by European investors."

38. *Wall Street Journal*, August 1, 1914, 1.

39. *New York Times*, August 2, 1914, 4.

40. Ibid. The "shorts" had good reason to worry. Prices were higher when the exchange finally reopened in December (see *Wall Street Journal*, December 15, 1914, 2).

41. *New York Times*, August 1, 1914, 5.

42. McAdoo 1931, 290.

43. McAdoo's disclosure appeared in his autobiography (1931, 290).

44. *New York Times*, August 3, 1914.

45. McAdoo 1931, 41.

46. Ibid., 97.

47. *New York Times*, August 1, 1914, 5.

48. Sprague (1915, 510) said "the disturbing effect of these [stock exchange] sales was almost wholly due to the fact that they were sales by foreign holders rather than [because of] the quantities offered for sale."

49. The industrial index declined by 11.3 percent and the railroad index declined by 8.7 percent between Thursday, July 23, the day of the Austrian Ultimatum, and Thursday July 30, the last day of trading before the closure.

50. See Comptroller of the Currency, *Annual Report*, December 7, 1914 (1915), 22. Gold reserves on the balance sheet, equal to the sum of gold coin, gold certificates of deposit, and clearing house certificates (see p. 25), totaled $626 million. Banks held an additional $377 million of reserves in the form of legal tender that could be converted into gold.

51. According to Friedman and Schwarz (1963, 781–82) legal tender, sometimes called lawful money, consisted of gold coin, silver dollars, fractional silver coin, U.S. notes (sometimes called legal tender notes or greenbacks), Treasury notes of July 14, 1890, and U.S. gold certificates and silver certificates.

52. According to Friedman and Schwarz (1963, 708) at the end of July, 1914, bank demand deposits (checking accounts) totaled $9,674 million and currency in circulation totaled $1,819 million. For a brief discussion of the growth in the use of checking accounts, see Friedman and Schwartz (1963, 122).

53. Ibid., 56.

54. Officer (1996, 41) says that Britain was on a de facto gold standard since the early 1700s.

55. Based on Officer's data (2001), you needed about £1, 18 shillings in 1914 to buy what £1 bought in 1714. By way of contrast, you needed about £56 in 2000 to buy what £1 could buy in 1914.

56. See Bordo and Rockoff 1996, 414–15.

57. Ibid., 393.

58. Ibid.

59. The total from the July 23 until July 29 was $27,850,000 according to the *Wall Street Journal* (July 29, 1914, 1). According to the annual reports of the U.S. Treasury, only May 1904, May 1908, and April 1910 had larger exports than $25 million.

60. Sprague (1910) discusses these panics.

61. *New York Times*, January 7, 1914, 7.

62. Ibid.

63. *Washington Post*, January 7, 1914, 3.

64. Ibid.

65. Ibid.

66. *Wall Street Journal*, August 3, 1914.

67. *New York Times*, August 1, 1914, 5.

68. Sprague 1910, 13.

69. Federal Reserve Board, *First Annual Report* (1915), 6.

70. *New York Times*, June 16, 1914, 14.

71. *New York Times*, July 22, 1914, 2.

72. Letter from McAdoo to Wilson, December 20, 1913, *Papers of Woodrow Wilson* (1979).

73. From the Diary of Colonel House, December 22, 1913, *Papers of Woodrow Wilson* (1979).

74. Letter from Wilson to Hulbert, March 15, 1914, *Papers of Woodrow Wilson* (1979).

75. McAdoo 1931, 274–75.

76. Letter from McAdoo to Page, May 4, 1914, Papers of William G. McAdoo, Library of Congress.

77. McAdoo 1931, 274–75.

78. Glass 1927, 100–110.

79. McAdoo 1931, 51–52.

80. Ibid., 105.

81. Lippmann 1927, 113.

82. *New York Times*, July 12, 1914, 1.

83. *Washington Post*, July 10, 1914, 1.

84. Ibid.

85. See Brocsamle 1973, 122.

86. *New York Times*, July 24, 1914, 1.

87. Warburg 1930, 20.

88. Ibid., 58ff.

89. Ibid., 97–98.

90. *New York Times*, July 14, 1914, 3.

91. McAdoo 1931, 285ff.

92. Papers of William McAdoo, Library of Congress.

93. Glass 1927, 131.

94. McAdoo 1931, 106.

95. Ibid., 122.

96. *New York Times*, July 29, 1914, 1.

97. *Washington Post*, August 3, 1914, 1.

98. *Washington Post*, August 1, 1914, 1.

99. *New York Times*, August 8, 1914, 6, and August 10, 1914, 6.

100. *Washington Post*, July 31, 1914, 5.

101. *Washington Post*, August 1, 1914, 2.

102. *New York Times*, August 5, 1914, 20.

103. *Wall Street Journal*, August 11, 1914, 8.

104. *New York Times*, July 28, 1914, 13.

105. *Wall Street Journal*, July 30, 1914, 8.

106. *Wall Street Journal*, July 29, 1914.

107. *New York Times*, September 25, 1869, 1.

108. Ibid.

109. See Friedman and Schwartz 1963, 7, 48, 83.

110. *New York Times*, December 18, 1878, 8.

111. Ibid.

112. According to Stedman (1905, 281) the gold department of the New York Stock Exchange was abolished on December 31, 1878.

113. See Chicago Board of Trade 1989.

114. Biographical details on Max May come from the *New York Times*, May 28, 1931, 27.

115. According to the *Wall Street Journal* (May 25, 1931), the other two members of the Big Three were John E. Garden of the National City Bank and James M. Donald of Hanover National Bank.

116. *Wall Street Journal*, July 29, 1914, 1.

117. *Wall Street Journal*, July 25, 1914, 8.

118. *Wall Street Journal*, April 16, 1910, 6.

119. The *Wall Street Journal* (July 31, 1914, 8), refers to $4.88 as the "ordinary gold export point," which is .28 percent above the mint parity of 4.8665.

120. With less than $35 million in capital in 1913, the Guaranty Trust Company bought and sold $1.8 billion of foreign exchange in London, $654 million in Germany, and $340 million in France. See *New York Times*, January 7, 1914, 7, and JP Morgan Chase Archives, JP Morgan Chase, New York.

121. For example, if it also cost .28 percent to ship gold from England to the United States, then the gold import point equaled $4.8529. Officer (1996, 174) indicates that the gold import point was larger in absolute magnitude than the export point.

122. *Wall Street Journal*, July 24, 1914, 8.

123. *Wall Street Journal*, July 25, 1914, 8.

124. See Andrew 1910.

125. The exchange rate of $4.92 times 42,477 British pounds equals $208,986.84 minus $206,718 for buying the 10,000 ounces of gold at the Treasury and minus the shipping costs of $578.81 equals $1,690.

126. Advertisement, *New York Times*, July 26, 1914, RP3.

127. *New York Times*, July 26,1914, 1.

128. Ibid.

129. Memorandum, August 3, 1914, in Keynes 1971, 12.

130. *New York Times*, March 19, 1891, 3.

131. Ibid.

132. *Wall Street Journal*, July 31, 1914, 8.

133. *New York Times*, July, 29, 1914, 3.

134. Officer (1996, 139) reports the .07 percent estimate. The gold export point of $4.8835 is .0035 (=.0028 plus .0007) above the mint parity of $4.8665. The *Wall Street Journal* suggests that the export point for coins equaled $4.89, but that still does not explain the $4.92 exchange rate.

135. *New York Times*, July, 29, 1914, 3.

136. Ibid.

137. The $500 estimate comes from the *Wall Street Journal* (April 16, 1910). The July 30, 1914, *Wall Street Journal* specifies the increase to $600 on the July 28.

138. *New York Times*, July, 29, 1914, 3.

139. *New York Times*, August 1, 1914, 3.

140. The new export point is $4.9298, which is .013 (= the normal .0028 shipping cost plus .0007 for coin abrasion plus .0095 for increased insurance) above the mint parity of $4.8665.

141. *Wall Street Journal*, July 31, 1914, 8.

142. *Wall Street Journal*, July 29, 1914, 8.

143. Lindert 1969, 18–19.

144. *New York Times*, August 1, 1914, 3.

145. *New York Times*, July, 29, 1914, 3.

146. August 2, 1914, 4.

147. *Wall Street Journal*, July 30, 1914, 1.

148. See *Wall Street Journal*, August 5, 1914, 1.

149. *Wall Street Journal*, August 3, 1914.

150. *Wall Street Journal*, August 5, 1914, 1.

151. *New York Times*, August 1, 1914, 3.

152. *Wall Street Journal*, August 1, 1914, 7.

153. Ibid.

154. *New York Times*, August 1, 1914.

155. *Wall Street Journal*, July 31, 1914, 7.

156. U.S. Treasury, *Annual Report*, 1914.

157. The data are from various annual reports of the U.S. Treasury.

158. *Wall Street Journal*, June 11, 1914, 8.

159. *Wall Street Journal*, June 18, 1914, 8.

160. *Wall Street Journal*, June 20, 1914, 6.

161. Ibid.

162. *Wall Street Journal*, April 24, 1914, 8.

163. Ibid.

164. McAdoo 1931, 290.

165. *New York Times*, August 3, 1914, 3.

166. Ibid.

167. Ibid.

168. *New York Times*, October 25, 1907, 1.

169. Ibid.

170. Siegel (1998, 183) reports a decline of 8.29 percent in the industrial average on March 14, 1907.

171. The Banking Act of 1933 created the Federal Deposit Insurance Corporation (see Friedman and Schwartz 1963, 435).

172. *New York Times*, October 23, 1907, 2.

173. Ibid.

174. Ibid.

175. *New York Times*, October 20, 1907, 1.

176. *New York Times*, October 21, 1907, 2.

177. The *Wall Street Journal* reported the following deposit totals: $52 million for the Knickerbocker Trust Company (June 19, 1907); $37 million for the Chase National Bank (June 10, 1907); and $75 million for the First National Bank (June 10, 1907).

178. *New York Times*, October 22, 1907, 1.

179. Ibid.

180. Ibid.

181. Ibid.

182. *New York Times*, October 23, 1907, 1.

183. Ibid.

184. Total deposits in the Trust Company of America were $46.7 million in June 1907 (see *Wall Street Journal*, June 19, 1907, 8).

185. *New York Times*, October 24, 1907, 2.

186. *New York Times*, November 9, 1907, 2.

187. Sprague 1910, 252.

188. *New York Times*, October 23, 1907, 5.

189. Chernow 1990, 122.

190. *New York Times*, October 24, 1907, 1.

191. *New York Times*, October 26, 1907, 1.

192. Ibid.

193. Ibid., 4.

194. Ibid., 5.

195. Ibid.

196. Ibid.

197. Ibid.

198. Ibid., 2.

199. Ibid.

200. *New York Times*, October 27, 1907, 2.

201. Ibid.

202. See Andrew 1908b, table I. Andrew defined large cities as those with a population greater than 25,000.

203. See Andrew 1910, table 4; Friedman and Schwartz 1963, 781.

204. See Andrew 1908a, 290. The two previous notes cite two of Andrew's other statistical descriptions of this period.

205. Ibid., 291.

206. Ibid., 292.

207. Based on Andrew 1910, table 17.

208. Andrew 1908a, 294.

209. Ibid., 296.

210. Ibid., 294.

211. Comptroller of the Currency, *Annual Report*, 1907, 70.

212. *New York Times*, October 24, 1907, 1.

213. *New York Times*, November 8, 1907, 3.

214. Friedman and Schwartz 1963, 157.

215. Ibid., 135.

216. Ibid., 179.

217. See ibid. Friedman and Schwartz (128–34) describe the origin of silver certificates.

218. Ibid., 179.

219. Ibid., 46.

220. The amount of greenbacks outstanding was fixed at $347 million by an act of Congress on May 31, 1878. See ibid., 24.

221. National bank notes outside the treasury totaled $280 million in 1867; the total declined to $162 million in 1893; and in 1900 the volume outstanding returned to its 1867 level and then rose to $542 million in 1906 (see ibid., 17, 130, 179).

222. See Andrew 1907.

223. *New York Times*, November 14, 1907, 2.

224. Goodhart (1969, 120) says "The Treasury's working balance had been reduced to approximately $$5 million." Also see Friedman and Schwartz 1963, 162n.

225. *New York Times*, October 29, 1907.

226. Ibid., 1.

227. Sprague 1910, 284.

228. See Friedman and Schwartz 1963, 158. They say that without the gold imports, the 5 percent decline in the stock of money between September 1907 and February 1908 would have been much greater (with a larger negative impact on the economy).

229. Goodhart 1969, 120.

230. Sprague 1910, 318.

231. *New York Times*, November 12, 1907.

232. Ibid.

233. George Cortelyou extended Shaw's precedent by mobilizing the Treasury's $25 million in a futile attempt to stem the crisis in October 1907.

234. See Andrew 1907, 565-66

235. *New York Times*, November 12, 1907.

236. *New York Times*, April 17, 1915.

237. *New York Times*, November 10, 1907.

238. See *Congressional Record*, 60th Cong., 1st sess., 1908, 504.

239. *New York Times*, January 15, 1908.

240. Laughlin 1908a, 94, 96.

241. *New York Times*, February 28, 1908.

242. Comptroller of the Currency, *Annual Report*, 1907, 74.

243. *New York Times*, February 2, 1908.

244. *New York Times*, January 30, 1908.

245. *Wall Street Journal*, March 18, 1907.

246. *New York Times*, March 18, 1907.

247. *Washington Post*, March 28, 1908.

248. *New York Times*, April 10, 1908.

249. *New York Times*, January 9, 1908.

250. *New York Times*, January 28, 1908.

251. See Andrew 1908c, 669.

252. Ibid., 668.

253. *New York Times*, January 13, 1908, 6.

254. *Washington Post*, May 6, 1908, 1.

255. Other securities consisted of *any* other securities held by commercial banks, subject to the approval of the secretary of the Treasury. Railroad bonds, which had been excluded from the Aldrich bill that passed the Senate, could now be acceptable through the "other securities provision" (see Laughlin 1908b, 505).

256. See Section 9, Andrew 1908c, 673.

257. See Section 3, Andrew 1908c, 671.

258. Section 5 of the bill limits the total amount of emergency currency to $500 million but restricts each bank's currency outstanding to its total capital and surplus. Section 7 instructs the secretary of the Treasury to distribute the emergency currency among states in proportion to the total capital of banks in each state relative to the total capital of all banks in the United States.

259. See Section 11, Andrew 1908c, 675.

260. See Sections 5 and 11, Andrew 1908c, 672 and 675.

261. See Friedberg 1964, 180.

262. See Section 17, Andrew 1908c, 676.

263. See Section 20, Andrew 1908c, 676.

264. *Congressional Record*, 60th Cong., 1st sess., 1908, 7069.

265. Ibid., 7068.

266. Ibid., 7221.

267. Laughlin 1908b, 490.

268. Ibid., 499.

269. Ibid., 513.

270. *New York Times*, June 11, 1908.

271. Ibid.

272. *New York Times*, July 17, 1910.

273. See Comptroller of the Currency, *Annual Report*, 1911, 76–77. The total capital and surplus of the 284 banks equaled $566 million and the total capital and surplus for all banks equaled $1,644 million (as of June 30, 1910).

274. *Washington Post*, August 1, 1914, 5.

275. See the memo written by Benjamin Strong, Albert Wiggin (Chase National Bank) and James Brown (Brown Brothers), November 2, 1914, box 1470, Board of Governors, Central Subject File, 1913–1954, National Archives II, College Park, Maryland.

276. See chapter 1.

277. See *Commercial and Financial Chronicle* 99 (August 22, 1914): 499.

278. The New York bankers worried especially about withdrawals of cash by country banks that held deposit balances in New York banks. See the memo by Strong, Wiggin, and Brown.

279. *New York Times*, August 4, 1914.

280. See Friedman and Schwartz (1963, 158) for the linkage between the gold drain that started in May 1907 and the October panic of that year.

281. McAdoo 1931, 290.

282. Both Hepburn and Vanderlip are quoted in the *New York Times*, November 11, 1907, as urging the establishment of a central bank in the United States.

283. *New York Times*, April 3, 1908.

284. *New York Times*, August 3, 1914.

285. A Committee of the Chicago Clearing House, also meeting on Sunday, had made the same decision (see *Washington Post*, August 3, 1914).

286. *New York Times*, August 3, 1914.

287. Ibid.

288. Ibid.

289. *Wall Street Journal*, August 1, 1914, 1.

290. *New York Times*, August 2, 1914.

291. *Washington Post*, August 3, 1914.

292. *Wall Street Journal*, August 3, 1914.

293. Withers 1915, 12–14.

294. *New York Times*, August 3, 1914. The relevant part of the moratorium read as follows (*Wall Street Journal*, August 15, 1914): "The presentation for payment of a bill of exchange, other than a check or bill on demand, which has been accepted before the beginning of the fourth day of August, 1914 . . . shall for all purposes . . . be deemed to be due and be payable on a date one calendar month after the date of its original maturity."

295. McAdoo 1931, 290.

296. Ibid., 56–57.

297. *Wall Street Journal*, August 1, 1914. Also see U.S. Treasury, *Annual Report*, December 7, 1914, 2.

298. Statement of the Members of the New York Clearing House, August 1, 1914 (*Wall Street Journal*, August 3, 1914, 8).

299. Ibid.

300. McAdoo 1931, 291.

301. Ibid.

302. *Washington Post*, August 1, 1914.

303. *Congressional Record*, 63rd Cong., 2 sess., 1914, 13067.

304. *Washington Post*, August 1, 1914.

305. *Congressional Record*, 63rd Cong., 2 sess., 1914, 13069.

306. *Washington Post*, August 1, 1914.

307. Ibid.

308. *Congressional Record*, 63rd Cong., 2 sess., 1914, 13169.

309. The entire quotation, from the *Congressional Record*, 60th Cong., 1st sess., 1908, 7069, appears in chapter 3.

310. *Congressional Record*, 63rd Cong., 2 sess., 1914, 13168.
311. Ibid., 13169.
312. Ibid., 13168.
313. Ibid., 13168–69.
314. Ibid., 13172.
315. Ibid., 13171.
316. Ibid.
317. *New York Times*, August 4, 1914.
318. *New York Times*, June 27, 1909.
319. *Washington Post*, August 6, 1914.
320. *Washington Post*, August 11,1914.
321. *Washington Post*, August 6, 1914.
322. See Comptroller of the Currency, *Annual Report*, December 7, 1914 (1915), 58 and 99.
323. Ibid., 99.
324. The call report for national banks showed $722 million in national bank notes outstanding on June 30, 1914. The three previous call reports (Comptroller of the Currency, *Annual Report*, December 7, 1914, [1915], 22) show national bank notes outstanding of $720 million, $725 million and $727 million. See the same *Annual Report*, 61, for the increase per annum since 1910.
325. The *Washington Post* (December 21, 1913) reported: "One of the last amendments agreed upon in the Senate extended this [Aldrich-Vreeland] emergency act until June 30, 1915, by which time the new [Federal Reserve] system, it is presumed, will be in full operation."
326. *New York Times*, June 12, 1913.
327. *Washington Post*, June 12, 1913.
328. Ibid.
329. Comptroller of the Currency, *Annual Report*, 1907, 74.
330. Kemmerer 1914.
331. *Wall Street Journal*, June 13, 1913.
332. *Wall Street Journal*, August 1, 1914.
333. Illiquid assets sell at an average discount of 30 percent (see Silber 1991).
334. U.S. Department of Commerce 1975, 2:1007.
335. *New York Times*, August 2, 1914.
336. Ibid.
337. *New York Times*, August 4, 1914.
338. See Silber (1977) for a discussion of the interrelationship between the liquidity of financial markets, financial institutions, and money supply.
339. *Wall Street Journal*, August 6, 1914.
340. Ibid.
341. Ibid.
342. *Wall Street Journal*, August 5, 1914.
343. Ibid.
344. *Wall Street Journal*, August 12, 1914.
345. See Comptroller of the Currency, *Annual Report*, December 6, 1915 (1916), 93. A table shows that, based on the 125 percent of capital limitation,

$1,493 million additional national bank notes could have been issued under the Aldrich-Vreeland Act.

346. Ibid., 45.

347. The data in this paragraph refer to June 30, 1914, as reported in U.S. Department of Commerce 1975, Part 2, Series X 410-419, 992.

348. See Friedman and Schwartz 1963, 781.

349. Sprague (1914, 184) observed: "With these emergency notes the banks satisfied practically all demands for additional money for domestic use outside the banks, thus safeguarding their reserves."

350. *Wall Street Journal*, August 13, 1914.

351. Based on Friedman and Schwartz 1963, 800, table B-3.

352. On October 31, 1914, the money supply totaled $16,532 million versus $16,135 million outstanding on July 31, 1914. See Friedman and Schwartz 1963, 708, table A-1.

353. According to Friedman and Schwartz (1963, 706, table A-1) the money supply measured $11,044 on December 31, 1907, versus $11,374 million on September 30, 1907. Friedman and Schwartz (p. 158) say: "The decline in the money stock from September 1907 to February 1908 has all the earmarks of a scramble for liquidity on the part of both the public and the banks." The monetary base actually rose over this interval, in part, because of the massive gold inflows from Europe that began in November 1907. Bank deposits declined, however, because the public increased its currency holdings and banks increased their holdings of reserves.

354. See Friedman and Schwartz 1963, 156–18.

355. *New York Times*, August 26, 1914, 8.

356. Ibid., 11.

357. Ibid.

358. Ibid.

359. See *Wall Street Journal*, August 12, 1914.

360. Ibid.

361. The money supply, from Friedman and Schwartz (1963, 704ff., table A-1), is measured as currency plus bank demand and time deposits. On December 31, 1914, the total equaled $16,319 million versus $16,136 million on July 31, 1914. The total outstanding on December 31, 1913, was $15,819 million versus $11,985 million on December 31, 1908.

362. The opening of the Federal Reserve Banks on November 16, 1914, may have contributed to the withdrawal of emergency currency. However, the total had already dropped by nearly $50 million before the middle of November.

363. Comptroller of the Currency, *Annual Report*, December 7, 1914 (1915), 51. By December the rate on commercial paper had dropped back to 4.50 percent, and in January 1915 it declined below the prewar level to an average of 3.75 percent (see Comptroller of the Currency, *Annual Report*, December 6, 1915 [1916], 106).

364. *New York Times*, August 8, 1914.

365. Comptroller of the Currency, *Annual Report*, December 6, 1915 (1916), 4.

366. Sprague 1915, 517, 519, 533.

367. *Commercial and Financial Chronicle* 99 (August 1, 1914): 292.

368. Ibid. (August 15, 1914): 432.

369. *Wall Street Journal*, August 1, 1914, 8.

370. Sprague 1915, 533.

371. McAdoo 1931, 284–85.

372. Letter from Wilson to Morgan, August 13, 1914, *Papers of Woodrow Wilson* (1979).

373. McAdoo (1931, 293) said: "This was the first publicly conducted conference of businessmen . . . that a government official had ever held in Washington.

374. *Wall Street Journal*, August 7, 1914, 8.

375. The *New York Times* (August 8, 1914, 5) reports that the National City Bank made the announcement on the evening of August 7.

376. Ibid.

377. *Wall Street Journal*, August 8, 1914, 4.

378. Noyes (1916, 92) reports $42 million in gold exports during the last week of July. Chapter 2 cited the *Wall Street Journal* estimate of $27 million in exports between July 23 and July 29. His study for the national monetary commission was *History of the National Bank Currency* (1910).

379. Noyes 1916, 94.

380. *New York Times*, April 23, 1945, 16.

381. Ibid.

382. An analysis of the threat to convertibility is found in Simon 1960.

383. See http://projects.vassar.edu/1896/crossofgold.html.

384. *New York Times*, August 23, 1914, SM16.

385. See *New York Times*, July 25, 1915, BR272, and July 7, 1915, 11.

386. Laughlin 1918, 345.

387. Letter from Bryan to Wilson, August 10, 1914, *Papers of Woodrow Wilson* (1979).

388. *Washington Post*, August 14, 1914, 1.

389. *New York Times*, August 3, 1914, 3.

390. Bordo and Kydland (1995, 424) say: "Under the rule, gold convertibility could be suspended in the event of a well-understood, exogenously produced emergency, such as a war, on the understanding that after the emergency had safely passed convertibility would be restored at the original parity."

391. According to Officer (1996, 43), Britain left the gold standard on February 26, 1797, and returned on April 30, 1821.

392. Keynes (from the *Morning Post*, August 11, 1914, in Keynes, 1971, 20–24) discusses the suspensions by Russia, Germany, and France.

393. Memorandum, August 3, 1914, in Keynes 1971, 7–15.

394. See Lindert 1969, 1, 17.

395. Memorandum, August 3, 1914, in Keynes 1971, 10.

396. Ibid., 12.

397. *Wall Street Journal*, August 1, 1914, 7.

398. *New York Times*, August 2, 1914, 4.

399. According to Charles Conant (*New York Times*, August 23, 1914, SM16): "The [emergency] notes are being taken out by New York banks in order to enable them to retain their gold and restore their reserves. With this object,

they pay out their new notes to meet demands for currency while retaining the gold in their vaults."

400. *New York Times*, August 23, 1914, SM16.

401. *Wall Street Journal*, August 3, 1914, 6.

402. *Wall Street Journal*, August 10, 1914, 8.

403. Ibid.

404. *New York Times*, August 8, 1914, 9.

405. *New York Times*, August 7, 1914, 5.

406. *New York Times*, August 2, 1914, 4.

407. *New York Times*, August 3, 1914, 3.

408. *Washington Post*, August 2, 1914.

409. Paish 1911, 176.

410. The New York City Clearing House issued consolidated figures for the weeks ending August 8 and August 15 (*New York Times*, August 9, 1914, X11, and August 16, 1914, X11). On August 15 total reserves—specie plus legal tender—equaled $382 million. The reserve deficiency is listed as $48 million on August 15. The week ending August 8 shows reserves equal to $386 million but does not list any explicit deficiency. Because total deposits remained unchanged at $1.9 billion on both dates, the reserve deficiency must have been $44 million on August 8, or about 2.4 percent below required reserves.

411. *New York Times*, August 4, 1914, 12.

412. *Washington Post*, August 8, 1914, 2.

413. Hepburn 1915, 439. On August 3, 1914 (see Comptroller of the Currency, *Annual Report*, December 7, 1914 [1915], 14) the New York Clearing House suspended the requirement that banks settle their obligations to one another in lawful money. The Clearing House accepted national bank notes and Clearing House loan certificates—credits granted at the Clearing House based on a bank's assets—in settling adverse check clearings.

414. *New York Times*, August 12, 1914, 10.

415. *New York Times*, August 3, 1914, 3.

416. *Commercial and Financial Chronicle* 99 (August 15, 1914): 499.

417. Ibid.

418. *New York Times*, August 13, 1914, 10.

419. Carosso 1970, 84 and 198.

420. *New York Times*, August 14, 1914, 14.

421. *Wall Street Journal*, August 15, 1914, 1.

422. *Wall Street Journal*, August 12, 1914, 4.

423. Ibid.

424. See chapter 2 for a discussion of how shipping gold creates pounds. The $4.90 gold export point is mentioned in a letter from Benjamin Strong to Treasury Secretary McAdoo dated September 14, 1914 (Papers of William G. McAdoo, Library of Congress). It is confirmed in the *Wall Street Journal* (October 27, 1914, 1): "A decline in exchange below $4.90 . . . shuts off gold exports. This was the gold export point since the Bank of England established the gold depository in Ottawa."

425. *New York Times*, August 12, 1914, 10.

426. *Wall Street Journal*, August 12, 1914, 4.

427. See Noyes 1916, 47. However, the *Economist* (August 15, 1914, 308) suggests otherwise: "In many cases these dividend postponements are due to the partial nature of the moratorium."

428. *New York Times*, August 12, 1914, 10.

429. *Wall Street Journal*, August 12, 1914, 1.

430. *Wall Street Journal*, August 15, 1914, 1.

431. *New York Times*, August 19, 1914, 10.

432. Ibid.

433. *New York Times*, August 27, 1914, 10.

434. *New York Times*, February 7, 1946, 22.

435. Lewis (1938, 531) cites George Paish's estimate of $2,996 million for British holdings as of December, 1913. Lewis (p. 533) reports L. F. Loree's estimate of $4,170 million for all foreign holdings on June 30, 1914. Wilkins (2004, 8) reports $7.1 billion of total long-term foreign investment in the United States as of July 1, 1914, including securities and direct investment.

436. See chapter 1.

437. Noble 1915, 11.

438. Ibid., 12ff.

439. *New York Times*, August 3, 1914, 12.

440. Sobel 1972.

441. *Wall Street Journal*, August 4, 1914, 5.

442. Ibid., 1.

443. Ibid.

444. Noble 1915, 34ff.

445. Ibid., 38ff.

446. *New York Morning Telegraph*, August 15, 1914.

447. Noble 1915, 40.

448. *Wall Street Journal*, August 1, 1914, 1.

449. *New York Times*, January 4, 1915, 13.

450. Noble 1915, 41ff.

451. *Wall Street Journal*, August 4, 1914, 1.

452. *Wall Street Journal*, August 18, 1914, 1.

453. *New York Times*, October 7, 1914, 12.

454. Noble 1915, 18.

455. Ibid., 42.

456. *Wall Street Journal*, August 13, 1914, 4.

457. Noble 1915, 43.

458. Steven Wheeler, archivist at the New York Stock Exchange, located the records and provided copies of some of the entries. The records total four binders, each of which is about one inch thick. They contain all of the public releases issued by the committee but do not describe any of its deliberations. In addition to the published price quotations, the records also contain news clippings reporting on the committee's activities.

459. Mitchell Stephens, of NYU's Journalism Department, provided the reference to Mott (1950, 658) which referred to the *New York Morning Telegraph* as a "theater and turf paper."

460. Close to 600 stocks were listed on the New York Stock Exchange in 1914. Van Antwerp (1913) reports 555 listed stocks in 1912 and 502 in 1907.

461. See Schenk 1994, 351–52.

462. The industrial index dropped by 6.9 percent and the railroad index dropped 5 percent.

463. *Wall Street Journal*, August 1, 1914, 1.

464. According to Noble (1915, 9), Montreal, Toronto, and Madrid closed on July 28. Vienna, Budapest, Brussels, Antwerp, Berlin, and Rome closed on the 29th. St. Petersburg, the Paris Bourse, and all the South American countries were shut on the 30th. London closed on the morning of the 31st before New York. According to Keynes (1914, 461), the "Paris *Parquet* remained . . . open to a certain extent up to the impending evacuation of Paris by the Government on September 2nd."

465. The *New York Times*' August 1, 1914, front-page headline read: "Czar, Kaiser and King May Yet Arrange Peace."

466. Siegel 1998, 191.

467. Ibid., 190.

468. *New York Times*, January 3, 1915, AF8.

469. See *New York Times*, October 10, 1914, 1, and October 11, 1914, 9.

470. *New York Times*, August 30, 1914, SM4.

471. *New York Times*, January 3, 1915, AF8: "At the height of its activity, the New Street market consisted of about thirty-five brokers who dealt for cash only. In the downward slant of prices in October, it was estimated that fully 40,000 shares a day were handled for a number of days, fairly well divided between 100 share lots and fractional amounts of stock. The average daily turnover during September, October and November was placed . . . between 8,000 and 12,000 shares." Note that the *Morning Telegraph* reported New Street prices on a daily basis but never offered volume figures.

472. Ibid.

473. The 250,000 daily average is based on the same seventy securities that were actively traded on New Street (see Silber 2005).

474. Lewis (1938, 533) reports an estimate of $4.1 billion held by foreigners as of June 30, 1914. The U.S. Department of Commerce 1975 (2:735) reports a total value of railroad securities equal to $20.2 billion at the end of 1914. Thus, $4.1 divided by $20.2 equals 20.3 percent.

475. See Noyes 1916, 94.

476. *New York Times*, August 2, 1914, 4.

477. Trading averaged 894,000 shares per day from Monday, July 27, through Thursday, July 30, for a total volume of 3,576,000 shares for the week. The $100 million worth of shares sold by foreigners at $62 per share translates into 1,612,903 shares. Thus, 1,612,903 divided by 3,576,000 equals 45 percent.

478. See chapter 2.

479. *New York Times*, April 1, 1913, 3.

480. *New York Times*, March 13, 1943, 1.

481. *Wall Street Journal*, August 24, 1914, 5.

482. *New York Times*, February 15, 1914, XX4.

483. See Letter to the Editor from Stuyvesant Fish, former president of the Illinois Central Railroad, *New York Times*, March 21, 1914.

484. Ibid.

485. Ibid.

486. *Wall Street Journal*, August 24, 1914, 5.

487. Lamont 1933, 174.

488. *New York Times*, April 19, 1914, 14.

489. Ibid.

490. According to Section 10, Federal Reserve Act, December 23, 1913: "The Secretary of the Treasury may assign offices within the Department of Treasury for the use of the Federal Reserve Board."

491. See Harding 1925, 5 and 7.

492. Ibid., 5–6.

493. See Meltzer 2003, 485.

494. Federal Reserve Board, *First Annual Report* (1915), 13.

495. Letter from Warburg to McAdoo, August 27, 1914, Papers of William G. McAdoo, Library of Congress.

496. *New York Times*, September 2, 1914, 5.

497. Ibid.

498. *New York Times*, September 3, 1914, 10.

499. *New York Times*, September 4, 1914, 10.

500. Federal Reserve Board, *First Annual Report* (1915), 13.

501. *New York Times*, September 4, 1914, 10.

502. Ibid.

503. Ibid.

504. Letter to Treasury Secretary McAdoo from the Committee, September 4, 1914, Papers of William G. McAdoo, Library of Congress.

505. *Wall Street Journal*, September 5, 1914, 1.

506. This quotation, and the others in this paragraph, come from a letter to McAdoo from J. P. Morgan, August 21, 1914, Papers of William G. McAdoo, Library of Congress.

507. Ibid.

508. Lamont 1933, 175.

509. See chapter 4.

510. See chapter 5 and *Commercial and Financial Chronicle* 99 (September 26, 1914): 850.

511. *Commercial and Financial Chronicle* 99 (September 26, 1914): 850.

512. See Andrew 1907, 536–40.

513. *Commercial and Financial Chronicle* 99 (September 26, 1914): 850.

514. Lamont (1933, 181) says: "The negotiations with the city were led by J. P. Morgan and Davison in person." Lamont implies (pp. 172ff.) that Davison played a greater role in the New York rescue. The August 21 correspondence between McAdoo and J. P. Morgan and subsequent meetings between the two on September 10, 1914 (Summary, September 10, 1914, Papers of William G. McAdoo, Library of Congress) suggest otherwise.

515. A copy of the letter, dated September 4, 1914, addressed to Comptrol-

ler Prendergast and signed by J. P. Morgan & Company and Kuhn, Loeb & Company, appears in the Papers of William G. McAdoo, Library of Congress.

516. New York City Mayor Mitchell's complaint is recorded in Summary, September 10, 1914, Papers of William G. McAdoo, Library of Congress.

517. *New York Times*, September 5, 1914, 10.

518. Ibid.

519. Ibid.

520. See the telegram from Benjamin Strong Jr. to McAdoo, and the response, September 8, 1914, Papers of William G. McAdoo, Library of Congress.

521. Summary, September 10, 1914, Papers of William G. McAdoo, Library of Congress.

522. *New York Times*, September 11, 1914, 8.

523. Press Release, Federal Reserve Board, September 11, 1914, Papers of William G. McAdoo, Library of Congress.

524. *Wall Street Journal*, September 14, 1914, 1.

525. Lamont (1933, 180) credits Davison with convincing the banks to join the syndicate. Lamont (p. 181) says that 126 banks participated but the *Wall Street Journal,* September 15, 1914, lists 124.

526. The allocation came to 4 percent of each bank's deposits. See the *Wall Street Journal*, September 15, 1914, for every bank's contribution.

527. The description in this paragraph is based on the *Wall Street Journal*, October 20, 1914.

528. *Wall Street Journal*, September 19, 1914, 1.

529. Letter from J. P. Morgan to McAdoo, September 18, 1914, Papers of William G. McAdoo, Library of Congress.

530. *Wall Street Journal*, September 15, 1914, 5.

531. *Wall Street Journal*, March 8, 1913, 7.

532. See chapter 4.

533. *Wall Street Journal*, September 15, 1914, 5.

534. *Wall Street Journal*, September 19, 1914, 7.

535. *Wall Street Journal*, September 21, 1914, 8.

536. McAdoo's press release (*Wall Street Journal*, September 21, 1914, 8) credits Strong, along with James Forgan, L. L. Rue, and A. H. Wiggin, with reviving the Gold Pool.

537. *New York Times*, August 19, 1914, 10.

538. *Wall Street Journal*, September 17, 1914, 8.

539. *New York Times*, August 11, 1914, 6.

540. *New York Times*, September 1, 1914, 8.

541. Ibid.

542. Ibid.

543. *New York Times*, September 2, 1914, 8.

544. Ibid.

545. Warburg's statement, issued on September 2, appeared in the *New York Times* (September 3, 1914, 9).

546. McAdoo 1931, 225.

547. The Memorandum to Senator Robert Owen and Samuel Untermyer, May 24, 1913, is reprinted in Warburg (1930, 639ff).

548. McAdoo 1931, 235.

549. See chapter 1.

550. McAdoo 1931, 280.

551. Letter and Memorandum, August 27, 1914, from Warburg to McAdoo, Papers of William McAdoo, Library of Congress.

552. Ibid.

553. Warburg 1930, 58–59; Lamont 1933, 97.

554. Warburg 1930, 59.

555. Glass 1927, 30.

556. Ibid., 82.

557. *New York Times*, September 1, 1914, 8.

558. See Silber 2006.

559. Chandler 1958, 26, 31.

560. *New York Times*, October 17, 1928.

561. Ibid.

562. Lamont 1933, 59.

563. Chandler 1958, 28.

564. Ibid., 30–31.

565. Lamont 1933, 97.

566. Chandler 1958, 32.

567. Ibid., 34.

568. Ibid., 35.

569. Ibid., 35.

570. Ibid., 36.

571. Ibid., 37.

572. *Washington Post*, August 1, 1914, 1. Also see chapter 1.

573. Chandler 1958, 38.

574. Chandler 1958, 83. The Federal Reserve Act required that the system hold gold reserves of 40 percent against its liabilities of Federal Reserve notes. According to Friedman and Schwartz (1963, 194–95), "Since the Federal Reserve was required to keep a gold reserve of 35 percent of its deposits [reserves of member banks], it could use any excess over that amount [the 35 percent] . . . to meet the 40 percent requirement for notes." Strong recognized that to provide for an "elastic currency" to meet the needs of commerce and to avoid panics, the system needed excess gold reserves.

575. Chandler 1958, 84.

576. Willis 1915, 158.

577. Ibid.

578. Letter and Memorandum, August 27, 1914, from Warburg to McAdoo, Papers of William McAdoo, Library of Congress.

579. See the previous chapter. 1.75 is slightly bigger than .085 divided by 4.90 (the gold export point).

580. Chandler 1958, 41.

581. Ibid.

582. Ibid.

583. Ibid., 61.

584. Letter, September 24, 1914, box 659, Board of Governors of the Federal Reserve System, Central Subject File, 1913–1954, National Archives II, College Park, Maryland.

585. Telegram, September 11, 1914, ibid.

586. Telegram, September 15, 1914, ibid.

587. McAdoo 1931, 299.

588. *Wall Street Journal*, August 25, 1914, 2.

589. See chapter 4.

590. *New York Times*, August 30, 1914, 5, and September 3, 1914, 5.

591. *New York Times*, September 12, 1914, 16.

592. *New York Times*, September 29, 1914, 4.

593. Ibid.

594. *New York Times*, October 3, 1914, 10.

595. *New York Times*, October 4, 1914, 27.

596. The Diary of Charles Hamlin, October 10, 1914, vol. 2, pp. 168–71, Library of Congress, provides an account of this meeting. All quotations are taken from Hamlin's handwritten notes.

597. Ibid., 168–69.

598. Ibid., 169.

599. Ibid.

600. Ibid., 170.

601. Letter, October 15, 1914, Papers of William McAdoo, Library of Congress.

602. Letter, October 13, 1914, box 1470, Board of Governors of the Federal Reserve System, Central Subject File, 1913–1954, National Archives II, College Park, Maryland.

603. Ibid.

604. October 15, 1914, Minutes of the Board of Governors of the Federal Reserve System, Records of Federal Reserve System, Central Subject File, 1913–1954, National Archives, College Park, Maryland.

605. See Transcript of the Conference, box 293, ibid.

606. Ibid.

607. *New York Times*, October 27, 1914.

608. The dialogue appears in McAdoo (1931, 289).

609. Chandler 1958, 61.

610. Ibid., 65.

611. *Wall Street Journal*, October 27, 1914, 1.

612. *New York Times*, October 27, 1914, 1.

613. Ibid., 2.

614. Ibid.

615. Ibid., 1.

616. The *Wall Street Journal* had reported on October 15, 1914, 3: "Exports of cotton thus far this season are about one-sixth as large as those of a year ago."

617. McAdoo 1931, 297.

618. *New York Times*, October 27, 1914, 3.

619. McAdoo 1931, 297.

620. U.S. Treasury, *Annual Report*, 1915, 14.

621. *New York Times*, October 25, 1914, XX11.

622. *Wall Street Journal*, August 1, 1914, 1.

623. *Washington Post*, September 26, 1914, 3.

624. Ibid.

625. See the first quotation in this chapter from the *New York Times*, August 11, 1914, 6.

626. *Wall Street Journal*, August 27, 1914, 1.

627. Diary of Charles Hamlin, October 30, 1914, vol. 2, p. 177, Library of Congress.

628. See Memo, November 2, 1914, box 1470, Board of Governors of the Federal Reserve System, Central Subject File, 1913–1954, National Archives II, College Park, Maryland. The memo was written by Benjamin Strong, Albert Wiggin of the Chase National Bank, and James Brown of Brown Brothers. These three had been designated by a committee of bankers to present an analysis of the current financial situation to Sir George Paish and Basil Blackett of the United Kingdom. They had all participated in the Treasury conference on October 23.

629. See also (unsigned) Memo, October 30, 1914, Papers of William McAdoo, Library of Congress. The memo is a draft of the November 2 memo from Strong, Wiggin, and Brown.

630. U.S. Treasury, *Annual Report*, 1914. Also see chapter 2.

631. McAdoo 1931, 278.

632. *Wall Street Journal*, November 13, 1914, 8.

633. Ibid.

634. See the consolidated balance sheet of the Federal Reserve Banks on November 20, 1914, in Willis 1915, 159.

635. Sprague 1914, 185.

636. Noble 1915, 83.

637. Ibid.

638. Ibid.

639. Memorandum against the Suspension of Gold, August 3, 1914, in Keynes 1971, 11.

640. Ibid., 10.

641. Paish 1911, 169–71.

642. Ibid.

643. Ibid., 175.

644. See Swoboda (1968), Chrystal (1977), and Krugman (1980), for the role of low transactions costs and economies of scale in producing a single international medium of exchange.

645. See Krugman 1980, 523.

646. Data on international currency reserves are not available for this period. However, Lindert (1969) constructed data for 1913. Based on the distribution of foreign exchange reserves by currency in 1913, he says (17): "London was clearly the primary reserve center on the eve of World War I. On the other hand,

the primacy of sterling among reserve currencies was not so unrivalled as some authors have implied. . . . Of the holdings reported by currencies, sterling accounted for more than French francs and German marks combined."

647. Lindert (1968, table 2) reports the following distribution of foreign reserve balances held in various countries in 1913: United Kingdom = $455 million; France = $275 million; Germany = $152 million; United States = $157 million. Almost all of the U.S. foreign balances were owned by Canadian entities.

648. *Wall Street Journal*, September 15, 1900, 1.

649. According to Noyes (1909), "New York took $28 million of the British exchequer loan of August 1900; applied for $150 million of the loan of May, 1901, and secured $100 million; it subscribed for $80 million of the loan of April 1902." Noyes does not report the amount allocated in 1902 but the *Wall Street Journal* reported (April 17, 1902, 8) that the American subscription will be £5 million or $24 million (£5 million times $4.8665). The total issued in New York sums to $152 million ($28 million plus $100 million plus $24 million).

650. Hovey 1912, 280–81.

651. See *Wall Street Journal*, May 7, 1904, 5, and May 11, 1904, 5.

652. See Carosso 1970, 80–81. Also see Young 1930, 10–11. Young also mentions loans to the governments of Cuba, Canada, and Mexico. These are less compelling examples of American leadership in international finance since these countries fall more easily under America's sphere of influence.

653. *Congressional Record*, 57th Cong., sess. 1, 1902, 2201.

654. Sprague 1910, 274.

655. For the denomination of British war bonds, see the *Commercial and Financial Chronicle*, August 11, 1900; May 4, 1901; and April 19, 1902. For the German bonds, see *Wall Street Journal*, September 19, 1900, 2.

656. The denomination of the Swedish bond appears in Equitable Trust Company of New York 1920a, 62.

657. See *Wall Street Journal*, May 11, 1904, 5.

658. Letter from Higginson to Wilson, August 20, 1914, Papers of William G. McAdoo, Library of Congress.

659. Ibid.

660. Ibid.

661. See chapter 7.

662. Sterling sold at $5.065 on September 1, 3.37 percent above $4.90. Sterling stood at $4.9025 on October 31, within .05 percent of $4.90.

663. *Wall Street Journal*, October 27, 1914, 2.

664. *New York Times*, November 1, 1914, 10, attributes the report to Sir George Paish, the representative of the U.K. Treasury.

665. *Washington Post*, November 9, 1914, 4.

666. *Washington Post*, November 10, 1914, 10.

667. The .51 percent decline in Sterling on November 12 has a t-statistic of 2.217.

668. *Wall Street Journal*, November 13, 1914, 8.

669. *Wall Street Journal*, February 17, 1915, 1, continued.

670. *Wall Street Journal*, February 16, 1915, 4.

671. *Washington Post*, January 5, 1915, 10.

672. *Washington Post*, January 8, 1915, 5.

673. The bond is listed as denominated in dollars in Equitable Trust Company of New York 1920a, 62.

674. *Washington Post*, March 15, 1915, 10.

675. *Wall Street Journal*, October 20, 1915, 5, and September 10, 1915, 8.

676. See Equitable Trust Company of New York 1920b, 5.

677. Lewis 1938, 354–55.

678. The total of £516 million times $4.8665 equals $2.5 billion.

679. *Washington Post*, January 18, 1915, 5.

680. Ibid.

681. Ibid.

682. Ibid.

683. See *Wall Street Journal*, September 11, 1915, 8, and November 17, 1915, 7.

684. *Wall Street Journal*, October 18, 1915, 8.

685. See Officer 1996, table 6.8.

686. See Brunner and Meltzer (1971) for the role of money in economizing on information and transactions costs.

687. Krugman 1980, 523.

688. *Wall Street Journal*, September 11, 1915, 8, and June 27, 1916, 2.

689. *Wall Street Journal*, November 30, 1918, 10.

690. Ibid.

691. Chernow 1990, 198.

692. *Wall Street Journal*, January 10, 1916, 8.

693. Moggridge 1969, 12–13.

694. Ibid., 14.

695. Brown 1940, 231, table 18.

696. *Wall Street Journal*, September 3, 1919.

697. Moggridge 1969, 49.

698. Moggridge 1972, 37–38. The formal name of the committee was The Committee on the Currency and Bank of England Note Issues. Bradbury succeeded Chamberlain after Chamberlain became secretary of state for foreign affairs.

699. Ibid., 39.

700. Ibid., 42.

701. *Wall Street Journal*, March 26, 1925, 8.

702. *Wall Street Journal*, December 19, 1928, 16.

703. The totals are for the years between 1926 and 1928. See Brown 1940, 618.

704. Young 1930, 104ff.

705. See the previous paragraphs and compare the *Wall Street Journal*, December 19, 1928, 16, with March 26, 1925, 8.

706. Conant (1915, 54) cites August 12, 1870, as the date the Chamber of Deputies authorized the Bank of France to suspend specie payments.

707. Bagehot 1873, 31–33.

708. See Bordo and Rockoff 1996.

709. Bagehot 1873, 32.

710. Memorandum, August 3, 1914, in Keynes 1971, 11.

711. Memorandum, January 17, 1917, in ibid., 220.

712. Moggridge 1969, 10.

713. Letter, July 25, 1924, in Keynes 1981, 271.

714. Noyes 1926, 86–88.

715. See Willis 1923, 981ff. Ferderer (2003) credits the increased liquidity of the banker's acceptance market with helping dollar exchange challenge the sterling bill. He also credits Britain's abandoning gold in 1919, while the United States remained on the gold standard, with contributing to the growth in dollar exchange.

716. See *Address of the Honorable Paul Warburg before the Pan American Conference* (Washington, D.C.: Government printing Office, 1915), 6, box 2, Papers of Paul Warburg, Yale University.

717. *New York Times*, August 3, 1914, 3.

718. *Commercial and Financial Chronicle* 99 (August 22, 1914): 499.

719. See chapter 5.

720. Diary of Charles Hamlin, October 10, 1914, vol. 2, 160, Library of Congress.

721. Ibid.

722. The transcript of Keynes's testimony is reprinted in Keynes 1981, 250.

723. Moggridge 1969, 32.

724. Friedman and Schwartz 1963, 315.

725. Bagehot 1873, 56.

726. Ibid.

727. Ibid.

728. See Meltzer 2003, 348.

729. *Federal Reserve Bulletin* (Washington, D.C.), 1931.

730. *Federal Reserve Bulletin* (Washington, D.C.), 1931 and 1932.

731. See Friedman and Schwartz 1963, 713. Friedman and Schwartz (318 and n. 19) note that the decline of "the money stock by 12 percent from August 1931 to January 1932" was the second largest decline ever over a comparable period in U.S. monetary history.

732. See Lindsey, Orphanides, and Rasche in Federal Reserve Bank of St. Louis Review 2005, 187ff.

733. See Neely 2003.

734. See Taylor 2002, 8.

735. See Meltzer in Federal Reserve Bank of St. Louis Review 2005, 167.

736. See Federal Reserve Bank of St. Louis Review 2005, 306.

737. Lippmann 1927, 116.

738. Ibid., 113.

739. *Wall Street Journal*, August 8, 1914, 4.

740. *New York Times*, August 26, 1914, 11.

References

Andrew, A. Piatt. 1907. "The Treasury and the Banks under Secretary Shaw." *Quarterly Journal of Economics*, August.

———. 1908a. "Hoarding in the Panic of 1907." *Quarterly Journal of Economics*, February.

———. 1908b. "Substitutes for Cash in the Panic of 1908." *Quarterly Journal of Economics*, August.

———. 1908c. "The Currency Legislation of 1908." *Quarterly Journal of Economics*, August.

———. 1910. *Statistics for the United States, 1867–1909*. U.S. National Monetary Commission. Washington, D.C.: Government Printing Office.

Bagehot, Walter. 1873. *Lombard Street: A Description of the Money Market*. Reprint, New York: J. Wiley & Sons, 1999.

Board of Governors of the Federal Reserve System. Central Subject File, 1913–1954. National Archives II, College Park, Maryland.

Bordo, Michael, and Finn Kydland. 1995. "The Gold Standard as a Rule: An Essay in Exploration." *Explorations in Economic History*, no. 32.

Bordo, Michael, and Hugh Rockoff. 1996. "The Gold Standard as a 'Good Housekeeping Seal of Approval.'" *Journal of Economic History*, June.

Broesamle, John J. 1973. *William Gibbs McAdoo: A Passion for Change, 1863–1917*. Port Washington, N.Y.: National University Publications, Kennikat Press.

Brown, William A. 1940. *The International Gold Standard Reinterpreted, 1914–1934*. Vol. 1. New York: National Bureau of Economic Research.

Brunner, Karl, and Allan Meltzer. 1971. "The Uses of Money: Money in the Theory of an Exchange Economy." *American Economic Review*, December.

Carosso, Vincent P. 1970. *A History of Investment Banking in America*. Cambridge, Mass.: Harvard University Press.

Chandler, Lester V. 1958. *Benjamin Strong, Central Banker*. Washington, D.C.: Brookings Institution.

Chernow, Ron. 1990. *The House of Morgan: An American Banking Dynasty and the Rise of Modern Finance*. New York: Atlantic Monthly Press.

Chicago Board of Trade. 1989. *Commodity Trading Manual*. Chicago: Chicago Board of Trade.

Chinn, Menzie, and Jeffrey Frankel. 2005. "Will the Euro Eventually Surpass the Dollar as Leading International Reserve Currency?" National Bureau of Economic Research, Working Paper 11510, July.

Chrystal, K. Alec. 1977. "Demand for International Media of Exchange." *American Economic Review,* December.

Committee on Government Operations. 1981. *Silver Prices and the Adequacy of Federal Actions in the Marketplace, 1979–1980*. Washington, D.C.: U.S. Government Printing Office.

Comptroller of the Currency. 1907, 1908, 1911. *Annual Report*. Washington, D.C.: Government Printing Office.

———. 1915. *Annual Report*, December 7, 1914. Washington, D.C.: Government Printing Office.

———. 1916. *Annual Report*, December 6, 1915. Washington, D.C.: Government Printing Office.

Conant, Charles A. 1915. *History of Modern Banks of Issue*. 5th ed. New York: G. P. Putnam and Sons.

Diary of Charles Hamlin. Library of Congress, Washington, D.C.

Eichengreen, Barry J. 1992. *Golden Fetters: The Gold Standard and the Great Depression, 1919–1939*. New York: Oxford University Press.

Eichengreen, Barry J., and Ricardo Hausmann, eds. 2005. *Other People's Money*. Chicago: University of Chicago Press.

Equitable Trust Company of New York. 1920a. *The National Loans of the World*. New York: Equitable Trust Company of New York.

———. c. 1920b. *Foreign Loans as Investments*. New York: Equitable Trust Company of New York.

Fay, Sidney B. 1928. *The Origins of the World War*. New York: Macmillan.

Federal Reserve Bank of St. Louis Review. 2005. *Reflections on Monetary Policy 25 Years after October 1979*. March–April, part 2.

Federal Reserve Board. 1915. *First Annual Report for the Period Ending December 31, 1914*. Washington, D.C.: Government Printing Office.

Ferderer, J. Peter, 2003. "Institutional Innovation and the Creation of Liquid Financial Markets: The Case of Bankers Acceptances, 1914–1933." *Journal of Economic History*, September.

Ferguson, Niall. 1999. *The House of Rothschild, 1849–1999*. New York: Viking, Penguin Group.

———. 2001. *The Cash Nexus: Money and Power in the Modern World*. New York: Basic Books.

———. 2006. "Political Risk and the International Bond Market between the 1848 Revolution and the Outbreak of the First World War." *Economic History Review*.

Flandreau, Marc. 2004. *The Glitter of Gold: France, Bimetallism, and the Emergence of the International Gold Standard, 1848–1873*. Translated by Owen Leeming. New York: Oxford University Press.

Friedberg, Robert. 1964. *Paper Money of the United States*. 5th ed. New York: Coin and Currency Institute.

Friedman, Milton, and Anna J. Schwartz. 1963. *A Monetary History of the United States, 1867–1960*. Princeton, N.J.: Princeton University Press.

Glass, Carter. 1927. *An Adventure in Constructive Finance*. Garden City, N.Y.: Doubleday, Page.

Goodhart, Charles A. E. 1969. *The New York Money Market and the Finance of Trade, 1900–1913*. Cambridge, Mass.: Harvard University Press.

Harding, William P. G. 1925. *The Formative Period of the Federal Reserve System*. Boston: Houghton, Mifflin.

Hepburn, A. Barton. 1915. *A History of Currency in the United States*. New York: Macmillan.

Hovey, Carl. 1912. *The Life Story of J. Pierpont Morgan*. New York: Sturgis & Walton.

Kemmerer, Edwin W. 1914. "Issue of Emergency Currency in the United States." *Economic Journal*, December.

Keynes, John Maynard. 1914a. "War and the Financial System, August 1914." *Economic Journal*, September.

———. 1914b. "The Prospects of Money." *Economic Journal*, December.

———. 1971. *Collected Writings of John Maynard Keynes*. Vol. 16: *Activities, 1914–1919*. Edited by Elizabeth Johnson. London: Macmillan.

———. 1981. *Collected Writings of John Maynard Keynes*. Vol. 19: *Activities, 1922–1929*. Part I. Edited by Donald Moggridge. London: Macmillan.

Kindleberger, Charles P. 1967. *The Politics of International Money and World Language*. Princeton Essays in International Finance, Princeton University, Princeton, N.J.

———. 1973. *The World in Depression, 1929–1939*. Berkeley: University of California Press.

Krugman, Paul. 1980. "Vehicle Currencies and the Structure of International Exchange." *Journal of Money, Credit, and Banking*, August.

———, ed. 2000. *Currency Crises*. Chicago: University of Chicago Press.

Lamont, Thomas W. 1933. *Henry P. Davison: The Record of a Useful Life*. New York: Harper & Brothers.

Laughlin, J. Laurence. 1908a. "The Aldrich Bill." *Journal of Political Economy*, February.

———. 1908b. "The Aldrich-Vreeland Act." *Journal of Political Economy*, October.

———. 1918. *Credit of the Nations*. New York: Charles Scribner's Sons.

Lewis, Cleona. 1938. *America's Stake in International Investments*. Washington, D.C.: Brookings Institution.

Lindert, Peter. 1969. *Key Currencies and Gold, 1900–1913*. International Finance Section, Department of Economics, Princeton University, Princeton, N.J.

Lippmann, Walter. 1927. *Men of Destiny*. Seattle: University of Washington Press.

McAdoo, William G. 1931. *Crowded Years*. Boston: Houghton Mifflin.

Meltzer, Allan H. 2003. *A History of the Federal Reserve*. Vol. 1: *1913–1951*. Chicago: University of Chicago Press.

Menger, Karl. 1892. "On the Origins of Money." *Economic Journal*, June.

Moggridge, Donald. 1969. *The Return to Gold, 1925: The Formulation of Economic Policy and Its Critics*. London: Cambridge University Press.

———. 1972. *British Monetary Policy, 1924–1931: The Norman Conquest of $4.86*. London: Cambridge University Press.

Mott, Frank L. 1950. *American Journalism: A History of Newspapers in the United States through 260 Years, 1690 to 1950*. Rev. ed. New York: Macmillan.

Mussa, Michael, James M. Boughton, and Peter Isard, eds. 1996. *The Future of the SDR in Light of Changes in the International Financial System*. Washington, D.C.: International Monetary Fund.

Neely, Christopher J. 2003. "The Federal Reserve Responds to Crises: September 11th Was Not the First." Federal Reserve Bank of St. Louis, Working Paper, October.

Noble, Henry G. S. 1915. *The New York Stock Exchange in the Crisis of 1914*. Garden City, N.Y., 1915. Reprinted in *Wall Street and the Security Markets* (New York: Arno Press, 1975).

Noyes, Alexander D. 1909. *Forty Years of American Finance*. New York: Putnam's.

———. 1910. *History of the National Bank Currency*. National Monetary Commission. Washington, D.C.: Government Printing Office.

———. 1916. *Financial Chapters of the War*. New York: Charles Scribner's and Sons.

———. 1926. *The War Period of American Finance*. New York: G. P. Putnam's Sons.

Officer, Lawrence H. 1996. *Between the Dollar-Sterling Gold Points: Exchange Rates, Parity, and Market*. New York: Cambridge University Press.

———. 2001. "Comparing the Purchasing Power of Money in Great Britain from 1264 to Any other Year Including the Present." *Economic History Services*, available at www.eh.net/hmit/ppowerbp.

Paish, George. 1911. "Great Britain's Capital Investment in Individual Colonial and Foreign Countries." *Journal of the Royal Statistical Society*, January.

Papers of Paul Warburg. Yale University Library, New Haven, Connecticut.

Papers of William G. McAdoo. Library of Congress, Washington D.C.

Papers of Woodrow Wilson. 1978, 1979, 1991. Edited by Arthur S. Link. Princeton, N.J.: Princeton University Press.

Remak, Joachim. 1959. *Sarajevo: The Story of a Political Murder*. New York: Criterion Books.

Romer, Christina D., and David H. Romer. 2004. "Choosing the Federal Reserve Chair: Lessons from History." *Journal of Economic Perspectives*, Winter.

Report of the Monetary Commission of the Indianapolis Convention. 1900. Indianapolis: Hollenbeck Press.

Roosa, Robert V., and Fred Hirsch. 1966. *Reserves, Reserve Currencies, and Vehicle Currencies: An Argument*. Princeton Essays in International Finance, Department of Economics, Princeton University, Princeton, N.J.

Schenk, Catherine. 1994. "Closing the Hong Kong Gap: The Hong Kong Free Dollar Market in the 1950s." *Economic History Review* 47, May.

Schmitt, Bernadotte E. 1930. *The Coming of the War, 1914*. New York: C. Scribner's Sons.

Siegel, Jeremy J. 1998. *Stocks for Long Run*. 2d ed. New York: McGraw-Hill.

Silber, William L. 1977. "The Optimum Quantity of Money and the Interrelationship between Financial Markets and Intermediaries." *Banca Nazionale Del Lavoro Quarterly*, March.

———. 1983. "The Process of Financial Innovation." *American Economic Review*, May.

———. 1991. "Discounts on Restricted Stock: The Impact of Illiquidity on Stock Prices." *Financial Analysts Journal*, July–August.

———. 2005. "What Happened to Liquidity When World War I Shut the NYSE?" *Journal of Financial Economics*, December.

———. 2006. "Birth of the Federal Reserve: Crisis in the Womb." *Journal of Monetary Economics*, March.

Simon, Matthew. 1960. "The Hot Money Movement and the Private Exchange Proposal of 1896." *Journal of Economic History*, March.

Sobel, Robert. 1968. *Panic on Wall Street: A History of America's Financial Disasters*. New York: Macmillan.

———. 1972. *Amex: A History of the American Stock Exchange, 1921–1971*. New York: Weybright and Talley.

Sprague, O.M.W. 1910. *History of Crises under the National Banking System*. Washington, D.C.: National Monetary Commission. Reprint, New York: Augustus M. Kelley, 1968.

———. 1914. "The War and the Financial Situation in the United States." *Quarterly Journal of Economics*, November.

———. 1915. "The Crisis of 1914 in the United States." *American Economic Review*, September.

Stedman, Edmund C. 1905. *The New York Stock Exchange; Its History, Its Contribution to National Prosperity, and Its Relation to American Finance at the Outset of the Twentieth Century*. Reprint, New York: Greenwood Press, 1969.

Studenski, Paul, and Herman Kroos. 1963. *Financial History of the United States*. 2d ed. New York: McGraw-Hill.

Swoboda, Alexander. 1968. *The Eurodollar Market: An Interpretation*. Princeton Essays in International Finance, Department of Economics, Princeton University, Princeton, N.J.

Taylor, John B. 2002. "A Half Century of Changes in Monetary Policy." Available at www.treas.gov/press/releases/docs/fried.pdf, November 8.

Temin, Peter. 1989. *Lessons from the Great Depression: Lionel Robbins Lectures for 1989*. Cambridge, Mass.: MIT Press.

U.S Department of Commerce, Bureau of the Census. 1975. *Historical Statistics of the United States*. Washington D.C.: Government Printing Office.

U.S. Treasury. 1914, 1915. *Annual Report*. Washington, D.C.: Government Printing Office.

Van Antwerp, William C. 1913. *The Stock Exchange from Within*. Garden City, N.Y.: Doubleday, Page.

Warburg, Paul M. 1930. *The Federal Reserve System: Its Origins and Growth*. Vol. 1 and 2. New York: Macmillan.

Wilkins, Mira. 2004. *The History of Foreign Investment in the United States, 1914–1945*. Cambridge, Mass.: Harvard University Press.

Willis, H. Parker. 1915. "American Finance and the European War." *Journal of Political Economy*, February.

———. 1923. *The Federal Reserve System: Legislation, Organization and Operation*. New York: Ronald Press.

Withers, Hartley. 1915. *War and Lombard Street*. London: John Murray.

Young, Ralph A. 1930. *Handbook on American Underwriting of Foreign Securities*. Washington, D.C.: Government Printing Office.

Index